D0046456

Assessing Personal and Social Development

Assessing Personal and Social Development: Measuring the Unmeasurable?

Edited by

Sally Inman, Martin Buck and Helena Burke

UK Falmer Press, 1 Gunpowder Square, London, EC4A 3DE
USA Falmer Press, Taylor & Francis Inc., 1900 Frost Road, Suite 101, Bristol, PA 19007

First published in 1998

A catalogue record for this book is available from the British Library

ISBN 0 7507 0762 3 cased
ISBN 0 7507 0761 5 paper

Library of Congress Cataloging-in-Publication Data are available on request

Jacket design by Caroline Archer

Typeset in 10/12pt Times by
Graphicraft Typesetters Ltd., Hong Kong.

Printed in Great Britain by Biddles Ltd., Guildford and King's Lynn on paper which has a specified pH value on final paper manufacture of not less than 7.5 and is therefore 'acid free'.

Contents

List of Figures

Acknowledgments

Ros Moger who has acted as a consultant editor to the book.

The editors would like to thank all those teachers, student teachers and LEA advisers who have been involved with the work of the Centre for Cross Curricular Initiatives. Their ideas and comments have greatly helped to develop our thinking. Thanks also to Judith Bretherton and Judith Gray whose, often invisible, administration of the Centre has enabled us to continue this work.

Preface

Patricia Broadfoot

Schools are under pressure. The advent of published league tables of examination results coupled with parental choice has focused their attention as perhaps never before on the academic attainment of their pupils. Moreover, as well as this pressure to compete in the market for pupils, schools will in the future also be required to meet targets concerning the examination results of their pupils which have been imposed upon them by Government.

In such a climate, the future for other aspects of education is likely to be bleak. To the extent that schools and individual teachers are forced to focus their energies on 'getting the scores up' so the time and enthusiasm for less readily measurable educational outcomes will inevitably be reduced. Personal and Social Development (PSD) is one of several such aspects of learning that are currently under pressure, both explicitly, for their space on the timetable, and implicitly in terms of their assumed value in the eyes of teachers and students. For the truth is that despite the anguished handwringing of politicians and policy-makers about the need for schools to take more responsibility for the moral, civic and spiritual development of the next generation in our society, 'what you test is what you get'. In practice, both individual students and the institutions responsible for teaching them, will prioritize those things on which they are judged. The more 'high stakes' that judgment is, in that its consequences are significant, the more this is likely to be the case.

During the past twenty years or so, this power of assessment to drive educational priorities has increasingly been realized by policy-makers around the world. Many countries have put in place some form of national assessment system or redesigned their public examination arrangements to act as a direct conduit for the educational priorities of Government. Successful as these initiatives have typically been in strengthening effective central control of priorities and practices within the education system, they have not come without a price. What Governments seem remarkably slow to recognize is that other key objectives — notably at the present time the preparation of students for lifelong learning and constructive citizenship — are actively inhibited by such developments.

It is not just a question of the necessary prominence being given to academic achievements under the current regime. More fundamentally the issue is one of *discourse* — the language we use to define our collective understanding of what education in the late twentieth century is and of how it should be delivered. Whilst the education system as a whole and individual schools, teachers and students within it find themselves constrained to pursue these external targets so intensively, alternative priorities and the practices implied by them can make little headway. Arguably we are poised on the threshold of a major revolution in the delivery of education which will be made possible by advances in information technology. Yet we find ourselves constrained perhaps more than ever before by the teaching, learning and assessment practices of an earlier age.

This is why *Assessing Personal and Social Development* is such an important and timely book. It represents a brave and constructive attempt to encourage debate about how the acknowledged power of assessment to drive curriculum priorities might be harnessed to support the pursuit of other key educational objectives. And it is also a highly practical book in providing concrete examples of how this *might be*, and indeed *has been*, done. If, as The European Commission suggests 'the main function of a school must be to guide the young people in its care in their personal and social development' (European Commission, 1995 quoted in Chapter 1) then we need to recognize that such a mission will not be taken seriously in practice until activities in this area are also the subject of formal assessment and accountability.

Any doubts that this is so can be readily dispelled by looking at the history of Records of Achievement in England and Wales. An initiative which had as one of its key goals, the development and reporting of young people's personal and social qualities and skills, it was much valued by many teachers and pupils during the years leading up to the 1988 Education Act. With the implementation of the National Curriculum and particularly, of National Assessment, the attention of schools was inevitably diverted towards meeting these new challenges. Gradually, this initially relatively superficial change in priorities has become transformed into a more profound change in the discourse of education itself and in the way in which we think about educational problems and solutions. Thus, despite the formal advent of a National Record of Achievement in 1991 as an entitlement for all pupils, the evidence is clear that it has made relatively little impact (NRA Review, 1997). In short, unless success in the personal and social development, as well as in the academic development of its students, is one of the indicators against which schools are judged, these aspects will not be given the prominent place in the curriculum that they merit. The omens are not good in this respect. As Inman, Buck and Burke point out in their postscript, the Labour Government's White Paper 'Excellence in Schools' offers no recognition of the different forms of young people's achievement nor that the continuing emphasis on traditional forms of testing will discourage and demotivate many less-successful pupils.

However, even if teachers, policy-makers, students and their parents could reach agreement on the general principle that PSD is vitally important, there would still be many issues to resolve in translating this agreement into practice. The first problem would be defining what we mean by personal and social education. Is it essentially an intellectual exercise involving curriculum coverage of key aspects of contemporary personal, social and civic life such as drug-awareness, parenting, multiculturalism or pollution? Or is it rather the development of personal and social *skills* as in the 'Pathways to Learning' initiative described in Chapter 6 and the many other similar initiatives? Or again, should it be centrally concerned with individual self-knowledge, the development of self-esteem and the attitudes required both for successful learning and successful future citizenship? Slade's description of how even young children's orientation to their learning is the starting point for everything else they do powerfully reinforces the importance of this latter perspective. Clearly though, there are no hard and fast divisions between these various emphases, all of which are important. However, in pursuing the question of how to assess such activities, it is essential that the approach chosen is in harmony with the learning outcomes sought.

These tension are clearly recognized in Buck and Inman's opening chapter. They themselves take student self assessment as the essential starting point since it is intrinsic to their definition of PSD (p. 20). However, they also recognize that assessment serves many other purposes which include diagnosing students' learning needs, establishing learning outcomes and potential, ranking students against each other and comparing performance across schools. There is a familiar, if implicit, distinction here between the formative and summative purposes of assessment, between the use of assessment *for* learning and assessment *of* learning. Herein lies the essential tension for assessment in relation to PSD although it is a tension which characterizes the assessment of other aspects of learning too. Is it possible to provide for the kind of student-centred and owned self-assessment which is now widely recognized as a necessary core feature of effective PSD and indeed of learning more generally whilst at the same time conducting the more external, formal assessment of performance — however widely defined – which is the essential basis for providing evidence of student achievement in this area?

Assessing Personal and Social Development is shot through with this tension. Some chapters such as Chapters 6 to 9, place great emphasis on the use of assessment as an intrinsic part of the learning process itself. Others, such as Chapter 10, which describes an approach to formally accrediting students' achievements in PSE at Key Stage 4, take a more strategic focus in terms of current educational policy developments, student and teacher motivation. It recognizes the corresponding need for PSD to adopt at least some part of the prevailing educational discourse with its notions of performance indicators and overt evidence of learning outcomes. These tension are well summarized by Helena Burke in Chapter 8:

> To assess PSD is essential but, as indicated in Chapter 1, assessment of PSD is not straightforward. There are a number of issues to consider here: can and should all aspects of PSD be assessed? What constitutes evidence of personal and social development? What forms of progression can we expect within PSD? How can we record assessment? (p. 125)

However the problem of finding an appropriate way to assess PSD is further exacerbated by the impossibility of reaching a consensus about its *content*, even if agreement could be reached about its primary purpose. In Chapter 7, the reader is brought face to face with the postmodern dilemma. How can moral education be defined if there is no cultural consensus? Should PSD involve the arbitrary imposition of the values of the dominant culture (as many politicians seem to want), and if not, how are we to decide what to teach and hence, what to assess?

In responding to this dilemma, the author stresses the key role of stories in helping students to make sense of their culture and to articulate their values and feelings. However, here again we come up against the same impasse. Given that the ability to construct a personal learning 'narrative' could be argued to be the basis for effective management of one's own learning and development, it might be suggested that it would be most appropriate for assessment to focus on the quality of the narrative itself, rather than its content, in much the same way that evaluation skills are assessed in GNVQ. Yet, as soon as such a narrative is perceived to have external value as part of a formal assessment, the learner is likely to tailor its production to the perceived criteria of the assessor rather than seeking to maximize its personal utility.

Assessing Personal and Social Development provides the reader with a comprehensive introduction to these dilemmas. It offers an exciting mixture of illustrations that demonstrate both the complexity of deciding what might fall within the definition of PSD and the correspondingly difficult challenge of developing appropriate assessment techniques. Furthermore, even when these questions have been resolved, there remain the more practical problems of how to ensure that the chosen assessment technique is applied in such a way that it does indeed fulfil its intended purpose. At a time when so much time and energy are necessarily devoted to other activities, the more radical, time-consuming, inter- and intra-personal assessment approaches are the most likely to suffer. As such, the book is likely to be read at two levels. It will be valued by those in school who seek practical guidance concerning what role assessment might play in PSD programmes of various kinds. More generally it will engage with a wider readership who share its concerns about the current stranglehold of a narrow range of assessment purposes on the curriculum. Hopefully it will also challenge the Establishment to consider how far the current obsession with measuring academic standards is stifling the growth of more modern assessment technologies; technologies which have the capacity to support the development of those personal insights, skills and qualities upon which the communities of the twenty-first century will depend for their health and prosperity.

Patricia Broadfoot
November 1997

Introduction

Sally Inman, Martin Buck and Helena Burke

This book is concerned with the assessment of personal and social development (PSD) in primary and secondary schools. We recognize from the outset that this is a hugely complex area, fraught with a range of intellectual and ethical problems. The book attempts to acknowledge and grapple with these problems rather than ignore them. In our view there are no easy answers as to how to assess PSD, such answers would be to render assessment in this area to technicism and this would be both inappropriate and potentially dangerous. Thus the reader seeking a 'blue print' for how to assess PSD will inevitably be disappointed. Some will argue that the assessment of PSD is either impossible and/or undesirable. We do not take that position. Despite the complexities, we are convinced of the need to explore ways forward, and all the contributions to the book, in their different ways, are an attempt to move our assessment practice on.

Chapter 1 is concerned with the status and role of PSD within the curriculum. Buck and Inman argue for a particular conception of PSD, one that makes it central to curriculum purpose. The chapter goes on to explore the need for assessment of PSD and explores some of the issues involved in determining appropriate assessment mechanisms for this area of human development. The chapter ends with some suggested principles for assessment practice in PSD. In Chapter 2 Trainor provides a national overview of the shifting place of PSD within the curriculum, drawing on past and current documentation from the National Curriculum and inspection agencies. Trainor explores assessment possibilities and suggests that, for assessment to be worthwhile, PSD must be given high status in the curriculum; and the larger society must trust teachers to make professional judgments of young peoples' development. Chapter 3 explores the relationships, processes and practices in schools that promote PSD. Lyseight-jones argues that these are as important as our assessment practices and give the latter purpose and meaning, both to the learner and to the external world. The chapter suggests that process based assessment must have a central place in assessment practices for PSD.

Chapter 4 is concerned with the establishment of appropriate learning outcomes for PSD. Buck and Inman review and evaluate some of the emerging national thinking about learning outcomes. They attempt to identify appropriate outcomes for PSD. They suggest that, for assessment purposes, we need to distinguish between the interrelated components of PSD — knowledge and understanding, skills and attitudes. The chapter goes on to explore issues of progression and, finally outlines some ways in which learning outcomes can be more explicitly embedded in our curriculum planning.

In Chapter 5 the focus is on pupils' attitudes and behaviour. Slee asks teachers, schools and policy makers to critically re-examine the way they understand disruptive behaviour and to adopt an educational approach to behaviour and discipline. By doing this he argues, we make pupils' behaviour central to their PSD and promote an ethos, curriculum, and structures that provide for a proper 'apprenticeship in democracy'.

Chapter 6 describes and evaluates a national project — 'Pathways towards adult and working life'. Harris discusses a curriculum initiative that has attempted to define a range of PSD learning outcomes, and to provide for progression in the learning of young people from 5 to 16. Harris argues that, for PSD initiatives to be successful, they must permeate the whole school.

Chapter 7 explores value formation in young children. Tandy describes work undertaken with children in nursery and infant classes to illustrate the use of stories in the development of pupils' attitudes and values. He goes on to suggest how work of this nature can promote PSD learning outcome, including those of SCAA's Desirable Outcomes and explores how we might begin to assess these outcomes in ways which take account of the complexity of the learning experiences.

Chapters 8 and 9 are both concerned with assessment practice for PSD. In Chapter 8 Burke describes and evaluates a piece of small scale action research in a secondary school. The focus of the research is teacher/pupil conferencing. Burke describes the strengths and weaknesses of the conferencing process to promote and capture aspects of PSD. Chapter 9 also looks at conferencing, but in the context of the infant school. Slade explores how we might adapt the conferencing already well established in many primary schools to enable teachers to use this form of structured dialogue to explore the PSD of young children. The chapter also raises some issues about conferencing, especially with young children.

Chapter 10 provides a case study of assessment practice drawn from the PSE curriculum in a secondary school. Pooley demonstrates how the learning outcomes for the PSE curriculum explicitly relate to the aims and ethos of the school, describes the assessment processes used, and then outlines the process of evaluating current assessment practice for this area of the curriculum.

The focus of the book is assessment of PSD. However, we are aware that a range of factors, many of which have been touched on but not fully explored in the book, determine effective assessment of PSD. The question of effective teachers for PSD is one important area for further exploration. The chapters by Slee, Lyseight-jones and Slade all raise questions about the kinds of attributes demanded of teachers. Clearly making effective provision for, and assessing PSD requires teachers who have had the appropriate training to undertake this kind of work with pupils. Some teachers may feel overwhelmed by the wide range of skills demanded of them. We should remember that much of this work has already begun and thus we can build on existing good practice. Notwithstanding this, there are implications both for Initial Teacher Training and the Continuing Professional Development of teachers.

In addition, as Slade suggests, this kind of work with pupils may sometimes require of teachers a level of self-reflection and personal insight that is difficult to acquire through conventional training programmes. Not all teachers may be able or willing to engage in the depth of self-reflection required and there may be a case for teachers having different roles within the assessment processes.

The book only touches on issues to do with the accreditation of learning in PSD. The reason for this is twofold: one is to do with constraints of time and space; the second is to do with the appropriate sequencing of developing assessment practice and accreditation systems. In our view there is much to do before we are near to developing appropriate assessment practice for PSD and this work will encompass reviewing and enhancing whole school provision. Once we have accomplished this daunting task we can then explore appropriate accreditation. Nevertheless, there is a range of recording and accreditation initiatives currently in use or being developed that will undoubtedly prove useful to this work. These include the many school and LEA initiatives in relation to Records of Achievement at primary and secondary level; the work produced by ASDAN (the Award Scheme Development and Accreditation Network) for the Youth Award Scheme, the revised National Record of Achievement currently being piloted. There is much scope in all these schemes to record and accredit pupils' learning within PSD.

One of the overriding concerns in putting this book together has been to attempt to situate all the contributions at the theory/practice interface. Our early discussions centred on the need to integrate theory and practice, and thus to speak to practitioners in ways that both required reflection and review of practice and, at the same time, pointed to new practical possibilities. We are aware that we have not entirely achieved this aim. It proved more difficult than we had thought. Nevertheless we hope that we have gone some way towards this position.

Finally, the book has been put together through collaboration between a group of teachers, LEA advisers, ex-HMI and tutors working in Initial Teacher Training and Continuing Professional Development. The collaboration has been possible because of long standing working relationships between many of the participants. Many of us have been previously involved in developing curriculum initiatives and providing professional development for colleagues at local and national levels. Whatever the final strengths and weaknesses of the book, we firmly believe such collaboration to be essential for successful curriculum development.

Chapter 1

Personal and Social Development at the Crossroads

Martin Buck and Sally Inman

Abstract

In this opening chapter we attempt to set the scene in relation to the assessment of personal and social development (PSD). The chapter explores the nature of PSD, particularly in relation to values and then examines its relationship to overall curriculum purpose, arguing that PSD must be central to that purpose, and explicitly underpin the curriculum. Finally, the chapter explores some of the issues involved in assessing PSD and suggests some tentative principles to guide our assessment practice.

Setting the context

This is a pertinent moment to review the position of the personal and social development (PSD) of pupils within schools. As we move increasingly nearer to the twenty-first century a range of voices, both from within education and from other areas of civil life, are asking some fundamental questions about the future. Implicit in the questions being asked is a feeling of concern and disquiet about many aspects of our current society and a worry about the kind of society that our young people will inherit. In contrast to the individualism that pervaded the 1980s there is renewed concern with the rights and responsibilities associated with collective living.

Underlying these concerns are a further set of questions concerning the education we shall provide in the twenty-first century. What kinds of schools will best serve that society? What will we ask of teachers in such schools? Central to these questions is a growing interest in the kinds of personal qualities we want to promote in our young people as they move into the next century and the responsibilities of schools to foster those qualities. In other words, the personal and social development of young people within our schools has taken centre stage.

As we have intimated, any discussion as to the place of personal and social development of pupils within the school curriculum should be put within the context of wider societal debate and concern about values and morality. During 1995 and 1996 we witnessed a growing interest in societal values and public morality and, within this, a renewed interest in the proper role of schools in the promotion of values and morality in young people. Much of this debate was triggered by particular events, some of which gave rise to 'moral panics' partly orchestrated and sustained by the mass media. The murder of a small child, Jamie Bulger (1993) by two young boys, the murder of school boy Steven Lawrence (1993) in South London, the violent killing of small children and their teacher at Dunblane in Scotland (1996), the fatal stabbing of the London headteacher, Phillip Lawrence (1996) and the murder of a teenage boy outside the gates of a South London school (1997) each served to demonstrate that all is not well within society.

Explanations for such behaviour and events were various and often conflicting. From within the media, the church, politics and education explanation and blame was sought in a variety of places and people. Explanations included: the apparent corruption and lack of moral values in national politics, government, and business, offering poor role models for the young. The influence of what has been described as the Thatcher idealogy was pinpointed by some; in particular the belief that there is 'no such thing as society', linked with self-interest and gain, rather than care and concern. The Chief Rabbi, Jonathon Sacks, for example speaking on Radio 4 said of Margaret Thatcher 'I think when she said there was no such thing as society she was making a terrible mistake, and we know exactly what happens when society begins to disintegrate' (quoted in *The Independent*; Bevin, 1996).

Others pointed to poor parenting and the apparent breakdown of morals and traditional values in the family (Hutton, 1997). This was linked by some to the decline of religious faith and influence of the church in peoples' lives. Yet others sought explanations within some of the political and economic changes emerging from the Conservative government of the time and suggested that deepening inequalities together with high rates of unemployment and shifts in welfare policy and practice left many young people alienated from their communities and from the wider society. Some Tory MPs took this view. The then backbencher Hugh Dykes, for example, is quoted in the *Independent* as saying

> Vast numbers of moderate and fair minded people in Britain feel strongly that we now have a modern society of gross unfairness and inequalities. (Bevin, 1996)

The debate over values became central to party politics in the run up to the election of May 1997, with the political parties keen to demonstrate an explicit set of values and a new moral code for the future.

The role of schools

This national concern and debate about values and morality has involved much public discussion as to the responsibilities of schools. Schools and teachers have once again been put in the spotlight for their responsibilities in forming young citizens, in particular their role in fostering moral and behavioural codes in young people. The teaching of values and morality and the promotion of self-discipline have become key issues for debate. Towards the end of 1996 the debate escalated when a number of events collided. The School Curriculum and Assessment Authority (SCAA) published a consultation paper concerned with values in schools and their communities (SCAA, 1996) and, at virtually the same time, two schools became the centre for intense media and public attention. The Ridings School in West Yorkshire, and Manton School in Nottinghamshire both hit the headlines over pupil behaviour and school discipline.

The consultation paper from SCAA had emerged from a long running but much less high profile debate over the role of schools in pupils' spiritual and moral development. This debate can be traced to earlier documents from the Office for Standards in Education (Ofsted) (Ofsted, 1994) and in a series of discussion papers, first from the then National Curriculum Council (NCC) and then SCAA, (NCC, 1993, SCAA, 1995, 1996). Nick Tate, Chief Executive of SCAA had also been raising the profile of the spiritual and moral development of pupils in a number of speeches to various professional associations during 1995 and 1996. In the early part of 1996 SCCA convened a national conference on spiritual and moral education. At the conference Tate made clear his concern with societal and schools' values. In his opening address he said:

> Philip Lawrence's death highlights what should be a central theme of our conference: the achievements of schools in this area of the curriculum and the need for society to give them more support than it is sometimes currently doing. Your papers give examples of what is already being done by schools to shore up the moral fabric of our society: schools laying down rules of good behaviour and suggesting to parents that these might apply in the home as well. (Tate, 1996)

This conference launched the notion of a national forum on values and it was the work of this forum that led to the publication of the SCAA November (1996) consultation paper. This paper set out a number of core societal values to which schools should adhere and outlined the principles for action associated with the core values. The publication gave rise to an intense, though short lived, media debate in which the document was both supported and attacked from a range of positions. A number of commentators, conventionally from the right, were largely condemning of the document, describing it as 'wishy washy', representing what were described as trendy platitudes about respect and equality and the environment. Some of these same critics demanded a strengthening of the document particularly in relation to marriage and family life. The then Secretary of State for Education and Employment aligned herself with this position and made clear that the revised document should redress this perceived weakness. Others were critical of the document for what they saw as an attempt to impose a set morality on young people. Such critics saw the processes and difficulties in reaching agreed societal values as problematic and posed questions about whose values were represented in the document. Further debate ensued as to whether morality is best 'taught or caught', and the implications of each position for schools and teachers in relation to their responsibilities for promoting moral development in young people. Despite the many criticisms, the document did serve to provoke useful debate about values in relation to schools, a point to which we return later.[1]

Meanwhile, the events at Ridings and Manton schools raised all sorts of issues. In particular, they raised issues about the responsibilities of schools for the behaviour of young people. At both schools some young people were portrayed as out of control in the school setting. The events gave rise to public debate about behaviour and school discipline and the responsibilities of parents in relation to their children. Solutions to the perceived problem of the behaviour of some young people included school/home contracts in relation to behaviour, and a return to corporal punishment in schools. During the course of the media coverage a new wave of public sympathy for teachers emerged, with teachers being portrayed as having impossible jobs in relation to pupils who were unwilling or unable to behave appropriately within a school setting.

PSD and values

Despite the high profile publicity given to a minority of so-called failing schools during the mid 1990s with respect to their academic performance and ability to inculcate appropriate values and behaviour, evidence from Ofsted Chief Inspector's Annual Reports indicates that the vast majority of schools are places where considerable effective practice has been developed in managing pupils' behaviour. Moreover, we contend that anyone currently involved with working in schools is likely to find the debate about the morality within them puzzling, as their direct experience would indicate that schools, on a daily basis, confront and deal with moral matters. Schools have nevertheless differed widely in the extent to which they have articulated explicitly a shared set of values with pupils and parents, which permeate the day-to-day life of the institution.

But what precisely are values? Halstead defines values as referring 'to principles, fundamental convictions, ideals, standards or life stances which act as general guides to behaviour or as general points of reference in decision making or the evaluation of beliefs or actions which are closely connected with personal integrity or personal identity' (Halstead and Taylor, 1996).

In short, values are concerned with the criteria by which we make judgments. This definition, however, raises the question of whether these criteria are absolute or relative, i.e. objective or subjective. Absolute criteria involve judgments which are applied in all situations across different times where circumstances do not alter the views on right and wrong. Relative criteria arise from a view that no set of values can be regarded as superior over another set of values, a view which is linked to a belief that judgments are simply an expression of personal opinions. The question of absolute criteria in relation to establishing a consensus on a values framework arises in the National Framework put forward by SCAA, which is discussed in more detail later in this section.

Are there some core democratic values? *Caring for the Earth* (IUCN, UNEP, WWF, 1991) advocated just such a set of core democratic values. These are:

respect for reasoning; respect for truth; fairness, acceptance of diversity; cooperation; justice; freedom, equality; concern for the welfare of others; peaceful resolution of conflict. These values spell out both the rights and responsibilities that citizens have towards each other and towards nature in striving for a more sustainable world.

O'Hear and White's publication in (1991) similarly gives emphasis to the importance of democratic values as the basis of a societal and education system. Drawing on White's (1990) earlier work on altruism (see appendix, p. 16) they give particular significance to the idea of self determination, including a 'sensitive concern for the well being of others' which requires, they argue, the removal of obstacles to a self determined life — including poverty, ill health, ignorance, inadequate upbringing, restrictedness of options, being subject to the will of others, absence of law and order and inadequate social recognition. The means for the removal of these obstacles, in their view, is through citizens working together to enable individuals to develop. In particular they give significance to the acceptance of cultural differences and an avoidance of discrimination arising from inequalities of power among different groups.

O'Hear and White also acknowledge the potential conflict of values both at a culturally opposing level (i.e. where the value position was established outside a liberal tradition) and within so called 'agreed value systems' where different emphasis is given to competing interpretations of how things are best applied.

How do schools relate to these liberal democratic and competing values? O'Hear and White assert that the role of education in a liberal democracy is to promote an entitlement to personal qualities, knowledge and competencies necessary for their (citizens') well being. They give specific significance to the role of the local state school providing a revised entitlement curriculum explicitly framed by a set of values which underpin those of a liberal democracy. Such schools must allow children to deal with conflicting values in which they can be helped to resolve conflict and to appreciate the different values at stake and to weigh them up against each other, as part of their development as individual citizens.

Whilst emphasizing this approach in helping students to resolve conflicts between family and wider values, O'Hear and White stress that teachers need to be sensitive to local values and to develop understanding between schools, parents and local religions and minority communities. However, they are clear that the choice must always be left to the student as to how to weigh 'self directness' against attachment to the local community or obedience to religious authority.

The SCAA 1996 document, *Values Education and the Community*, referred to earlier, appears to accept implicitly some of the precepts outlined above of a liberal democracy. The National Forum from which it arose advocated a values framework linked to the wider society, relationships, the self, and the environment. Without assuming agreement on their source or application, these values are considered by SCAA to have a wide societal support. SCAA emphasized that these values are not to be regarded as definitive or complete, nor do they claim to offer any new perspective. In particular, the document views the principles outlined below as being more general than the specific shared values of particular religious or cultural groups.

SCAA Values in Education and the Community

Society:	We value truth, human rights, the law, justice and collective endeavour for the common good of society. In particular we value families as sources of love and support for all their members and as a basis of a society in which people care for others.
Relationships:	We value others for themselves, not for what they are or what they can do for us, and we value these relationships as fundamental to our development and the good of the community.
The Self:	We value each person as being of intrinsic worth, with potential for spiritual, moral, intellectual and physical development and change.
The Environment:	We value the natural world as a source of wonder and inspiration, and accept our duty to maintain a sustainable environment for the future.

Each value statement has an attached set of principles for action. For example there are eleven such principles attached to the values statement for society. Two of these are:

- understand our responsibilities as citizens;
- help people to know about the law and legal processes.

These value statements can be read in a variety of ways; as idealized or even native or conversely as normative and controlling, depending on the context in which they are read and applied. The statements clearly make no reference to the key element of a liberal democracy, self-determination for each citizen, as articulated by O'Hear and White. Not surprisingly, the SCAA values framework fails to address a number of the obstacles to self-determination, particularly those concerned with poverty and ill health as well as inequalities in power.

Despite this important weakness, SCAA has begun a discussion with schools and the wider society on the importance of a values framework in helping schools make explicit some of the purposes of education. The SCAA document does acknowledge the fact that the majority of schools are already working within a framework of values as identified in mission statements and sets of school aims, as well as in their policies and practices. The purpose of the document according to SCAA, is to support schools with a 'secure basis for the provision of spiritual, moral and social education' with 'a strong desire to link values and behaviour'.

Of equal importance in SCAA's view is the significance of the framework in strengthening SCAA's own position in its support of schools, with the opening of a debate on the ways that other societal institutions can assist teachers in delivering the framework. The former goal will be supported through a two year pilot study supported by guidance materials, illustrating shared values into practice, including approaches to learning and assessment.

The SCAA document also offers a reference point through a national framework, for schools to discuss and clarify their own values and make them explicit. However, the framework is deceptively simple in apparently gaining consensus on a set of absolute values. Those many schools already working actively in the area of values development will recognize the complexity of operating these in practice. A list of values principles could encourage schools to adopt these in an uncritical manner, particularly if they are adopted as a yardstick for values development in a yet again revised Ofsted Framework. Halstead, following O'Hear and White, argues that

> Schools must pay attention to the diversity of values in the communities they serve (which are themselves in flux) as well as in society at large and to the legitimate expectations of interested parties. They must examine their aims and their curriculum provision and practices to see what practices lie embedded there and must reflect on the justifiability, appropriateness and coherence of these values. In the end the statements of value that emerge may be ambiguous, provisional and less than totally clear. (Halstead and Taylor, 1996)

We believe that it is essential that schools undertake a process of making their values explicit and in doing so develop a clarity of vision. This process requires pupils to understand the link between the wider school values and their own personal values development. In making values live within an institution and offering students an opportunity to explore conflicting values, some clarifying and understanding of the statements of value may be that much less 'ambiguous and provisional'.

This process requires, we believe, a clear distinction to be made between the values themselves and the processes and tools necessary to develop this understanding and experience. It is the knowledge and understanding, skills and attitudes that should be central to the design of a school's approach to personal and social development, sustaining the values through lived experience.

Personal and social development

The personal and social development of pupils refers both to the processes of development within pupils and to the outcomes of that development. The three elements of knowledge and understanding: skills promotion and attitudinal interrelatedness of the elements exploration in an interrelated approach are all of equal importance.

- Knowledge and understanding involves a focus upon — self, interpersonal, societal and global dimensions, all of which are interdependent.
- Skills development, involving interpersonal and social communication, along with critical and reflective awareness.
- Attitudinal development involving a positive disposition and behaviour towards the self and others, known and unknown, which can sustain values of fairness, justice and equality.

To be committed to fairness, for example, requires tools, knowledge and understanding of what fairness and unfairness means within the self, local, national and international contexts as well as understanding the interconnectedness of these dimensions. It requires skills to promote effective communication and decision making to promote fairness and it requires attitudes towards respect and tolerance of the self, and others.

As we have stated elsewhere (Buck and Inman, 1992),

> Personal and Social Development involves engaging pupils in thinking about, enquiring into and discussing issues that have profound importance both at a deep, personal and at a social level. It is the constant interplay between the personal and the social that should inform our work with pupils. This requires recognition that personal growth, involving increasing self-awareness, self-esteem and confidence is a complex and even painful process which requires an understanding of the immediate, societal and global contexts in which the individual is located.

In other words personal growth always has a critical social dimension.

PSD and curriculum purpose

The title of this chapter implies that PSD could, as it were, go one way or another in the near future. Some of the difficulty in knowing where PSD might go lies in the unresolved nature of where it stands in relation to the central purpose of schooling. This is not a new question, there is a long tradition of educational thought and curriculum development concerned with the place of PSD within our schooling system. The debate has never been resolved, and the question as to the role and status of PSD is now in urgent need of answering as we move into the next century. As we and others have argued elsewhere, (Buck and Inman, 1993, Whitty, Rowe and Aggleton, 1994) despite the framing of the 1988 Education Reform Act (ERA) and the introduction of the cross curricular elements, the major preoccupation of the early 1990s was the National Curriculum and subject assessment. Any serious consideration of where provision for pupils' personal and social development should stand in relation to the overall purposes of education has, until recently, remained low on the national education agenda.

The way in which we conceive of PSD will determine its place and role within the curriculum. We have chosen to define PSD in terms of three interrelated elements: knowledge and understanding, skill promotion and attitudinal development.

These elements relate to both the personal and the social and the interplay between them.

PSD and educating the whole person

Is provision for PSD the same as educating the whole child, are they transferable terms? There has been a tendency to talk about 'educating the whole person' and PSD as if they are one and the same thing. In our view this is not the case. What is nearer the truth is that we cannot claim to educate the whole person unless provision for PSD is central to that education. The education of the whole person is to do with developing a number of capacities that encapsulate the defining characteristics of a whole person. Pring, for example, suggests that a whole person is defined by the following characteristics: knowledge and understanding; intellectual virtues; imagination; intellectual skills; self-reflection; moral virtues and habits; social and political involvement; integrity and authenticity. Pring argues that since these attributes are deeply dependent upon learning, schools must play a vital role in their formation (Pring, 1984). Clearly, not all the attributes suggested by Pring are encapsulated by PSD; there are areas of knowledge and understanding and intellectual skills that are important in their own right. PSD gives that knowledge and skills a human purpose, one that very much relates to the particular social, ethical and political structures and processes within which we live.

PSD as a curriculum strand

We can talk about the need for PSD to be central to education without being clear as to where it stands in relation to the whole curriculum. One version is to view it as one, albeit important, strand of the whole curriculum. PSD can then be set alongside other strands, and provision can be made for its development within the wider context of the other aspects of young peoples' development. It seems to us that one of the dangers of this perspective is that cognitive and intellectual development can become somewhat divorced from PSD. The latter will be seen more in terms of skills and attitude formation. This poses difficulties as it can seem to imply that, for example, spiritual, moral, social and cultural development (SMSC) does not involve the development of knowledge and understanding or the acquisition of intellectual skills. That is, that the spiritual, moral, social and cultural aspects of development do not themselves contain intellectual properties. At the simplest level the first position has often led to a curriculum model in which PSD is a strand of the whole curriculum but does not give shape and purpose to the whole. In secondary schools this has often meant that PSD equates to the pastoral curriculum or the PSE course, with subjects having little defined responsibility for this development. PSD becomes, in effect, another subject on the school curriculum, one which often enjoys low status from pupils and staff. Pring warns us of the dangers of this model when he says:

> There is no doubt in many peoples' minds that the personal, social and moral development should be a major concern of schools. But it is mistaken to conclude that the way of translating this concern in curriculum terms is to put another subject, namely PSE, into the timetable. (Pring, 1984)

While Pring's warning was written some years ago, it remains relevant today. The divorce of the intellectual from PSD also gives rise to other problems. Clearly subjects are concerned with the development of knowledge, understanding and skills that cannot be described as PSD, but it should be the contribution from PSD that gives human purpose and value to that development. As we have emphasized earlier, to become a whole person one needs to integrate the intellectual skills of reasoning, inquiry and debate with purpose and value. The dangers in separation are serious — examples abound within science and medicine where the frontiers of knowledge and understanding have become divorced from moral, social and spiritual concerns. Current examples can be found in the sphere of genetics where science has the capacity to do things that have profound moral, social and spiritual implications. The debate over cloning and choosing the gender of babies are two obvious examples of the areas of debate.

PSD as central to the task of schools

The other position is to view the PSD of pupils as the most important task of schools. In the words of the European Commission the main function of schools must be 'to guide the young people in its care in their personal and social development' (European Commission, 1995). To take this view necessitates a coherent whole school framework that specifies how PSD explicitly permeates all the work of the school. Within this model PSD is everyone's responsibility and the subjects of the curriculum must be partly defined in terms of the contributions that they can make to this development.

The second model implies that if PSD is central to curriculum purpose, then it will need to permeate a school's aims, ethos, teaching and learning, the formal and hidden curriculum etc. To use a well-worn slogan it will need to be a whole school approach in which all aspects of school life make a demonstrable contribution. Only in this way can we see schools fostering the attributes needed for the citizens of tomorrow. This is not to argue that a properly constructed PSE course does not have a place within the whole school provision, particularly within secondary school. Rather it is to say that such a course must have a clear and definable purpose which explicitly articulates with, and enhances, provision across the school.

It should be clear to the reader that we ourselves would advocate this second model of PSD. However, PSD defined in this way does not fit easily with the curriculum models that have emerged from the 1988 ERA and subsequent reforms and revisions. As we have argued earlier, despite the well known aims of the ERA to provide breadth, balance and relevance and preparation for adult life, the reality has been a curriculum dominated by subject knowledge and assessment. Even primary schools which have long been concerned with the whole child, have found it increasingly difficult to keep PSD at the centre of their work. With SCAA now publicly articulating concern for personal and social development of pupils in schools we are clear that the solution cannot be to invent new guidelines and curriculum areas for PSD, e.g. courses in citizenship as yet another addition to an already overcrowded school curriculum. The lessons of what happened to cross curricular themes and dimensions need to be remembered (Whitty, Rowe and Aggleton, 1994). We need a more radical rethink of the curriculum in relation to purpose rather than more piecemeal solutions.

Assessing PSD

This section explores some of the issues and possibilities involved in thinking about the assessment of PSD as we have defined it. In spite of the inherent difficulties involved in devising appropriate assessment mechanisms for such a complex area of human growth, we are convinced that schools must assess their pupils' progress. We cannot hold PSD to be central to the purpose of schools and, at the same time, claim that we cannot assess the effectiveness of the provision we make for it. As Pring argues:

> There is something paradoxical in holding a view that personal, social and moral development is the most important aspect of education, whilst at the same time arguing that there are no criteria either for selecting what is significant in this development or for assessing what counts as having developed successfully. If there are no such criteria then anything counts as development and there is no point in teaching or fostering one kind of development rather than another. (Pring, 1984)

Further, PSD, as we have argued earlier, essentially involves critical reflection by pupils and teachers and the development of those learning skills that are to do with self-evaluation and the setting of targets. Thus, intrinsic to PSD is a form of self-assessment whether that be made explicit through our assessment practices or not. In other words, at the simplest level, whether we like it or not, assessment must be central to PSD.

The Scottish Office Education Department has clearly taken this view. We have elsewhere referred to the curriculum initiatives in Scotland with respect to PSD (Inman and Buck, 1995). These initiatives have included development work on learning outcomes and the assessment of PSD in Scottish schools. In the national guidelines for PSD the Scottish Office states:

> It is as important in personal and social development as in other subject areas to include assessment as an integral part of the learning and teaching process. (Scottish Office, 1993)

However, it is one thing to argue for the necessity of assessing such development and quite another to find mechanisms that both adequately capture the complexities of that development and reflect the values and principles of PSD. Later chapters in this book attempt to demonstrate in some detail how we might go about this task, but at this point we shall restrict ourselves to outlining some of the issues and principles involved in assessing PSD. Before we do this it is worth reminding ourselves that while the debate over the formal assessment of PSD is relatively new, teachers have always made judgments concerning the personal and social development of their pupils. These judgments have also been recorded and reported by teachers, sometimes informally, but also through school reports and records of achievement. The latter have also involved pupils in their own self-assessment of their personal and social development. What is new and different is the attempt to make the criteria and evidence base of these judgments more rigorous, explicit and public.

Determining some principles for assessing PSD

There are a number of issues that we need to tackle in determining the principles that should underpin our assessment of PSD. These include:

1. Defining our purposes

There is wide agreement that assessment fulfils a number of different purposes. These include: establishing what knowledge, understanding, skills pupils demonstrate; diagnosing learning difficulties; planning future curriculum opportunities; ranking pupils in terms of their development; and comparing performance across schools. In terms of PSD we need to be clear as to whether assessment should fulfil all these purposes and, if not, which purposes are appropriate. In our view assessment of PSD can be appropriately used to establish the development point of pupils, it can help us to diagnose problems and can inform our curriculum planning. What is much more contentious is the use of such assessment to rank pupils or to compare performance across schools.

2. Recognizing the complexities in PSD

Our assessment must take full recognition of the different, yet interrelated areas of growth within PSD and the implications of these differences for the assessment strategies we use. The development of knowledge and understanding and skills is different from the development of attitudes and this must be recognized. As HMI made clear in their 1994 discussion paper (Ofsted, 1994) attitude development is complex in the extreme. By its very nature it is non-linear and can be determined by a host of factors many of which lie outside the control of the school. The potential effects of factors such as class, culture, gender and family circumstances cannot be overestimated. Thus, while we can draw on established good practice within assessment to devise strategies for assessing knowledge, understanding and skills in PSD, when we come to attitudes and values then our judgments will need to take account of the complexity of the development. Our judgments and the evidence base of those judgments can never be fixed or absolute, rather they will inevitably be tentative, interpretative, and set within underlying values.

3. Consistency of practice

Our assessment of the PSD of pupils must be consistent with the nature of the subject itself. If PSD includes involving pupils in self-reflection at a deep and complex level; the development of their self-esteem and confidence; the ability to give dignity to, and respect for others then our assessment processes must also demonstrate and further promote these qualities. Thus assessment must involve pupils in their own assessment, taking their reflections and evaluations seriously. They must promote pupils' confidence and self-esteem and adequately reflect our own ability to give dignity and show respect to them as well as capturing their developing capacity to do this to others. An assessment process which fails to do this will in itself act to block pupils' development.

4. School culture

Assessment which attempts to embody the qualities above will necessitate a school culture which reflects and promotes such qualities on an everyday level. Thus the formal assessment procedures will need to be accompanied by on-going relationships and ways of behaving between teachers and pupils, teachers and teachers and pupils and pupils which are consistent with the principles. Pupils must experience their voices being taken seriously in other aspects of school, and must be treated with respect and dignity. A school will need to ensure that appropriate policies and procedures are in place for these to happen (Taylor, 1996).

5. External voices

If PSD takes place as much out of school as it does within it then we need to establish how we can gather and record evidence from other external sources. The voices of parents/carers and other significant adults will need to be brought to bear in the assessment process. The parent/carer conferencing processes established in many primary schools is one vehicle for doing this. However, there are potential difficulties in bringing in a range of voices — what happens if the evidence provides a conflicting picture of pupil's development or if the criteria cannot be agreed? Schools will need to develop assessment and recording processes that can take account of differing and sometimes conflicting evidence and judgments.

6. Ownership of records

The previous issue leads us to some important ethical issues around ownership and control of assessment particularly in terms of the recording of development. The issues are to do with who the records belong to, where they go, who has access to them and for what purposes. Some have argued that the potential dangers involved in recording assessment of PSD are so great that we should not engage in formal assessment and recording processes, particularly with respect to moral and spiritual development (Merttens, 1996). We would not wish to underplay the dangers, particularly with regard to issues of ownership and control over written records. We do need to take seriously how records are written and agreed. Similarly, we need to think carefully about where records go and what part a young person should play in this decision. It may be that some parts of a record are best left as confidential, with the pupil retaining the right to decide how to use it.

Principles for assessing PSD

Exploration of these issues naturally leads us to a number of principles which we believe should underlie assessment practices with respect to PSD. These can be summed up as follows:

1. The purposes of assessment should be explicit to teachers, pupils and parents/carers. These purposes should comprise: the establishing of points of development for individual pupils, the diagnosing of difficulties; and informing future planning. Comparisons between pupils and schools should not form part of the agenda.
2. Assessment processes must be appropriate to what is being assessed. We must distinguish between those learning outcomes to do with knowledge and understanding and skills on the one hand and those to do with attitudes on the other.
3. Assessment must distinguish between development that is roughly 'linear' and that which is clearly sometimes non-linear in nature.
4. Pupils must be engaged in self-assessment including dialogue with adults that is both valued and used and takes place over time.
5. Assessment processes must themselves reflect and promote the PSD of pupils.
6. Assessment must involve a range of appropriate adult voices and evidence as well as that of pupils.
7. Whole school culture embodied in policy and day-to-day practices must be consistent with PSD and the assessment processes used to establish development.
8. There needs to be a partnership in the ownership of records of assessment. That partnership must be agreed between pupils, teachers and parents or carers.

Conclusion

This chapter has argued that PSD must be central to curriculum purpose. We have suggested that PSD comprises the acquisition of interrelated knowledge and understanding, skills and attitudes and that these together help to enable young people to sustain values within their lived experience. The assessment of PSD must capture these interrelated components, thus providing a rich portrait of a young person's development. This is a daunting task and one that has only just begun. The principles for assessment in PSD outlined in this chapter are one contribution to moving in this direction.

Note

1 Perhaps less publicly aired but significant in these events was the role played by the teaching union, the NAS/UWT.

References

BUCK, M. and INMAN, S. (1992) *Curriculum Guidance No. 1: Whole School Provision for Personal and Social Development*, Centre for Cross Curricular Initiatives, London: Goldsmiths College.

BEVIN, A. (1996) 'The 11th Commandment: Thou shalt not pass the buck', *The Independent*, 28 October 1996.

BUCK, M. and INMAN, S. (1993) *Curriculum Guidance No. 2: Re-affirming Values*, Centre for Cross Curricular Initiatives, London: Goldsmiths College.

EUROPEAN COMMISSION (1995) White Paper on Education and Training.

HALSTEAD, M. and TAYLOR, M. (1996) *Values in Education and Education in Values*, London: Falmer Press.

HUTTON, W. (1997) *The State to Come*, London: Vintage.

INMAN, S. and BUCK, M. (ed.) (1995) *Adding Value*, Stoke on Trent: Trentham Books.

IUCN, UNEP, WWF (1991) *Caring for the Earth*, Gland: Switzerland. Earth Scan.

MERTTENS, R. (1996) 'Children's personal development: The ethical implications', in HALSTEAD, M. and TAYLOR, M. *Values in Education and Education in Values*, London: Falmer Press.

NCC (1993) Spiritual and Moral Development: a discussion paper, York: NCC.

OFSTED (1994) Discussion Paper on Spiritual, Moral, Social and Cultural Development, London: Ofsted Publications.

O'HEAR, P. and WHITE, J. (1991) 'A National Curriculum for all: Laying the foundation for success', Education and Training Paper No. 6, Institute for Public Policy Research.

PRING, R. (1984) *Personal and Social Education in the Curriculum*, London: Hodder and Stoughton.

SCAA (1995/96) Discussion Papers No. 3 and No. 6 on Spiritual and Moral Development, London: SCAA Publication.

SCAA (1996) *Values in Education and the Community*, London: SCAA Publications.

SCOTTISH OFFICE EDUCATION DEPARTMENT (1993) *Personal and Social Development 5–14*, Edinburgh: Scottish Office.

Tate, N. (1996) Speech to the SCAA National Symposium Education for Adult Life.

Taylor, M. (1996) 'Voicing their values: Pupils' moral and cultural experiences', in Halstead, M.

White, J. (1990) *Education and the Good Life*, London: Kogan Page.

Whitty, G., Rowe, G. and Aggleton, P. (1994) 'Subjects and themes in the secondary school: Curriculum research papers', *Education*, **9**, 2.

Appendix

John White (1990) warns against making a virtue of moral education within education for democracy in favour of a focus upon education in altruism. He argues that morality brings with it 'rigidity, a tendency to fanaticism, an unwillingness to compromise and a pervasive tendency to blame oneself and others for moral defects'. He argues instead for the development of altruistic dispositions which involve:

- being attached to those close to one;
- having less intimate but still warm relationships with those with whom one comes into infrequent contact;
- being well disposed to strangers with whom one has face to face contact;
- being attached to one's local community;
- being attached to institutions of which one is a member and which one sees as conferring benefits on others;
- being disposed to fulfil special obligations one incurs in a social role e.g. parent;
- being disposed to honour the general obligation one occurs in making promises or contracts;
- being impartial between claims between one's own and other's claims amongst those of others;
- being disposed to protect others' well being in general;
- being prepared to promote others' well being in general; and
- possessing altruistic virtues.

Chapter 2

Personal and Social Development within the National Context: A Review of Recent and Current Initiatives

David Trainor

Abstract

The purposes of education are hotly debated but always at the centre of disagreement is the emphasis that should be given to transmitting subject knowledge. Some models highlight the importance of personal fulfilment through the discovery of self. Other views set personal happiness and fulfilment against the need to turn out a useful economic citizen and consider the community. This chapter traces the struggle between the different views of education. It identifies a strong tradition for balancing the economic, social, moral and personal within education but shows how, despite enshrining such noble aims in law, the current concern with standards measured in subjects, teaching method and accountability, have marginalized many of these highly prized elements of the curriculum and the means of achieving them.

Background theory

From Plato and Aristotle onwards the debate about the nature and purpose of education has raged. This is not the place for an in-depth review. In brief the key issues have been:

- The importance of knowledge cf the skill of problem solving;
- The relative importance of attitudes and personal qualities, cf. the acquisition of specific subject knowledge and skills;
- Whether education should pursue knowledge and wisdom for its own sake (educating the individual) or should concentrate on the needs of society;
- Should education be primarily for the few or for all?

Though these themes endure, the division of opinion has become sharper and the need to find solutions in a world of rapid change is more urgent. The older educational philosophers must be seen in context and we must not be too easily seduced by their resolution of the argument. When education was provided only for the few, individual tutors or groups of a very small size were the norm. The essential content of the curriculum was limited and it was possible to integrate the learning of this basic knowledge and skill with developing personal qualities. There was no problem of 'getting a quart into a pint pot'. The methods of instruction could be flexible and suited to individual need. After a long period of economic and technical change, the situation is now very different.

Today we find it difficult to select from the enormous corpus of current knowledge, that which is essential to a good education. The pressure to cover all the desirable knowledge makes it difficult to fit in other aspects of education. Yet much of what is deemed invaluable never seems to come to our aid in life, while we are constantly having to learn new things. The pressure on the curriculum means that there is often little time to indulge in a programme of personal development and we are forced to seek ways of achieving such goals on the back of teaching subject matter. Since much personal development depends on particular knowledge and skill, a fresh tension arises; if more content or different content is needed, something must be ditched and the agony of determining the National Curriculum continues to reflect these problems. Such problems have become greater in the modern era because we no longer educate just a few select pupils in small groups.

Today's teacher knows that it is important to develop the individual not just for their own sake but because society needs that talent; yet because **all** pupils must be educated, it is necessary to teach (relatively) large groups together and often to subserve their individual needs to the group goal. We have not always got the balance right and the debate has been particularly intense in the past twenty years.

It is worth noting that the debate is going on world wide and that those countries which are identified as 'doing well' in one way or another are often dissatisfied with aspects of their own performance. It is of particular interest that while England casts envious eyes on the levels of achievement in Japan, especially in mathematics, the Japanese are envious of the creativity and flair generated in England. Most of the leading Japanese manufactures are reported to be buying the majority of their design/styling from the UK and there has been an upsurge of interest among many Japanese families in buying an English education for their children. The reasons for this are doubtless complex and do not mean that our curriculum is 'right' or that our personal and social development (PSD) provision is universally good, but we should beware throwing some of the baby out with the bathwater!

Some of those who have sought to improve the educational outcome have said that the problem arises from an over-concern for subjects. They believe that the pressure on curriculum time is due to an over specification of subject content and that it leads to a predilection for a didactic teaching style which is inimical to the best PSD. This chapter does not seek to challenge the organization and delivery of the curriculum through subjects. We may not always have the right subjects and sometimes there is a case for a change in the prescribed content of a subject, but it is difficult to see how a public education system could function without subjects. A public education system has to use structures, both for reasons of economy and accountability, and however curriculum content is packaged some form of subject structure is inevitable.

The great debate

A growing interest in the nature and purpose of education and the standards achieved at the end of compulsory schooling was evident in the mid 1970s. Her Majesty's Inspectorate (HMI) was determined to use its professional expertise and knowledge of the system to provide a lead. The Curriculum Publications Group (CPG) was established by the new Senior Chief Inspector, Sheila Browne, in May 1975 and this enabled HMI to make an informed and thoughtful response to the 'Great Debate' launched by Prime Minister James Callaghan's Ruskin College speech in October 1976. It is instructive to re-read some of the documents.

Educating Our Children was published by the Department of Education and Science (DES) to inform debate at a series of regional conferences held in February and March 1977. The subjects of debate were:

- The School Curriculum 5–16
- The Assessment of Standards
- The Education and Training of Teachers
- School and Working Life

It will be immediately apparent that these themes have continued to direct debate up to the present day. Not surprisingly there are some important principles stated. In paragraph 2.1 we read:

> In addition to establishing basic skills, the curriculum should enable children, as part of their essential general education to understand the society of which they are a part, including the economics of everyday life and the role of industry and commerce in sustaining our standard of living. Our society is changing rapidly; not only is technology constantly advancing, but we now live in a multi-cultural and multi-racial society which the curriculum needs to reflect.

The paper helpfully goes on to balance the need for greater specification of the curriculum at national level, and a guarantee of national standards, with the need to retain the diversity which should arise when teachers use their particular gifts and the resources available locally, to meet children's needs. A sentence from paragraph 2.4 should not be forgotten: 'It is unlikely, however, that a common core, or even a common curriculum, described solely by reference to subject names, will advance us sufficiently far in the analysis of needs'.

These issues are teased out further in *Curriculum 11–16* — the so-called 'Red Book' — which established the baseline for a practical partnership in curriculum development between HMI and some schools in five LEAs over the period 1977 to 1983. Section 1 of these papers arguably sets out the best and most comprehensive justification for a wide ranging programme of education; but the individual subject papers, which were supposed to illustrate how the curricular ideal could be achieved showed just how diverse opinions were in HMI and how not everyone was prepared to sacrifice the pure goals of subject teaching to this common goal. It is possible that some did not fully understand this goal, and in particular the eight areas of experience which were to be the template for curriculum construction. It is certain that not all shared the same vision.

These problems reverberated in the partnership activity. There were many objectives common to subject departments in the participating schools. In particular, to develop and foster:

- An understanding of society;
- personal and social skills;
- study skills;
- communication skills;
- decision-making skills;
- the ability to make reasoned judgments; and
- an awareness and respect for the environment.

There was a strong philosophical commitment to the notion of a curriculum defined in eight 'Areas of Experience'. Despite this, schools and teachers clung tightly to specific subject knowledge and skills, the delivery of which often prevented such wider objectives being achieved. It was difficult to develop commitment to Areas of Experience at the chalk face. For example, an internal review found that the 'creative' area corresponded to art and that the creative aspect which runs across disciplines was largely ignored.

The conflict between subjects and areas of experience was most strongly seen in respect to the aesthetic/creative, the ethical and the social/political.

In the developing national debate there was increasing criticism of early specialization and 'breadth and balance' became watchwords of those judging the curriculum. Pressures of time prevented all subjects being given reasonable time in all years of schooling, but if something had to be dropped, would it be possible to achieve a justifiable coverage? To what extent might art or music or one of the design and make subjects provide a parallel experience and make an equal contribution to developing the individual? Similar questions were posed in relation to the role of history, geography and RE and the ethical and social/political areas.

Some schools offered optional choices, others developed integrated courses. Integrated humanities was popular across the secondary age range and creative arts courses developed strongly under TVEI (see below). Pressures on such developments came from many sources and were based mostly on fears that children of the future would not have specific knowledge that could be traditionally tested. A change in subject content always gives rise to fears of falling standards. These criticisms might have been averted if HMI had more loudly proclaimed 'Whether or not it is found that standards have remained constant, risen or fallen over some past period is less important than whether the standards which are being achieved today correspond as nearly as possible to society's requirement' (*Educating Our Children*, paragraph 3.3).

Another possible solution, widely discussed, was for subjects to have very different time allocations in different years; in some years a subject might not appear at all. There is much merit in such ideas and arguably the desire to see subjects equally represented is responsible for much of the current pressure on the primary school curriculum. Then, as now, it received short shrift mainly because the pay and prestige of subject teachers is based upon the allocation of time to their subject. Furthermore in secondary schools 'developing a sound body of factual material and a good attitude towards the subject such that they might regard it as a foundation for continuing study and interest' (unpublished geography review in Red Book project) is widely responsible for keeping going the traditional approaches and content of academic disciplines.

Despite these difficulties, belief in the broad objectives of education remained strong in the period up to 1985. *A Framework for the School Curriculum* (DES, 1980), *A View of the Curriculum* (HMI, 1981), *The School Curriculum* (HMSO, 1981), the White Paper 'Better Schools' (Cmnd. 9469, 1985) and 'The Curriculum from 5 to 16' (*Curriculum Matters 2*, an HMI series) are just some of the papers that carried the torch as the nation continued to seek agreement. The precise phraseology varied but the purposes of learning stated in paragraph 44 of 'Better Schools' are sufficient to illustrate the strength of commitment to a programme of PSD.

1. to help pupils to develop lively, enquiring minds, the ability to question and argue rationally and to apply themselves to tasks, and physical skills;
2. to help pupils to acquire understanding, knowledge and skills relevant to adult life and employment in a fast changing world;
3. to help pupils use language and number effectively;
4. to help pupils to develop personal moral values, respect for religious values, and tolerance of other races, religions, and ways of life;
5. to help pupils understand the world in which they live, and the interdependence of individuals, groups and nations;
6. to help pupils appreciate human achievements and aspirations.

Technical and Vocational Education Initiative (TVEI)

Many of these concerns became prominent in the Technical and Vocational Education Initiative (TVEI) which was launched in 1983, and after a short pilot phase was extended to all LEAs during the 1980s. TVEI was funded by central government in an attempt to make education more directly relevant to adult and working life. Initially it was shunned by many schools and teachers who perceived TVEI as a move towards narrow vocational training. It rapidly became apparent that what employers wanted was a review of the curriculum which would seek greater relevance in the content of subjects and a commitment from schools to developing those attitudes, values and personal qualities which make for a good citizen and employee.

It is important to note that most employers did not seek a ready-trained employee; they wanted people who were likely to be trainable quickly and who would be dependable and responsible. They recognized too that it was in their own best interests for society to remain stable and peaceable.

TVEI was responsible for promoting changes and developments of a kind which linked with some aspects of the Red Book exercise. In particular, TVEI sought to explore and promote:

- courses with an applied or practical bent. (Business studies received a particular boost, but technology, caring, catering, agriculture and creative arts were also stimulated);
- a change of attitudes to gender stereotyping;
- links between subjects and the place of cross curricular themes;
- teaching styles and assessment techniques which would bring some objectives not measured by current examinations more sharply into focus;
- a broader base to the post-16 curriculum.

Not all TVEI developments were a success and not all that were deemed successful survived the changes wrought in the 1988 Education Reform Act (ERA). However, it was possible to see that with different teaching styles and with different approaches to course structure and assessment, standards could rise and pupils could have their personal development enhanced. The firm belief of industry in these outcomes was to prove vital in the evolution of the National Curriculum (NC).

The coming of the 1988 Education Reform Act

Draft proposals for the ERA, published in 1987, reflected a public and political impatience with the failure to resolve the tensions in the education system. It was decided that a National Curriculum should be closely defined in subject specific terms and there was no mention of the broader PSD objectives. This caused concern to many interest groups, not least industrialists involved in the TVEI project. As a result of their many and strong representations, Section 1 was added to the bill. This states:

> The curriculum for a maintained school satisfies the requirements of this section if it is a balanced and broadly based curriculum which:
> (a) promotes the spiritual, moral, cultural, mental and physical development of pupils at the school and of society; and
> (b) prepares such pupils for the opportunities, responsibilities and experiences of adult life.

The National Curriculum Council (NCC) set about meeting this legal requirement by establishing a Whole Curriculum working group. The group tackled its remit with vigour and eventually a series of ten helpful booklets were produced and five 'Cross Curricular Themes' were identified. All the problems evident in the previous debate are to be seen in this work, with the added problem that ERA had changed the culture. We already knew that auditing subjects to identify cross curricular opportunities was difficult, and effective delivery was even more so; now teachers had their eyes firmly on the completion of the NC subject orders and schools and governing bodies were beginning to be exercised by test results and impending league tables.

Given the need to raise standards and the desire to 'get the new curriculum right' it is not surprising that there was little enthusiasm for the five themes. Faced with the eternal problem of how much of the wide PSD agenda depended on teaching additional content and how much was about developing skills, attitudes, values and personal qualities, the NCC erred towards content. This is hardly surprising since the prevailing wind was in favour of clearly defined content which could be tested. Teachers wanted the clarity so they would not inadvertently fail in their duty; others wanted this clarity because the only reliable testing to provide a basis for evaluating the success of the ERA and establish a baseline for league tables would have to be based on content. It left schools faced with five themes that looked like five additional subjects. This not only posed problems about time allocation but raised questions about available teaching expertise.

Change in the 1990s

In view of these developments, it is not surprising that the draft of the 1992 Education (Schools) Act should have concentrated on establishing an inspection regime based on standards in subjects and value for money. However with the NC settling down there was a growing recognition among parents and public that 'ethos and values' were important, even if they could not be measured easily. Many surveys purported to show that parents chose between schools on the basis of such intangibles. This may not be strictly true because examination success matters to such parents, but certainly in comparing schools with like standards it is the values and personal development which often determine choice. Anyway, whatever the cause, the Northbourne amendment to the bill in the House of Lords introduced a requirement for the newly created Ofsted to report on what schools do to promote 'the Spiritual, Moral, Social and Cultural, development of pupils at those schools', (Education (Schools) Act, 1992, section 2). SMSC, as it became known, thus emerged as the most difficult challenge facing Ofsted as it developed the framework for the inspection of schools.

Immediately all the old issues re-emerged. How would schools deliver SMSC, and where would inspectors look to find it? Would it be taught (and therefore inspected) by a team of specialists using timetabled lessons, or would it be found across the curriculum (in which case how would subject inspectors cope)? There was, however, one overriding issue and that was to define each of the terms. From

Red Book onwards a certain looseness in the interpretation of PSD objectives and themes had been evident; from now on it would be necessary to have greater clarity. The new framework for inspection was designed to measure the success of each school in meeting national expectations and there would not be room for the kind of reporting related to individual circumstances which had characterized some former inspection practice.

Ofsted and SMSC

The Ofsted approach to SMSC holds up well to scrutiny. The first framework had to be in place for September 1993. Consultation was as widespread and detailed as possible, but in an area as difficult as this there was no pretence that a good solution had been found. Definitions and criteria were given, but it was acknowledged that much more work, in the light of experience, was needed. My own job description required me to explain Ofsted thinking; to examine the outcomes of inspection; to listen to, and note, comments from schools; and to debate possible change and improvement in both definitions and criteria. The first HMCI, Professor Stewart Sutherland, had a keen personal interest in the area and addressed a number of the very many conferences held. A consultation document was written within Ofsted and after the text had been debated with an invited group of people with varying interests and expertise, was published in February 1994 ('Spiritual, Moral, Social and Cultural Development' an Ofsted discussion paper, February, 1994).

The consultation document was sent to all schools and widely circulated elsewhere: over 40,000 were eventually distributed. A review of the framework was in hand and in order to get as many useable responses as possible in a short time, a questionnaire was issued and responses requested within six weeks. This strategy was regrettable for it gave many people the impression that Ofsted was not serious in its intent. Nothing could be further from the truth! In the event a sufficiently large number of individuals and schools replied to make the exercise very worthwhile. I personally read about 1,000 responses, some of which came from individuals and some from organized group consultations. Some came from 'experts' but in the main they reflected the concerns and views of heads, teachers, governors, local elected members and diocesan education committees.

The foreword to the discussion paper articulates the issues well. In recognizing the importance of values in education it is seen to lie within the tradition established by HMI in the Red Book and all that followed; it makes it clear that personal development and the transmission of values are not easy and require a whole school commitment. 'Put simply, personal development cannot be hived off into one segment of school life, confined to such activities as assemblies, acts of collective worship, or classes in religious, personal or social education . . . if schools have a general statutory duty to encourage moral development, then that surely applies to those teaching, say, history or science, just as much as to those taking assemblies'. But it also raises issues pertinent to the 1992 Act and the new system of inspection.

Inspection of SMSC

The 1992 Act and the new system of inspection were unashamedly about judging the outcomes achieved by schools and despite the many obvious pitfalls in seeking to reach such judgments in SMSC, the first framework was internally consistent in its approach. It was, after all, reflecting a public mood which sought to measure school effectiveness and increase accountability. By the time the discussion paper was produced it was clear that this line had to be moderated for SMSC. Thus the discussion paper sought to open up the question of how much attention should be given to outcomes.

> It is tempting, but mistaken, to suggest that inspection should focus only on provision. If inspection fails to lead to any judgment of the effects and effectiveness of the educational processes, it is not performing its full function. (Ofsted, 1994)

If professional inspectors felt that they ought to be able to reach some view about the quality of SMSC outcomes, so too did many teachers. However, teachers were concerned that judgments which are difficult for them when taken in the context of a full knowledge of the pupils and their background, and over a long period of time, are simply not possible in the context of a week's inspection. The major concerns expressed could be summed up under four heads:

1. Is development in SMSC a linear process from which we might expect to see some clear progression?
2. How can the contribution of the school be isolated from influences at home and in the locality?
3. Where will inspectors seek their evidence?
4. How will SMSC be interpreted by inspectors? Will there be a consistent approach? If there is a clash of values, whose values count?

There was an overwhelming belief that inspection should focus on processes rather than outcomes; as the law put it, on 'what schools do to promote' SMSC development.

If Ofsted was genuinely concerned to explore and resolve such problems, there were some glaring procedural errors. SMSC was expected to be a cross curriculum issue but the guidance given to subject inspectors did not offer such prompts and the lesson observation pro-forma did not encourage reportage of SMSC activity. Almost from the outset the responsibility for SMSC matters was placed in the hands of one member of the inspection team and it did not always benefit from a wide-ranging whole team discussion. Although Ofsted worked hard to dispel the myth that spiritual development was not to be confined to assemblies and RE lessons, the framework pulled in that direction and required a judgment on the legality of the provision of collective worship in the section on the spiritual.

It rapidly became clear from the reports on inspections that a narrow and somewhat 'religious' view of the spiritual was the norm. It was also clear that there was considerable confusion between the moral and the social. Good moral development was most often equated with a pleasant ethos and good relationships and there was little evidence that the positive development of values and their application to complex issues was expected to feature in a curriculum. Likewise there appeared to be little expectation of specific attention to the links between social development and the knowledge and skills of a good citizen. The cultural suffered from an over easy equation with 'multi-cultural' and occasionally from a narrow view of high culture. Many schools declared that they were unhappy with the inspection coverage in SMSC.

Change and development in the framework

Strenuous efforts were made to improve the situation through guidance notes, training courses and conferences but the much needed improvement had to wait for the revised framework which came into operation in April 1996. Keen observers will note that there are significant changes in the criteria and guidance which reflect well on the consultation process but the pressures for a reform of the framework came from many quarters and sadly not all the most desired changes came to pass. In particular the changes to the recording of lessons inspected and the reporting of subjects still did not encourage a proper whole school approach to SMSC.

The 1992 framework grouped spiritual and moral together in Section 5.3 and social and cultural were joined in Section 5.4. This unhelpfully blurred the distinction between the parts of each pairing and at the same time suggested that there was a real gulf between the two sections. The criteria were understandably vague but sought outcomes: e.g. 'An evaluation of pupils' spiritual and moral development' and 'An evaluation of pupils' awareness and understanding of social and cultural matters'. Other prompts required inspectors to comment on the way that the curriculum and other aspects of school life contributed to the quality of the school community and pupils' attitudes to people, property etc. All this is perfectly proper but there was a strong feeling that in the context of the whole framework, too much emphasis was being placed on judgments of behaviour and attitude over which a school might have little influence.

The 1994 revision gave ample evidence that Ofsted had been actively engaged in a consultative process. A fuller and more helpful definition of each of the four terms was provided and they were linked together in a single section, 5.1. Each of the criteria began with 'is to be judged by how well the school promotes' and this shift towards the processes of PSD made the requirement to seek and judge 'how pupils respond to that provision' more acceptable to all concerned.

The current framework, revised in 1995, continues the shift of emphasis made in 1994. In continuing the shift away from the original focus on outcomes to a focus on what schools do to promote pupil development, it is noticeable that reference to pupil response is dropped and that the focus is firmly on active promotion by the school; i.e. ethos and atmosphere alone are not enough. In elaborating the criteria each section begins 'Does the school' followed by 'teach', 'provide', 'encourage'. There is a strong reminder to all concerned that the four elements of SMSC will inevitably interlink and that evaluation should reflect this. These changes are supported by changes in other parts of the document. Particular improvements in the new framework, all of which were pressed in the consultation are:

- A wider more inclusive view of the spiritual which sees the religious dimension as a part of a broad approach to the human condition; the requirement to report on the legal compliance with the law on collective worship is reported in a different section. There are important references to receiving and valuing pupils' ideas across the curriculum which have implications for teaching styles.

- A stronger definition of the moral which emphasizes the importance of ethical principle in determining moral behaviour rather than the fear of punishment or reward. This establishes an important distinction from compliant social behaviour, in which people obey the law despite the fact that they may disagree with the morality on which it rests. The guidance also suggests that pupils' ability to apply moral reason may differ from their observed behaviour; this is very important in reaching a sound judgment, not least when a school makes good provision which challenges accepted values in a so-called difficult neighbourhood.

- An introduction of the word 'citizenship' into the criteria for the social, along with references to group work and cooperation which again have consequences for teaching styles.

- The criteria for 'cultural' seek to balance 'their own and other cultural traditions', a matter which many schools sought to emphasize in the consultation. There is a need to start from where pupils are — i.e. an appreciation of their local culture — before moving outwards. It is perhaps a pity that the exemplars still hint at a high cultural perspective and neglect to emphasize the ways in which politics, law and technology, for example, shape our culture.

There were two other changes of significance. The first was the creation of a separate section (4.2) on Attitudes, Behaviour and Personal development. There was much debate about where different aspects should sit within the framework. There is no one simple solution, but by separating the reporting of behavioural outcomes from SMSC provision the revised framework makes it likely that inspection will more clearly identify what schools do in their curriculum to promote SMSC. It should also mean that there will not be the same tendency to equate schools in so-called 'good' catchments with 'good' SMSC and vice-versa. The second was to give schools the opportunity to set part of the inspection agenda in Section 3.1. Without compromising the function of inspection as external audit, this change does allow a school some room to draw its particular problems and plans into the inspection focus. Those schools which complained that their inspections neglected some good and interesting work on SMSC will in future have only themselves to blame if they do not use Section 3.1 to highlight their aims and then monitor the inspection team to see that they deal appropriately with such matters.

With these changes the framework is probably as good as it can be at this point in time. We are dealing with a difficult area and it will take time for inspectors and schools to reach a consistent view on where and how evidence may be sought and interpreted. With clearer criteria in place the most likely cause of inconsistency of inspection judgment will be the balance struck by a team between process and outcomes. There is much ambivalence in schools here, for though they welcome the shift towards an evaluation of process, teachers are aware that they have some outcomes in their objectives and that they make frequent subjective assessments of pupils' current state and recent progress. Further improvement will be dependent upon better national guidelines from SCAA. Only when the specification of the curriculum and the Orders for each subject take account of PSD can we expect to see a greater consistency of provision, more clarity in the divide between process and outcomes, and more consistency in the judgments of inspectors.

National dissonance

Two parallel developments did not help SMSC. They were the revision of the National Curriculum (The Dearing Review) and the national concern about effective teaching styles.

There was considerable pressure for a reduction in the subject specifications within the NC but in its published comments to SCAA on the review, Ofsted said:

> Some statement of the principles underpinning the NC and of the values it seeks to foster and develop through individual subjects would appear to be timely. Such a statement could form part of an overview statement about the curriculum as a whole and, in this way, help to develop a sense of unity of purpose among the teachers of the various subjects and their pupils. The advantages of a unifying set of educational principles to which all of those involved in education can subscribe are overwhelming. Such a set of principles should be drawn up so that the spiritual, moral, social and cultural goals which the curriculum is in law charged with serving will be made more explicit and linked more closely to the work of individual subjects. (Ofsted response to SCAA consultation on draft proposals for the National Curriculum: July 1994, para. 30)

Most practitioners and commentators feel that with no such principles declared, the revised NC is even less helpful than its predecessor to those seeking help with SMSC. The slimming of the orders, in the main, removed those few prompts to SMSC within subject teaching. Many people felt that science in particular had become somewhat mechanistic and that the absence of SMSC pegs impoverished the subject, as well as the curriculum. In setting in motion the Values Forum and announcing its intention to address such matters at the next NC review, SCAA has given a welcome and important signal.

Teaching styles have always been a matter of legitimate concern and regardless of the success or otherwise of the different approaches it is clear that some methods work well with any teacher and others do not. HMI have indicated time and again that a variety of teaching styles is needed, firstly because some intended outcomes depend on particular methods, and secondly because not all pupils learn effectively in the same way. This concern is reflected in the guidance on judging teaching in Section 5 of the present framework. If there is a weakness from the SMSC perspective it is that these criteria do not recognize that the best methods for securing mastery of NC subjects may not always secure good PSD. Pupils will not develop responsibility and initiative if their work is always heavily directed by teachers: likewise they will not learn to collaborate and work in groups unless given the opportunity. Individual self-knowledge and self-esteem of the kind that are important in spiritual development will depend on some recognition of an individual who is not always swept along in the tide of whole class teaching.

That said, we know that well planned and directed class teaching is a cost effective way of developing basic subject skills and knowledge. Recent work on the teaching of reading has emphasized the virtues of formal, whole class teaching (*The teaching of reading in 45 Inner London Primary Schools*, Ofsted*, 1996). Unfortunately, such subtleties are often missed in public debate and with the strong pressure for improved standards many of the teaching methods needed for successful SMSC are being rejected in favour of a formal, whole class approach. The significance of league tables and measurable outcomes is such that few heads or governors can ignore those methods which might bring improved success. Although most people value SMSC, it is not yet possible to establish a measure which might be of use to a school in establishing its status. It is like the dilemma facing a sports team — is winning **all** that matters or do style and entertainment also matter?

Personal and social education

The PSE curriculum

It is as a result of the above dilemma that recent years have seen a growth of separate PSE provision. Schools recognize the need to do something, but the pressure to deliver 'pure' subject outcomes allied to the acknowledged difficulty of achieving success in cross curriculum delivery, makes for a separate timetable slot. This is immediately self-defeating since pupils then regard such lessons as deviant to the main thrust of the school. There is ample evidence to suggest that putting attitudes and values in a separate box, the content of which is not examined and is rarely included in reports, and which is taught sometimes by teachers lacking expertise, does not give PSE lessons appropriate status. If, in addition, the teachers use different teaching methods in those lessons, which are rarely if ever used in the main subject curriculum, the problem is compounded. In any attempt to raise the status of PSD/SMSC it will be necessary to try to improve cross curriculum teaching (a matter which now awaits the next SCAA review) and/or to make some progress with assessing PSD outcomes. These matters are explored in other chapters but a few comments are appropriate here.

Assessing PSD

Whatever the reason, that which is regarded as important by society is that which is tested and accredited. There is no doubt that PSE frequently has low prestige with pupils and that schools and teachers give it very low priority, even when they claim to be fully supportive of the idea. In an attempt to combat such problems attempts have been made to accredit personal skills and qualities and thus to put PSE on a par with other subjects. Notable among such moves have been the efforts of the vocational bodies, with City and Guilds in particular working with schools on its course 365 and successors. TVEI saw numerous attempts to advance the cause, not least with unit accreditation and profiled records of achievement. The National Youth Awards typify another of the approaches.

As yet no development has really captured public confidence nationally, though there have been some examples of particular schools gaining some credibility for a scheme with some local employers. Apart from the difficulty which always attends the acceptance of new certification, the particular problems in PSD derive from the essentially subjective nature of the judgments. These are issues which always arise once we cease to test pure knowledge or to assess outcomes of measurable quality. Amongst the things it would be good to accredit are: determination; initiative; ability to plan and make decisions; to find and handle information; to manage time; and to work with others in a team. The difficulty for the assessor is to separate such judgments from the outcome. Schools also have to decide whether any such assessment should be confined to the work done in PSE time or whether account should be taken of PSD evidenced across the curriculum. The ideal must be to treat PSD as a whole curriculum issue and assess accordingly, but since many of the substantive areas of learning (e.g. drugs, citizenship and the world of work) are at present found in PSE lessons only there is also a strong case for starting from there.

For example, what both the pupil and any certificate user want to know is not whether action steps can be planned, timescales set and adhered to, but whether in following the plan something of quality emerges; not whether information is found in a wide variety of formats and used, but what quality of information is found and how well it is used. These are the kind of issues facing SCAA and NVQ in developing GNVQ. A close inspection of the skills and qualities which have regularly come to the fore would probably reveal that they could be put into two groups. In the one would go all those abilities which really cannot, and should not, be assessed away from the assessment of the quality of outcome. In the other would go those assessments of the individual which have validity on their own — so long as the user is prepared to trust the assessor's subjectivity — because the outcome itself is not capable of easy objective measurement.

There are skills and abilities which are only valid in the context of the outcome. For example, 'determined and well planned attack on the painting of a house, though the job lacked a good quality of finish and took two days too long'. There is no reason why such integrated profiles should not be produced. If two people can produce an equally good outcome, why should we not know which of them achieves this result with a good grace and demonstrating the flexibility that suggests the skill could be transferred? But there are also the more detached and subjective matters. For example, the effective group operator will not always win the day and an assessment of the ideas contributed, negotiated and refined, or of the effect of that person on group morale will depend on an observer — perhaps confirmed by the group itself. In like manner the important characteristics of self-control, initiative, personal behaviour, and the ability to be critically aware of self and able to remedy defects must depend on an observer. In this list are qualities which will have positive outcomes when nothing happens! For example, **resisting** taking drugs or joining in destructive gang activity.

There are two requirements for such subjective assessment to be widely accepted. They are: that society trusts teachers to make such judgments; and that the school gives status to those activities which provide the opportunity for the skills and qualities to develop. Both are difficult at the present time. Recent education reforms have challenged teacher assessment and the obsession with external tests as the only valid means of accreditation will take time to change. Giving status to SMSC is equally difficult, for, as explained in this chapter, there is no easy solution to cross curriculum delivery, little stimulus within existing NC orders, and some of the teaching styles necessary for success in personal development are perceived to be out of favour.

There is no denying that some of the necessary improvement will depend on changes at national level. Teachers should recognize that much useful development in the past has arisen from work done at the chalk face. As schools begin to seek ways of making their educational vision a distinctive part of their marketing, it will become necessary to show how the achievement of that vision is evaluated. Progress will depend upon teachers conducting experiments and sharing their results with parents and employers until a cost effective solution is found.

References

Department of Education and Science (1977) *Educating Our Children: Four subjects for debate*, London: DES.

Callaghan, J. (1976) 'Towards a National Debate', Speech at Ruskin College, October 1976.

Department of Education and Science (1980) *A Framework for the School Curriculum*, London: DES.

Department of Education and Science and Welsh Office (1981) HMSO *The School Curriculum*, London: HMSO.

DES (1988) *Education Reform Act 1988*, London: DES.

DES (1992) *Education Schools Act 1992*, London: DES.

HMI (1977) 'Curriculum 11–16', working papers by HM Inspectorate: a contribution to current debate, December.

HMI (1985) HMSO *Better Schools*, Cmnd. 9469, London: HMSO.

HMI (1985) *The Curriculum from 5 to 16*, HMI Curriculum Matters Series No. 2, London: HMSO.

HM INSPECTORATE (1991) *A View of the Curriculum*, London: HMSO.

NATIONAL CURRICULUM COUNCIL *Curriculum Guidance Series* (1990) ten booklets in all, numbers 4,5,6,7 and 8 deal with cross-curricular themes. York: NCC.

OFSTED (1992/1995) *Framework for the Inspection of Schools*, Her Majesty's Chief Inspector of Schools, August 1992; Revised May 1994. New Edition 1995. London: OFSTED.

OFSTED (1994) 'Response to SCAA consultation on Draft Proposals for the National Curriculum', July. London: OFSTED.

OFSTED (1994) 'Spiritual, Moral, Social and Cultural Development', an Ofsted discussion paper, February. London: OFSTED.

Chapter 3

'It's Not a Good Time for Children' — Assessment Issues within Personal and Social Development

Pauline Lyseight-jones

Abstract:

This chapter looks at a number of issues related to assessment and personal and social development. It contends that methods of assessing in personal and social development are possibly the least problematic aspects of this work. The chapter opens with a brief discussion about current national assessment practice which has moved from initial attempts to assess the process of learning and provide information which was relevant to the learner and teacher, as well as the parent, towards an assessment of a narrower range of outcomes, in the name of reliability and accountability. The chapter goes onto explore presumptions which underlie effective personal and social development and asserts that these are also the conditions which need to be present in the school setting if effective work is to be done.

Introduction

'It's not a good time for children' said the father whose son was about to transfer to secondary school. Our education system remains in a state of change but, at its core, the focus remains academic achievement. Yet, both children and adults need a wide range of skills and knowledge to be reasonably effective. The school system tends to focus on literacy and numeracy as the premier paths to achievement. All too often other talents are overlooked. This is wasteful. It must lead to those whose gifts lie in other directions leaving school with a nagging sense of failure, a feeling of not having fulfilled their potential.

Assessment practice today

Current assessment practice is moulded by the demands of the National Curriculum or external assessment bodies. This means that assessment tends to be linked to a taught curriculum. The current National Curriculum emphasizes English, mathematics and science. These three subjects are formally assessed at the end of Years 2 and 6 and assessment practice has developed to meet the externally decided assessment tests and tasks.

The history of National Curriculum assessment tells us an interesting story. The original intention of test developers (Sainsbury, 1996) was to produce authentic assessments which would have the capacity of assessing process elements of the National Curriculum in English, mathematics and science as well as assessing subject knowledge. Process based assessment is based on the assumption that learning is complicated, multi-faceted and non-linear. Nursery and reception teachers will plan for teaching, with a range of developments in mind; emotional, spatial, intellectual and so on. They will present curriculum through a range of means, through music, writing, movement, exploration. They will also assess, over time, through the collection of work samples, noting significant events, words or actions or taking account of other adults' experiences with the child. Their reports on the child's progress will set intellectual and academic development in the context of other development and will consider the full range of children's achievements.

However staff who had to administer the first National Curriculum process based assessments found it hard to manage them in the classroom. They required time to plan, implement and analyse and the constraints on teachers' time and the high value given to performance tables, meant that only the most committed staff were able to put them into practice adequately. The reactions of many teachers suggested that process based assessment was best suited to teacher assessment, running alongside formal tasks and tests. Successive revisions of the curriculum and the assessment process have led to a narrowing of the type and range of the assessments. Typically, the assessments are written and, as far as possible, pose questions to which there are specific answers or solutions. This type of assessment runs counter to all that we know about the way people learn and the way in which people express their understanding of what they have learned.

1. A presenter or bureaucracy decides what is to be learned.
2. The presenter teaches and makes up the test.
3. The participants study what they think will be in the test.
4. The participants take the test.
5. The presenter grades the test, based on what [he or she] decided was important.
6. The participants usually forget what they studied a few hours/days after the test.
7. The cycle repeats itself. (Jensen, 1996)

This cycle creates stress for the learner and stress for the teacher. It runs counter to good teaching and learning practice.

If we believe that people are a consequence of the interconnection of their elements, it is difficult to see how a child's academic development can be brought to its optimum without due regard and attention to other domains of experience. This is why personal and social development is crucial.

Personal and social development — some attributes

Personal and social development happens, with or without assessment; its quality and direction may be affected by the insight which assessment might bring. The attributes which we would wish to develop within personal and social development would include:

- independence;
- making judgments and decisions;
- learning from past actions and practices;
- cooperation;
- collaboration, developing the ability to link one's interests with those of the immediate community;
- developing the ability to plan and then to act on social and moral issues;
- developing the ability to plan and act on plans which are about situations outside of first-hand experience;
- developing an understanding of the role of the news media, political systems and pressure groups; and
- identifying bias.

In assessing these areas we are presented with a different set of concerns than would arise if the assessed area were an element of the mathematics curriculum, for example, 'recognize rotational symmetry of 2D shapes'. This is because the prerequisites for the assessment of these attributes in personal and social development are a further set of personal aspects. These aspects would include the development of confidence and self-esteem; we are starting to move perilously close to assessing the conscious self — and if it were found wanting, what then?

This issue is echoed in the assessment of religious education. As SACREs were devising their religious education syllabuses so the matter of assessment needed to be discussed. The debate goes like this — religious education has its place in the curriculum. It is a compulsory subject; other subjects describe what needs to be achieved at points in a child's school career; to know whether the child has reached a particular sign post, testing or assessment has to occur; progress in each subject has to be reported to the parent; we must make sure that religious education can be assessed as well. Unfortunately, assessing science achievement and assessing the extent to which a child, through learning from religion, has gained 'curiosity about the world we live in and the meaning of life' are very different activities and need to be recognized as such. Assessment in and of personal and social development has similar difficulties.

Assessment and personal and social development

The assessment of elements which link with a child's personal and social education brings us face-to-face with our own psychological health, our view on family structures, sanctions, belief systems and ultimately, our view of the current structure of the schooling system. Modelling systems tends to be a way to have others emulate them, having understood their value; it remains difficult to assess the elements which relate to children's personal and social development. If healthy examples are not able to be observed in the classroom, school or local community, including the home; it becomes an abstract exercise.

Spiritual, moral, social and cultural development

An integral part of personal development is expressed through the composite term, spiritual, moral, social and cultural development but these terms are not interchangeable. The four main questions which relate to these areas, as expressed in the framework for the Inspection of Schools, OFSTED 1995 are:

> Does the school provide its pupils with knowledge and insight into values and religious beliefs and enable them to reflect on their experiences in a way which develops their self-knowledge and spiritual awareness?
>
> Does the school teach the principles which separate right from wrong?
>
> Does the school encourage pupils to relate effectively to others, take responsibility, participate fully in the community and develop and understanding of citizenship?
>
> Does the school teach pupils to appreciate and develop their own cultural traditions and appreciate the diversity and richness of other cultures? (Ofsted, 1995)

Dealing with these is far from easy and local education authorities describe aspects of each development area more fully in their guidance on religious education for schools (for example, Harrow, 1995; Appendix). Even so, the assessment of these aspects is far from straightforward. It requires clarity about the nature of each particular term so that teachers can provide the context for progress. The outline below attempts to provide this clarity.

Spiritual development • *recognize breakthroughs*
• *build on enthusiasm and creativity*

thereby increasing the possibility that children experience awe, wonder and mystery. Spiritual development has within it the capability for 'eureka' moments, where children are lost for words because they have been uplifted by joy or brought to a sudden understanding — the teacher role is to consider the kinds of activities that might promote this.

Moral development • *establish a framework for fair decision-making*
• *develop forums for discussing the moral implications of school activities*

thereby beginning to use the outcomes of assessments to alter personal circumstances. Through good assessment in this sector children can begin to look at justice systems, personal, school and national, in a more realistic way.

Social development • *evaluation of the role of team membership*
• *contribution of the individual self to the whole*

thereby starting to decide individual goals within a context of knowledge about personal strengths. Children should be better able to be ambitious about their futures.

Cultural development • *valuing the range of cultures*
• *coming to an understanding of connections*
• *developing a clearer idea about personal choices*

thereby developing a firmer sense of belonging based on personal confidence and developing a personal view about quality. This area should lead to children being able to make links between cultural icons, artefacts, events, rituals and phenomena and being able to come to a personal appreciation of them.

To assess these areas effectively we have to use a range of assessment strategies, frequently and regularly, we have to agree that fulfilment of these aspects will be found in a variety of settings, both in class and elsewhere and that the accuracy of the assessment is more likely when the child is a part of the assessment system or endorses the outcome.

Elements in assessing for personal and social development

A key to assessing effectively in personal and social development (PSD) is to accept that the basic framework for assessment has to be broadened and built upon. The strategies, settings and involvement of children which are listed below are examples of the range.

Strategies
- examinations of children's work
- classroom observation
- observation in other settings

Settings
- in class
- in assemblies
- at play

- marking work
- talking to children
- setting specific assessment
- tasks or activities — role play
  debate
  written account
  evaluations
  self assessment
  group assessment
- taking photographs
- using video recording
- using audio recording

- on visits
- at lunch
- in small groups
- in pairs
- as an individual
- with a teacher
- with an adult other than a teacher

Involvement of children
- choosing what is to be assessed
- recording own views formally — on assessment record
  on the work
- building up a personal portfolio
- choosing a range of work to be in the portfolio
- annotating the work in the portfolio
- devising assessment criteria and measuring own progress
- writing/recording own commentary on annual report to parents
- deciding personal targets

But taking random parts of the range makes little sense unless the range itself is set in a clearer context. A suggested context is discussed below.

Talents and intelligences

Children tend to do their best when they are free from stress, when they feel safe and when they have feelings of personal capability and a trust in the group. The class setting and the curriculum have to be developed with these elements as central factors. In addition, the teacher has to keep a constant eye on the effect of the setting and the curriculum on children's learning. The teacher needs to be prepared to make necessary changes to improve matters. The work on multiple intelligences (Gardner, 1983; Lazear, 1994) can contribute much to this debate. This area is one which repays careful study, but briefly, the contention is that there is not one intelligence i.e. that which is measured by intelligence tests, but there are several. The intelligences which have been identified so far are;

1. **Linguistic**: a facility with language, patterning and systems
2. **Mathematical and logical**: likes precision and enjoys abstract and structured thinking

3. **Visual and spatial**: thinks in pictures and mental images, good with maps, charts and diagrams, uses movement to assist movement
4. **Musical**: sensitive to mood, enjoys rhythm, understands complex organization of music
5. **Interpersonal**: relates well to others, mediator, good communicator
6. **Intrapersonal**: self motivated, high degree of self knowledge, strong sense of values
7. **Kinesthetic**: good timing, skilled at handicrafts, likes to act and touch, good control of object (Smith, 1996)

Smith goes on to list further characteristics of each intelligence.

Effective teachers need to recognize that these groups of intelligences or talents exist (and that there might be more intelligences, as yet undefined. Clearly, there is overlap between the characteristics of each intelligence. In recognizing the intelligences it is also necessary to accept that people's preferred learning styles may also fall into one or several of these categories. In many ways, the multiple intelligences approach brings together much of what teachers, children and others have been saying over a number of years. The recognition that people have identifiable, distinct but interlocking or interconnecting intelligences is sensible. What is of more concern is the viewpoint that two of the seven currently identified intelligences predominate in the school value system — the areas of logical-mathematical intelligence and verbal-linguistic intelligence (Lazear, 1991). This means that only the children with talents which match the presentation and assessment of the curriculum will appear to succeed. Other children may find school depressing, unsettling or confusing. Many may be demoralized and will lose their confidence, as they move from being the 3-year-olds who knew that they could paint to the 11-year-olds who know who the class artists are (and it's not them).

Self esteem, self belief and stress

Lack of self esteem and self belief creates losers. The central work of those in personal and social education is to help people to realize their potential. Self belief and self esteem are necessary prerequisites in this task. Smith (1996) writes,

> The development of positive self-esteem and self-belief in learners contributes to the physical condition of relaxed awareness which optimises learning. It allows learners to set realistic and achievable goals whilst having a sense of one's own strengths and limitations. Learners with positive self-esteem are less likely to be plagued by self-doubt and the negative self-talk which comes with it. They are less likely to go into stress [. . .]. A school, college or training organisation which intervenes, at all levels, to build and maintain positive self-esteem and self-belief in learners, takes an important step in increasing the likelihood that new skills and knowledge will be transferable and lifelong. (Smith, 1996)

The reference to stress by Smith needs to be expanded somewhat. Challenge and determination are stressful but they are not necessarily bad, in the same way as pressure may be a spur or a hindrance to action. In our schools, there is a need to consider the systems — including assessment — which contribute to stress in children and try to humanize the systems. Jensen (1996) writes about positive stress (or eustress) which occurs when we feel we have, as he says:

- desire to solve the particular problem;
- the ability to resolve a problem;
- some control over a situation;
- sufficient rest between challenges; and
- perceived a solution to a problem. (Jensen, 1996)

This list is instructive as it puts both teachers and children in the same emotional field. For teachers, the range of education initiatives can lead to frustration, powerlessness and feelings of anger and failure. Children, increasingly, are put under pressure to perform well in English, mathematics and science, and little else. Older children could be forgiven for thinking that no grades matter at GCSE other than A, B and C and that any other grade means failure. Looking at employing effective assessment in a personal and social development context will support the teacher at least as much as it will support the child. This is because to do such assessment well, good conditions for teaching and learning have to be in place.

The necessary development of assessment practice

It could be said that the actual circumstance of assessment practice today indicates that we value what we assess and not the contrary. The assessments which we are increasingly expected to value are those which can appear in rank-ordered tables. As noted before, the areas assessed tend to be concerned with particular priority subjects and specific elements of those subjects — particularly subject knowledge. Access to better assessment practice needs to be improved. This is because our children will take their lead from us. Our responsibility is to identify and to assess what we value — even if it is complicated or time-consuming. The likely consequences of such an approach are so hopeful, so essential to the mental health of many of us, that it is difficult to see how we can continue to give succour to such a narrow, national approach to both assessment and education.

Lazear (1994) examines old and new assessment paradigms in the context of multiple intelligences. He notes as an example of the old assessment paradigm, that 'there is a clearly defined body of knowledge that students must master in school and be able to demonstrate or reproduce on a test' and of the new paradigm 'teaching students how to learn, how to think, and how to be intelligent in as many ways as possible, (that is, creating lifelong learners) is the main goal of education.'

The points which he makes are practical starting points when reviewing teaching, learning and assessment systems. The difficulty is to take the time to build better assessment systems and put them into practice. Lazear (1994) gives many practical examples of ways in which the whole child may be assessed, so that the range of their talents may be recognized. The realization of many of the schemes would take much teacher time in and outside of class. Even so, one of the practical aspects about having to consider assessing across at least seven intelligences is that the tools or methods through which the assessments will need to take place will need to match those intelligences. Therefore, the assessment schedules also show the wide scope of possible differentiation in classroom work. Differentiation in planning for teaching is a problematic area for many teachers. By making clearer the approaches which can be used to assess each intelligence, teaching practice is also clarified. The quality of information about children's learning would be improved and teachers' teaching might be better targeted, but manageability and time have become at least as important to many teachers as authentic assessment of the whole child. Authentic assessment implies assessment which is devised alongside and is integral to the curriculum. While this does not preclude the current assessment regime and the tools which that regime uses, authentic assessment expects that demonstration or 'performance' (Wiggins, 1984) is a valid means of expressing achievement or learning. Lazear (1994) encapsulates the notion well.

> If we are concerned with students' deep understanding of what they are learning in school, I believe we must provide them with opportunities to be examined in a wide variety of ways on the same information, all with the purpose of giving them opportunities to 'show off' what they have learned — to demonstrate or 'perform' their understanding — rather than using testing as occasions to tell them where they have failed and what they don't know.

Of course, the presumption is that the curriculum would have within it tasks and topics which would appeal to the learning preferences of children.

What assessment cannot do

Personal and social development is intimately concerned with the individual and how and why the individual negotiates their way through systems and how and why the individual works alone and with others. PSD attributes, such as self-confidence and the capability to analyse, can be identified in a school setting, and can be built upon through judicious planning and good teaching. Taking full account of children's talents or intelligences when planning for teaching will inevitably take into account personal and social development. Intrapersonal and interpersonal intelligences are crucial in this respect. Planning for teaching in this way will need to have assessment at its core. The assessment practice will have to have the capability of recognizing what kind of learning styles are preferred by individual children. If such a planning and assessment system were successfully employed we would like it to have made some difference, for the better, for the individual learner, when that learner was in school or elsewhere. But even good assessment cannot change current family systems or other institutions; children who have learned about fairness and justice, who are valued members of teams, who have discovered their own talents for making music or who have a growing appreciation of their individual selves in a social world may find that these attributes are not welcomed or understood in their homes. That said, some parts of the taught curriculum which have raised a number of moral issues have had and do have an effect on children and their home lives. The growth of environmental education which can incorporate discussion of conservation leads to discussions about the conditions of the planet and animal welfare. Many children take a personal journey and become vegetarians and/or recyclers following such work in schools and can be as firm in their adherence to the practice of vegetarianism or recycling as a zealous reformed smoker. The benefit of work in personal and social development is its potential for contributing to changing the outlook of individual children, which may lead to stronger, clearer thinking, more responsible adults. Assessment does not achieve this. The system into which the assessment is incorporated may achieve it.

The demands on teachers

There are a number of considerations for teachers as they try to put in place a curriculum for personal and social development and its allied assessment.

Modelling PSD

The most pressing need is for teachers to put the school aims into practice and ensure regular review. This tends not to pose a problem for the academic aims or parent-partnership aims, but is less secure in respect of those aims 'ensuring that each child fulfils their potential' or 'helping a child to be confident and caring'. As indicated earlier, the key to this issue is the extent to which the internal working of the school models the behaviour that it wishes children to emulate. Children learn about: social, moral, emotional and other issues by their own experience and by the way in which they see such issues interpreted around them. Many schools describe their overall aims for their children in esoteric terms. This vague and idealistic approach can be a gift when applied to PSD, the scope is so wide. Precisely because of this, teachers have to have done some personal work, and be committed to continuing this, as they build a personal and social development curriculum. As in other educational areas where ideas intertwine and become connected to personal and community values, the teacher should expect to be aware of an ideological construct towards which they should be trying to move their schools. This is modelling with meaning and commitment.

School self-image

The second area to be considered is the view which the school community has of itself. The image held is mirrored in children's attitudes about the school and about themselves as learners. One of the effects of the prominence of national task and test results is that it seems to be creating a greater polarization of views about what is a good or successful school and what is a school that is poor or unsuccessful. Ofsted inspections bolster this growing tendency to label the quality of schools on a range of criteria using instruments of measurement which would not pass muster, in their current state, if offered as integral parts of an education research programme. There is the danger of unnecessary animosity and undue complacency developing in the profession as external indicators, such as those above, are taken out of context. Teachers in schools which top the performance tables may perceive themselves to be good teachers. Teachers whose children do not do well may see themselves as poor teachers. The discussion is not whether teaching quality is directly and positively linked to national assessment results in English, mathematics and science. The discussion is about how teachers convince their children, in this competitive climate, that they can be effective learners — whether they are in a 'good' school or not. One of the most difficult acts for staff is to ensure that children remain optimistic and keen learners even when their school is at or near the bottom of national or local performance tables. The reflection on achievement, the how, why and what value needs to be orchestrated by staff. For staff to do this effectively they must be successful learners. Schools which truly embrace Investors in People need to show that staff development is at the core of their activities and that means all staff not only teaching staff.

Teachers' expectations

The third area of consideration is the expectation of children by teachers. All too often the determining factors in such expectations are the social and economic setting of the school. The work on value-added is both a strength and a weakness, in this respect. The use of contextual features, like the socio-economic background of children, explains more of children's achievement than other factors, such as birth dates. Even so, the proportion of academic success that is explainable, in any case, is limited and much of the variance in academic performance of groups children remains unexplained — just as it was when Plowden reported in 1967. This means, in effect, that there is all to play for — teachers should expect to make a difference and a compassionate glass ceiling should not be imposed on the achievements of socially and economically disadvantaged children. A perceptual and, possibly, an ideological shift on the part of some education professionals is necessary.

Valuing children

The fourth, and most **important** demand on teachers is that they conscientiously seek to develop the self-esteem and confidence of the children whom they teach. The link between low achievement, disaffection and a low self-image is well made. Emphasizing the importance of personal and social development by assessing it might help to avoid such situations.

> One of the reasons children don't want to be in school is because they experience a sense of failure, which is obviously talking about curriculum issues — the appropriateness of the curriculum and the level of teaching for individuals. I think it is one of the key areas — how do you make all children feel valued, even those who are not academically able. *Educational Psychologist*, (Kinder et al., 1995)

In addition, teachers have to ensure that they meet current assessment and reporting requirements which will shortly be expanded by the implementation of compulsory baseline assessment for children who are beginning school. Teachers will be making assessments on children's achievements in National Curriculum subjects and religious education. They will be writing and assessing targets for individual children through individual education plans and they will be assessing children's English language needs, if children are potential candidates for extra support. Clearly, this represents a considerable task for the individual teacher.

Ways forward

The overall premise in this chapter is that the key to children's personal and social development is the way in which they view themselves, the extent to which they see their own individual and group identity. Assessment in this area cannot concern itself solely or even mainly with end products but with the complex processes of the development of critical awareness of the self. A climate and a context have to be set which provides a fertile environment for personal growth. Children will then have the strength to look outside of themselves, to take on responsibility and to work with others.

Work in special educational needs is often the most enlightened when looking at ways in which children's personal and social development may be enhanced. Hendrick Keefe (1996) provides an excellent example, discussing notions of the learner and the learner's environment as well as how to use the assessment data which has been gleaned from small-steps planning, effective teaching and good record-keeping. These are elements of most systems of good practice in teaching and learning.

We need to

- try to find out what our children think and need;
- involve children in designing their environment;
- help children to teach each other and to learn from each other;
- encourage group tasks and activities;
- record achievement; and
- try to find out what our children think and need.

Circle Time and schools' councils can be of use here but other structured approaches may be helpful. Lawrence (1996) devised the Lawseq questionnaire which can help teachers to assess children's self-esteem and can be used both before and after implementing a self-enhancement programme in school. Rowland (1984) emphasizes the worth of discussions with children and of listening well. His transcript of a discussion about God between three children and himself is an illuminating example of the teacher accepting children's suggestions about the accuracy of his recordings, the conclusions which can be drawn and the next steps which could be taken. Discussions about devising school or class rules can also contain these elements. Radnor (1994) discusses the use of talk as a focus of enquiry and as an assessment tool and lists as the four principles underpinning such talk as:

1. personal development;
2. the stressing of individual uniqueness;
3. the articulation and appraisal of achievement; and
4. the assessees being responsible for assessing themselves.

This arose from a wider project on 'Assessing Achievement in the Arts' and represents a clear aim to use the process within dialogue as an assessment tool.

Involve children in designing their environment

Weindling (1987) discusses the changes which secondary headteachers make in the first days and months of their headships and the way in which staff perceive these changes; staff make a clear distinction between cosmetic or superficial change and change which has a positive impact on their work and the work of the school. Children are no different and can perceive the difference between tokenistic, busy work and real involvement. So, tasks such as redesigning the playground, developing a wild area or re-organizing the classroom can show children that they can make a difference. The evaluation of their work is the quality of the daily realization of their plans being put into practice.

Help children to teach each other and to learn from each other

Many schools have systems that do just this. The systems include paired reading, writing and illustrating books and making toys for younger children and children booking lesson time to read a newly enjoyed story or poem to the class.

Encourage group tasks and activities

Cooperative learning is a major element in personal and social development. Le Métais and Jordan (1996) list five main principles which apply to this style of learning. Group tasks and activities can be planned to develop children's social skills like negotiation, and be linked with pleasure and cultural development as well as delivering aspects of the curriculum, for example, theatre trips, residential visits, fund-raising and music, drama or dance performances.

Record achievement

Teachers already record a range of aspects of children's achievement and development either within curriculum records or in pastoral profiles. The final record tends to be written or it might be the inclusion of examples of the child's work, appropriately annotated. Yet children's achievement may be evidenced in other ways. The practice, common amongst teachers of younger children, of using a clipboard or sticky paper tabs, focusing on a specific child or activity and writing quick, contemporaneous notes of significant achievement can lead to the development of better observation on the part of teachers and to improved planning for teaching. Audio and video recording have a part to play in understanding the wider range of children's achievement such as turn-taking in discussion or play. Setting tasks which require children to evaluate their own work, and to keep a record of that evaluation, are also valuable. Photographs can provide a record of work in process that no other record is able to do, sometimes giving clues to the ways in which individual children approach practical tasks and how they solve practical problems.

Conclusion

The discussion on assessment in personal and social development cannot avoid including thoughts about the type of schools we want for our children and the kind of teachers we want children to be taught by. The range of assessment tools is wide but of all of the possible methods of assessment the most crucial is observation. Nutbrown, 1996 writes,

> Children need well-educated educators with knowledge at their fingertips, adults working with them who:
> - **see** what is happening
> - **understand** what they see and
> - **act** on what they understand.

This seems to be a reasonable set of pre-conditions for staff who wish to enable children to fulfil their emotional, academic and intellectual potential.

References

Creemers, B. (1997) *Effective Schools and Effective Teachers*, Occasional Papers Centre for Research in Elementary and Primary Education, Warwick University, UK.

Department of Education and Science (1967) *Children and their primary schools*, London: HMSO.

Department of Education and Science (1995) *Framework for the Inspection of Schools*, London: HMSO.

Gardner, H. (1983) *Frames of Mind: The Theory of Multiple Intelligences*, New York: Basic Books.

Harrow Education Advisory Service (1995) *Religious Education, Curriculum Guidelines for Schools: Harrow Agreed Syllabus*, London Borough of Harrow, Education Advisory Service.

Hendrick Keefe, C. (1996) *Label-free Learning — Supporting Learners with Disabilities*, Maine: Stenhouse Publishers.

Jensen, E. (1996) *Brain-based Learning*, California: Turning Point Publishing.

Keys, W., Harris, S. and Fernandes, C. (1995) *Attitudes to School*, Windsor, Berks: National Foundation for Educational Research.

Kinder, K., Harland, J., Wilkin, A. and Wakefield, A. (1995) *Three to Remember: Strategies for Disaffected Pupils*, Windsor, Berks: National Foundation for Educational Research.

Lawrence, D. (1996) *Enhancing Self-esteem in the Classroom (2nd edition)*, London: Paul Chapman Publishing.

Lazear, D. (1991) *Seven Ways of Knowing: Teaching for Multiple Intelligences*, Illinois: Skylight Publishing.

Lazear, D. (1994) *Multiple Intelligence Approach to Assessment*, Carmarthen: Zephyr Press.

Le Mètais, J. and Jordan, D. (1996) 'Groups or rows? — a cooperative learning perspective', *Topic*, **15**, Spring.

Nutbrown, C. (1996) 'Wide eyes and open minds — observing, assessing and respecting children's early achievement', in Nutbrown, C. (ed.) *Respectful Educators — Capable Learners — Children's Rights and Early Education*, London: Paul Chapman Publishing.

Radnor, H. (1994) 'The problems of facilitating qualitative formative assessment in pupils', *Topic*, **12**, Autumn.

Robson, M. (1997) 'How teachers can help children manage stress', *Topic*, **17**, Spring.

Ross, M., Radnor, H., Mitchell, S. and Bierton, C. (1993) *Assessing Achievement in the Arts*, Milton Keynes: Open University Press.

Rowland, S. (1984) *The Enquiring Classroom*, London: Falmer Press.

Sainsbury, M. (ed.) (1996) *SATs — The Inside Story*, Windsor, Berks: NFER.

Smith, A. (1996) *Accelerated Learning in the Classroom*, Stafford: Network Education Press.

SCAA (1995) *Spiritual and Moral Development*, London, SCAA: Schools Curriculum and Assessment Authority.

Weindling, D. and Earley, P. (1987) *Secondary Headship — The First Years*, Windsor, Berks: NFER-Nelson.

Wiggins, G. (1984) in Lazear, D., *Multiple Intelligence Approach to Assessment*, Carmarthen: Zephyr Press.

Appendix — The Contribution of RE to Spiritual, Moral, Social and Cultural Development

A pupil's spiritual development might include;

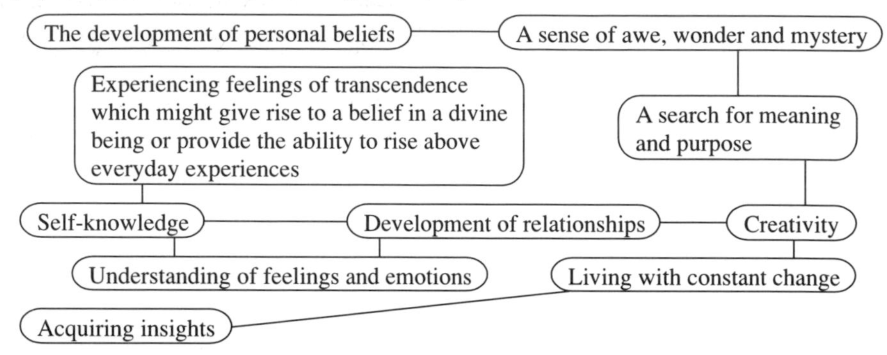

A pupil's moral development might include;

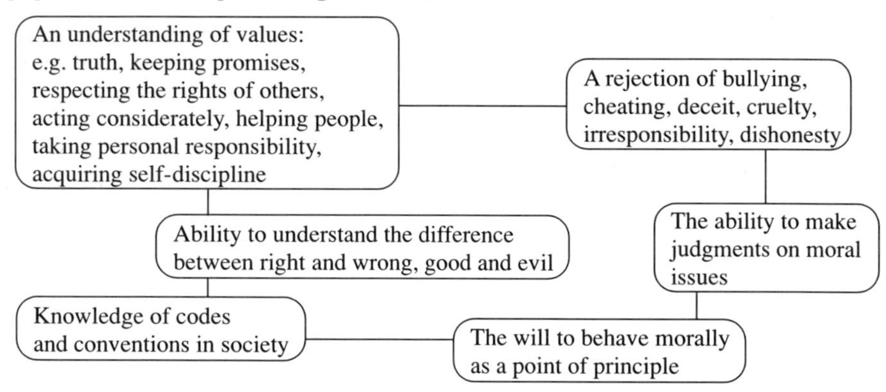

A pupil's social development might include;

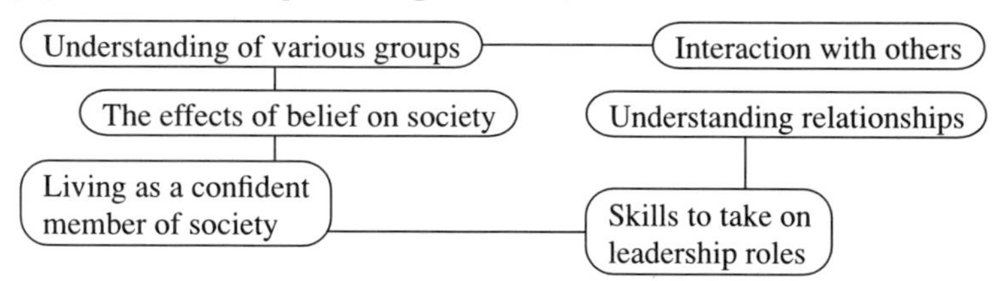

A pupil's cultural development might include;

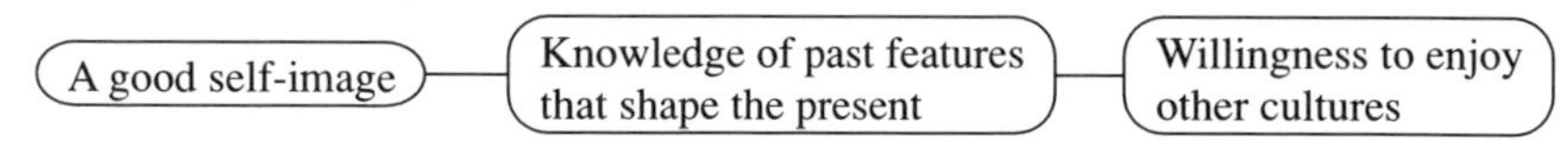

Attainment Targets 1 and 2, the programmes of study and learning experiences in the Harrow Agreed Syllabus of Religious Education take account of all these and give opportunities for development.

Reproduced by kind permission of the London Borough of Harrow — School Development Services.

Chapter 4

Learning Outcomes for Personal and Social Development

Sally Inman and Martin Buck

Abstract

Earlier chapters have made the case for assessing personal and social development (PSD) and explored some of the issues involved in establishing an appropriate system of assessment. In this chapter we focus on learning outcomes for PSD. We review recent and current thinking about learning outcomes for PSD as reflected in SCAA and Ofsted guidance and requirements and then outline what *we* believe to the appropriate learning outcomes. Finally, we focus on the relevant curriculum planning taking the reader through a professional development exercise reviewing policy and practice on anti-bullying as an example of how we might most effectively plan for, and assess, PSD learning outcomes.

In Chapter 1 we provided a definition of PSD and its role within the whole curriculum and suggested that PSD comprises the knowledge and understanding, skills and attitudes that young people will need if they are to sustain agreed values. Put another way, PSD is essentially about some very complex but specific learning outcomes.

Schools' aims as stated in mission statements will almost invariably include reference to PSD learning outcomes. The following example is not uncommon. 'Our mission is to ensure an education which promotes excellence and provides all our students with **the confidence and skills** to meet the challenges of the twenty-first century'. However, there is often still a gap between these high-level aims and the necessary policy and practice required to enable such aims to be realized. Part of the filling of that gap lies in the precise identification of the PSD learning outcomes, which should enable schools to make them more explicit to the learner, teacher and parent, and to enable judgments about development to be more authentic, verifiable and accountable.

Learning outcomes for PSD — changing requirements

Much of the discussion about PSD has, until recently, tended to be predominantly concerned with provision rather than product. However, the HMI (1989) paper

Figure 4.1: SCAA — Steps to spiritual development

- recognizing the existence of others as independent from oneself
- becoming aware of and reflecting on experience
- questioning and exploring the meaning of existence
- understanding and evaluating a range of possible responses and interpretations
- developing personal views and insights
- applying the insights gained with increasing degrees of perception to one's own life

began to rehearse some possible learning outcomes for PSD (HMI, 1989) and we can trace the development of HMI thinking through subsequent Ofsted papers and in the Ofsted Framework (Ofsted, 1993, 1994 and 1995). In our own early work in this area we attempted to spell out some generic learning outcomes for PSD (Buck and Inman, 1992). In retrospect these were a curious mixture of knowledge and understanding, skills, attitudes and values. At the time we were less clear than we are now of the difference between PSD and values and thus the two were sometimes conflated in this early work. Nevertheless, we were attempting to define some of the essential attributes required from emerging new citizens and the work proved useful in helping schools to review and evaluate their own shared values and learning outcomes for PSD. In the early 1990s the Scottish Office Education Department produced guidelines for learning outcomes for PSD 5–14, (Scottish Office, 1993). Elsewhere we have referred to the significance of this piece of curriculum development (Inman and Buck, 1995). The emergence of the Ofsted Framework for the inspection of schools in its changing form (Ofsted, 1993, 1994, 1995) and the Ofsted discussion paper of 1994 (Ofsted, 1994) provided further exploration of outcomes, with a particular focus on the learning outcomes associated with spiritual, moral, social and cultural development. While there were problems with the Ofsted view of PSD learning outcomes within the discussion paper (Buck and Inman, 1995), there is no doubt that the attempt to specify knowledge and understanding, skills and attitudes sharpened the thinking about PSD and helped to set the scene for later developments around assessment. The most recent Ofsted Framework distinguishes between provision and outcomes and specifies the outcomes associated with particular areas of PSD. These areas are those defined within section 4.2 of the current Framework, 'Attitudes, Behaviour and Personal Development'. The NCC and later SCAA have also begun to take the issue of outcomes seriously. The NCC (1993) discussion paper attempted to specify outcomes for moral development (NCC, 1993; reprinted SCAA, 1996, No. 3). The SCAA (1996) paper went further in suggesting points of progression in outlining what it described as steps to spiritual development (see Figure 4.1).

Also in 1996, as a part of the Desirable Outcomes for children's learning, SCAA produced some PSD learning outcomes for young children. These are

Figure 4.2: Desirable outcomes on entry to compulsory schooling: PSD (SCAA, 1996)

- children are confident
- show appropriate self respect
- are able to establish effective relationships with other children and with adults
- they work as part of a group and independently
- are able to concentrate and persevere in their learning and to seek help where needed
- they are eager to explore new learning
- show the ability to initiate ideas and to solve simple practical problems
- they demonstrate independence in selecting an activity or resources and in dressing and personal hygiene
- they are sensitive to the needs and feelings of others
- they show respect for people of other cultures and beliefs
- they take turns and share fairly
- they express their feelings
- they behave in appropriate ways
- they develop an understanding of what is right, what is wrong and why
- they treat living things, property and their environment with care and concern
- they respond to relevant cultural and religious events
- they show a range of feelings, such as wonder, joy, or sorrow, in reponse to their experiences of the world

described as an important component of the 'goals for learning for children by the time they enter compulsory education'. The document also describes the key features of progression for the learning outcomes, which can be seen in Figure 4.2.

Parallel to these initiatives others in the field were also taking more interest in learning outcomes. Chapter 6 in this book describes one such national project, Pathways towards Adult Life and Working Life. This project specifies learning outcomes for a range of areas of PSD and also provides Key Stage progression points.

In summary, a number of agencies have begun to take the issue of learning outcomes for PSD more seriously and common to all these initiatives is the attempt to define appropriate knowledge, understanding, skills and attitudes more closely. Where they differ is in the level of specificity in determining these outcomes; and in the extent to which they attempt to deal with progression.

Defining appropriate learning outcomes for PSD

If we are to tackle the issues around assessment of pupils' development then our learning outcomes need to be defined in ways that make the assessment process

Figure 4.3: Guidelines for planning assessment in PSD

Knowledge and understanding

Spiritual
- Knowledge of philosophical and religious ideas and practices
- Understanding of expectations and interpretations of origin and meaning of universe
- Understanding one's own beliefs

Moral
- Knowledge of the ideas and language of morality
- Know the difference between right and wrong
- Understanding the nature and purpose of moral discussion
- Understanding of the self and one's own personal values in relation to personal, interpersonal, local, national and global issues

Social
- Knowledge of the functioning and organization of societies
- Understanding of personal relationships and how individuals relate to others in situations
- Knowledge of how institutions function
- Understanding of rights and responsibilities within a social setting

Cultural
- Knowledge of one's own cultural traditions and practices
- Knowledge of other major cultural traditions
- Understanding of the diversity of cultural and political traditions

Skills

Spiritual
- The ability to give an account of our own beliefs

Moral
- The ability to articulate values
- Able to persuade others through moral reasoning
- Listening to others
- Sensitivity and respect for others' viewpoint
- Able to make moral decisions based on reason
- Ability to form moral judgments

Social
- Capacity to adjust to a range of social contexts, to show appropriate and sensitive behaviour
- Able to take on different roles — leader, team worker
- Can exercise initiative
- Can exercise responsibility
- Cooperates with others
- Make a strong contribution to the well being of social groups
- Forms effective relationships

Cultural
- Skilled in a range of cultural fields
- Able to relate school knowledge to wider cultural structure

Attitudes and values

Spiritual
- Attitudes which promote consistency between belief and action
- Personal response to questions about the purpose of life — to pain, beauty, suffering
- Derive values from one's beliefs

Moral
- Desire to persuade others through moral reasoning
- Desire to listen to others
- To have personal values in relation to the self — on a personal, interpersonal, local, national and global level
- Belief in rights, duties, responsibilities
- Disposition to act in accordance with one's own values

Social
- Attitudes which show the ability to adjust to a range of social contexts
- Disposition to make a strong contribution to the well being of social groups

Cultural
- Appreciation of the wider cultural aspects within society
- Valuing of own and others' cultural achievements

Figure 4.4: Breakdown of learning outcomes

Personal and social development learning outcomes*

- self knowledge and understanding including own beliefs, values and cultural traditions (KU)
- knowledge and understanding of the beliefs, values and cultures of others (KU)
- critically informed about local, national and global issues (KU)
- can make moral decisions and judgments and distinguish between right and wrong (KU,S,A)
- takes responsibility for own actions and the effect of own actions on others (KU,S)
- forms and sustains effective interpersonal relationships within a moral framework (S,A)
- cooperates with others (S,A)
- shows respect for the beliefs, values and cultures of others (A)
- reflects on and questions the taken for granted assumptions and beliefs of self and others (KU,S)
- thinks analytically (S)
- works collaboratively and autonomously (KU,S,A)
- has high self esteem (A)
- confident (A)
- has a commitment to treating others with fairness, justice and equality (A)
- shows care and concern for all forms of life now and in the future (A,S)
- desires to contribute to the well being of the social group (A)
- engages in questions about the meaning and purpose of life (S,A)
- evaluates own learning and is eager to explore new learning (S,A)

* KU refers to knowledge and understanding, S to skills, A to attitude

possible. This requires us to begin to distinguish between the interrelated components, i.e. knowledge and understanding, skills and attitudes embedded within the generic outcomes. This will enable us to focus more clearly on what we are trying to assess and to acknowledge the significant differences in our capacity to 'measure' knowledge, understanding and skills, as opposed to attitude development. The SMSC formula, as outlined by both SCAA and Ofsted in various discussion papers and in the Framework of Inspection, can be broken down into the different components. Our attempt to do this can be seen in Figure 4.3. While we recognize that some of the distinctions are in reality less clear than they appear and that some of the categories are not necessarily mutually exclusive, the distinctions can prove useful in planning for assessment within PSD.

A further problem with the above is the lack of what we might call a critical edge; the formula restricts PSD to those components covered through SMSC as defined through SCAA and Ofsted and in doing so seems to omit some of the knowledge, understanding, skills and attitudes that promote a more critical and questioning approach. In our own work on learning outcomes we have attempted to widen the conception of PSD to include those more critical qualities that we believe to be essential for effective citizenship. Figure 4.4 shows our attempt to provide a breakdown of the knowledge, understanding skills and attitudes comprising PSD. In doing this we have drawn from a variety of sources: Ofsted, SCAA, the Scottish Curriculum Council, as well as our own earlier work.

Figure 4.5: Interrelated elements of the learning outcome

attitudes: desire to work with others; respect for others; valuing oneself and others

skills: listening; articulate own ideas and beliefs; form and sustain effective interpersonal relations

knowledge and understanding: knowledge and understanding of self; knowledge and understanding of rights and responsibilities; knowledge and understanding of diversity of culture and belief

collaborate

However, whilst the breakdown of outcomes is useful for purposes of assessment, we are not arguing for a mechanistic mode of assessment which denies the interrelationship of the various components. Such an approach can be too easily seen in some current models of assessment such as statement banks, checklists and crude forms of profiling. Our concern is with holistic development but one which is open to analysis and scrutiny in relation to its constituent parts and its capacity to provide a proper balance between those parts. By doing this we can begin to provide a more explicit and rigorous evidence base for judgments in this complex area.

An example of how we might breakdown component parts and at the same time show their interdependence is shown in Figure 4.5 where we take the learning outcome 'works collaboratively' and show the interrelated elements of this outcome, but we should be mindful that it is only when these interrelated components work in harmony that the outcome is fully realized, i.e. that the person works collaboratively.

Issues of progression

One of the central questions we face is how we can determine progression in learning in this area. Progression is not simple in more conventional curriculum areas, but the difficulties become daunting when we are dealing with PSD, particularly since we are dealing with progression across the whole curriculum. Central to the problem is the fact that some aspects of PSD are essentially non-linear, there is no smooth and continuous process of development that we can capture. We know that the outside world is a critical factor in PSD and that regression as well as progression is sometimes a critical feature of the process. For example, very young children are often self-confident, have high self-esteem and demonstrate the capacity to make moral judgments, albeit at a simple level. These same children at 12 and 13 can often seem to have regressed in some of these areas, sometimes for reasons which are beyond our control or even understanding. Explanations for regression often have to be sought in life experiences related to family circumstance, gender, class, race. The wealth of evidence as to how the external world impinges on girls' development, for example, needs to be understood (Gilligan, Lyons and Hanmer, 1990). The influence of school is also critical. Teachers and schools can help move pupils on in their development but they can also undermine and block that development. There is a further problem in that conceptions of development in aspects of PSD, particularly those to do with attitude development, may vary across cultures. For example, in the complex area of attitudinal development in relation to gender relations there are some distinct cultural differences that need to be understood.

While recognizing and taking account of these complexities, we do need to find ways of saying something worthwhile about how young people might progress in their PSD. One way forward might be to adopt the principles embodied in the Scottish Office guidelines; to devise a broad, flexible framework for progression that can be adapted and translated at local level. Such a framework could then provide national guidelines for development that are sensitive to individual and local circumstances and thus do not attempt to legislate for standardized development. This would enable schools to be at the centre of any development in this area, supported by LEAs and national guidelines. It may be possible for schools to work collaboratively with other schools, including cross-phase groupings or pyramids, to establish agreed progression points for their pupils. Clearly some form of monitoring across schools and LEAs will be necessary so as to ensure appropriate support structures against agreed benchmarks.

Providing contexts to develop learning outcomes

So far we have discussed learning outcomes for PSD without reference to the school provision required to realize such outcomes. In this section we explore how we might provide suitable contexts for pupils to develop the knowledge, understanding, skills and attitudes of effective PSD. Our own earlier work was concerned with the planning of provision at whole school level. It involved the development of what came to be described as a framework of central questions. The questions were intended to be 'at the very heart of pupils' personal and social development' (Inman and Buck, 1995). They sought to enable pupils to explore areas of our lived experience that we believe to be essential for meaningful development. The framework was originally conceived as a high-level planning tool for schools. It went through several revisions as a result of the legitimate criticisms levelled at it by teachers and others. (See Appendix for a full discussion of the criticisms.)

We have once more revised the framework so that it embraces the issues we believe to be at the centre of PSD. We now see the framework as a vehicle for ensuring that all pupils have access to areas of the personal and social world that we believe are critical in the formation of the knowledge, understanding, skills and attitudes necessary for effective citizenship. The revised framework comprises nine central questions. Taken together the questions provide a framework for ensuring that pupils engage in areas of experience that are essential, not only for that aspect of PSD known as SMSC, but also other aspects — in particular the emotional and, in more indirect ways, the physical. We are aware that many schools will be

Figure 4.6: A framework of issues giving meaning to PSD outcomes

Issues	Spiritual	Moral	Social	Cultural
1. What should our rights and responsibilities be towards each other?		✓	✓	
2. On what basis should we influence and control others?		✓	✓	
3. How should we cooperate with others and resolve conflicts?	✓	✓	✓	
4. Why do we categorize others, on what basis should we do this?		✓	✓	✓
5. How do we acquire our values and beliefs, how do we change them?	✓	✓	✓	✓
6. How should we live together in communities?		✓	✓	✓
7. How can we best ensure the welfare of ourselves and others?	✓	✓	✓	
8. How should we relate to the non-human world?	✓	✓	✓	✓
9. In what ways can we give meanings to our lives?	✓	✓	✓	✓

exploring the issues raised through the questions; through the taught curriculum, collective worship, and extra-curricular activities. However, the framework enables schools to develop a more comprehensive and coherent approach, so that all pupils explore and confront what we believe are a set of issues at the heart of our existence. We are now clear that the framework is not a planning document for PSD but rather a framework of issues that give meaning to the PSD outcomes described earlier in this chapter. We would envisage that schools would use it as one basis for discussion around PSD; in the context of whole staff Inset, work with governors, meetings with parents and with pupils themselves.

However, it may be that some schools will themselves choose to use the framework for more explicit curriculum planning, particularly for PSE within the secondary sector. Figure 4.6 shows the revised framework.

Planning for PSD learning outcomes

If learning outcomes for PSD are to be realized then they must be explicitly and rigorously planned for within all aspects of the school. Within the taught curriculum planning for subjects has undergone extensive review in the light of National Curriculum requirements. The result has been a much more rigorous and detailed planning for learning outcomes within subject areas. However, it is also the case that learning outcomes have been defined in somewhat limited ways, the emphasis being on knowledge and some aspects of skill development. Assessment mechanisms have compounded this limited view of development, yet despite these reservations, there is evidence of much more rigour in curriculum planning. In contrast, planning for PSD has tended to remain somewhat low level, with relatively ill-defined learning outcomes. If we are to assess the PSD learning outcomes referred to earlier in this chapter then we must explicitly plan for these outcomes. Vague and general statements about promoting tolerance or knowledge of other cultures are not in themselves sufficient, but will need to be unpacked into more detailed, precise and assessable outcomes.

Planning for PSD outcomes: A case study of work on bullying

We have been concerned so far with curriculum planning for learning outcomes at a somewhat abstract level. We now attempt to make concrete some of these ideas by focusing more directly on issues of learning outcomes within the context of a specific area of PSD. What follows is essentially a staff development exercise with a focus on the planning and assessment of learning outcomes with reference to bullying. The exercise is in the form of a curriculum review of policy, procedures and curriculum provision with respect to anti-bullying. The aim is to evaluate current practice and to move forward. The exercise is offered as an illustration of some of the steps involved in reviewing assessment practice.

There is no need to rehearse the reasons why the theme of bullying is central to all schools. In earlier work (Buck and Inman, 1993) we spelt out some of the reasons why the issue of bullying requires a whole school approach, including provision for anti-bullying work within the taught curriculum. Others have done more extensive work in this area (DFE, 1994; Foster, Arora and Thompson, 1990; Smith and Sharp, 1994).

Reviewing anti-bullying measures

Our major concern in this exercise is with the taught curriculum. However, in reviewing their policy and procedures schools will also want to establish performance indicators for other aspects of whole school provision. Thus as a prelude to reviewing the taught curriculum we would suggest that schools would want to evaluate the success of current policy and procedures in terms of some agreed performance indicators. The performance indicators are to be seen as techniques to enable us to obtain a broad picture of the effectiveness of current practice through a combination of quantitive and qualitative data. Such indicators may include:

- a reduced rate of reported bullying;
- confidential student attitude surveys indicate a lowering of the rate of actual bullying; and
- active participation of students in developing anti-bullying school ethos measured through, for example, involvement in mentoring schemes, use of school council.

The taught curriculum

Work on bullying within the taught curriculum will inevitably take a variety of forms depending on factors such as age phase, curriculum organization. In the primary school work may be within the context of a theme or topic or might be the focus of a discrete block. In the secondary school bullying will be explored predominantly through the PSE/pastoral curriculum. Whatever the particular form the work takes there will be some common steps to any review of the taught curriculum. These might include the following examples.

1. Specifying the learning outcomes

Teachers will need to specify the explicit learning outcomes, i.e. knowledge and understanding skills and attitudes, currently fostered through the taught curriculum work on bullying. It may be helpful to compare any list with our own list of learning outcomes for bullying. These are in Figure 4.7.

Figure 4.7: Learning outcomes for bullying

1. Knowledge and understanding

- self knowledge — increased knowledge and understanding of own attitudes and beliefs as to what bullying is; who are the bullies, who are the 'victims'; what could be done about it? Reflection on and questioning of these attitudes and preconceptions
- increased knowledge and understanding of varieties of bullying, the different forms and contexts; awareness of why people bully others and the effects of this on others and the bully
- understanding of wider societal context of bullying
- increased knowledge of appropriate strategies to deal with bullying

2. Skills

- articulate own attitudes and viewpoint
- respect for others' viewpoint
- take responsibility for own actions
- forming and sustaining effective interpersonal relationships

3. Attitudes

- high self esteem and confidence
- attempting to be consistent between attitudes and behaviour
- showing respect for the beliefs of others
- commitment to treating others with fairness and justice

2. To review progression

It is clearly not straightforward to establish progression points but we may want to establish some flexible markers of development. These could include:

- Expanding knowledge and understanding of the types and range of bullying as a phenomenon. For example, from the more narrow focus of family, friends and school to the more sophisticated forms of bullying seen within workplaces, institutions and between nations.
- A more sophisticated understanding of ways of dealing with bullying and the confidence to use such procedures.
- Shifts of attitude in which young people become more valuing of others and more respecting of others' rights and their own responsibilities.

While these might prove useful markers of development, we should be aware that there will be understandable differences between pupils related to factors such as family circumstance, cultural background and previous experience of bullying.

Setting up learning activities on bullying: outcomes and assessment

Having established some general learning outcomes for curriculum work on bullying and begun to identify some points of progression we can then explore how we locate these within specific learning activities. Further, we can explore suitable assessment and recording mechanisms for such activities. What follows are two examples of such learning activities on bullying, accompanied by our attempt to:

1. suggest ways in which we might assess individual and group development in relation to the identified learning outcomes;
2. explore the nature of the evidence we would seek to support the assessment; and
3. explore how we might go about recording and accrediting the developments.

Both the activities are located within taught curriculum work on bullying. The activities can be modified across the age range and particular forms of curriculum organization. The activities are designed to enable teachers to contribute towards the promotion and assessment of a limited number of learning outcomes within the wider context of more extended work on bullying. Both activities are designed to be used as ways of enabling pupils to demonstrate their knowledge and understanding, to apply this to different contexts and to reflect and evaluate. In addition, particular skills will need to be exercised in the process of engaging in the activities, and the activities are designed to promote particular kinds of attitudes in relation to bullying. The activities provide opportunities for pupils to explore some of the issues outlined earlier in the chapter. In addition, both activities contribute towards a range of more generic skills — these include listening, working collaboratively, decision making.

Figure 4.8: Activity 1: Using objects to explore issues of abuse of power

Rope	Lightbulb
Handcuffs	Newspaper cuttings
Passport	Toy gun
Credit card	Medical card
Artefacts from a range of cultures	Soft toy
Photographs	

Activity 1: Using objects to explore issues of abuse of power

This activity provides opportunities for students to focus on how we define and understand bullying. Students are put into groups of five or six. Each group is given a range of objects either in a bag or a box. Figure 4.8 gives some examples of the types of objects that can be used. They are required to look at each of the objects in turn and come to an agreed decision as to whether these demonstrate *abuse of power* and then they are asked to report to the others in the class on:

- which of the objects demonstrate abuse of power and why;
- what other objects they would have included to give a fuller representation of the issues.

Figure 4.9 shows some suggested learning outcomes for this activity.

Figure 4.9: Learning outcomes for Activity 1

Knowledge and understanding

- Increased self-knowledge and understanding in terms of own attitudes and beliefs as to what bullying is; who are the bullies; who are the 'victims'; what can be done about bullying.
- Reflection on and questioning of existing knowledge, attitudes and preconceptions.
- Increased knowledge and understanding of varieties of bullying, the different forms and contexts.
- Increased understanding of why some people bully others and the effects of this behaviour on the 'victim', others and the bully.

Skills

- The ability to articulate our own attitudes and viewpoint.
- Respect for others' views and experiences.

Attitudes

- Commitment to treating people with fairness, justice and equality.
- Making moral judgments and distinguishing between right and wrong.

Figure 4.10: Sources of evidence

Sources of evidence

- appropriateness of choices and rationale given for choices to give insight into knowledge and understanding
- observation of discussion providing evidence of collaboration, listening skills, sensitive to others
- written accounts from group members of rationale and processes of decision making
- peer oral evidence
- oral and written self assessments

Figure 4.10 shows some suggested types of evidence that we might use to assess individual pupils and groups both during the activity and in their presentations to the class.

Recording assessment

Figure 4.11 gives some suggestions as to how we might record the evidence.

Figure 4.11: Recording the evidence

- records of self and peer assessments
- inclusion in portfolio
- checklist with written observations under headings
- video or audio tape of process and product
- agreed statements between teacher and pupil under headings

Activity 2: Using freeze drama to explore anti-bullying strategies

The theme for this activity is resistance to bullying. It provides opportunities for pupils to focus on strategies for dealing with bullying behaviour. Pupils are put into groups of 5 or 6. Each group is asked to undertake a number of steps. These are:

1. discuss and identify what they define as appropriate forms of resistance to bullying
2. decide on a context and particular situation in which bullying takes place

Figure 4.12: Learning outcomes for Activity 2

Knowledge and understanding

- Increased knowledge and understanding of varieties of bullying, the different forms and contexts
- Awareness of why people bully others and the effects of this on others and the bully
- Increased knowledge of appropriate strategies to resist bullying and to deal with incidents of bullying when they happen

Skills

- The ability to articulate one's own attitudes and viewpoints with respect to bullying
- Co-operating with others

Attitudes

- Increased respect for others' beliefs, values and cultures
- Making moral judgments and distinguishing between right and wrong

Figure 4.13: Sources of evidence

Sources of evidence

- appropriateness of choice and rationale given for choice
- observation of discussion process and drama
- oral and written self-assessment by individuals and groups

3. work at a frieze to represent both the bullying and the resistance to that bullying
4. prepare to show the frieze to the rest of the group

We have identified the learning outcomes for this activity. These can be seen in Figure 4.12.

Figure 4.13 shows some suggested types of evidence that we might use to assess individual pupils and groups both during the activity and in their presentations.

Figure 4.14 gives some examples of how we might record the evidence.

While we have chosen to use bullying as our theme, we believe that the processes described above will be similar for reviewing any area of PSD. The identification of learning outcomes, assessment and recording mechanisms for PSD provides a rigour to the planning, teaching and review process that has too often been lacking in this area of the curriculum.

Figure 4.14: Recording assessment

Recording assessment

- records of self- and peer assessment
- portfolio
- video of process and drama
- agreed statements

Conclusions

This chapter has been concerned with learning outcomes for PSD. For us, learning outcomes are the key to moving forward on assessment practice. The establishment of the three central, interrelated components of PSD should enable us to plan for more explicit assessment opportunities. The issues around progression are, and will remain, complex. It is our view that work needs to be done on the development of a flexible national framework that is sensitive to the needs of individual schools and pupils.

References

BUCK, M. and INMAN, S. (1992) *Curriculum Guidance No. 1: Whole School Provision for Personal and Social Development*, London: Centre for Cross-Curricular Initiatives, Goldsmiths College.

BUCK, M. and INMAN, S. (eds) (1993) *Curriculum Guidance No. 2: Re-affirming Values*, London: Centre for Cross Curricular Initiatives, Goldsmiths College.

BUCK, M. and INMAN, S. (eds) (1995) *Adding Value*, Stoke on Trent, Staffs: Trentham Books.

DES (1989) *Curriculum Matters 14: Personal and Social Education from 5–16*, London: HMSO.

DFE (1994) *Don't Suffer in Silence*, London: HMSO.

FOSTER, P., ARORA, C. and THOMPSON, D. (1990) 'A Whole School Approach to Bullying', *Pastoral Care in Education*, **8**.

GILLIGAN, C., LYONS, N. and HANMER, J. (1990) *Making Connections*, Cambridge MA: Harvard University Press.

MORRISON, K. (1994) *Implementing Cross-curricular Themes*, London: David Fulton.

OFSTED (1994) *Discussion Paper on Spiritual, Moral, Social and Cultural Development*, London: OFSTED.

OFSTED (1993, 1994, 1995) *Framework for the Inspection of Schools*, London: HMSO.

SCAA (1995) *Discussion Papers No. 3: Spiritual and Moral Development*, London: SCAA.

SCAA (1996) *Discussion Papers: No. 6 Education for Adult Life: The Spiritual and Moral Development of Young People*, London: SCAA.

SCAA (1996) *Desirable Outcomes for Children's Learning*, London: SCAA.

SCOTTISH OFFICE EDUCATION DEPARTMENT (1993) *Personal and Social Development 5–14*, Edinburgh: Scottish Office.

SMITH, P. and SHARP, S. (ed.) (1994) *The Problem of School Bullying: Insights and Perspectives*, London: Routledge.

Appendix

Our work in the early 1990s was largely concerned with planning for PSD within the taught curriculum. Central to this early work was the development of what became known as a framework for planning PSD. The framework was first written in 1992 (Buck and Inman, 1992) and has undergone several revisions since that time (Inman and Buck, 1995). In retrospect one of the inherent problems with the framework was to do with the lack of explicit reference to the teaching and learning processes implied by the questions. Consequently, it could be read almost as a syllabus of knowledge required for PSD. While we provided examples of the range of learning activities one might adopt in using the framework for planning and delivering (Buck and Inman, 1993; Inman and Buck, 1995) the development of skills remained implicit in the framework. A further related problem lies in the somewhat descriptive nature of some the questions. As Morrison pointed out:

> One notices that the questions deal in what and how but do not include why. (Morrison, 1994)

Lastly, because of the way they were phrased, the questions do not necessarily call for an exploration of the moral issues which clearly abound within the areas covered by the questions.

The revised framework is now more limited in its task; it represents an attempt to specify the areas of knowledge and understanding that are central to PSD.

Chapter 5

Educating for Personal and Social Development: A Question of Discipline?

Roger Slee

Abstract

Discussions of school discipline and disruptive student behaviour are commonly reduced to considerations of schools' punitive and regulatory policies and procedures. This chapter distances itself from this form of behaviourism to argue that discipline is an educational goal. In this respect, school discipline is central to the project of personal and social development and invites educators to embark upon developing and providing what Tony Knight has called 'an apprenticeship in democracy'. Such a reorientation of our thinking about discipline and student behaviour implies reform of curriculum, teaching methods and the organization of schools in order to increase student commitment and attachment to schooling. Current educational policy in the United Kingdom, and elsewhere, undermines the promise of reform.

Discursive tensions in talking about discipline, education and social development

Following McGoughlin's (1992) frames of reference which distinguish *minimalist* models from *maximalist* models of citizenship education, Buck and Inman (1995) eschew the narrow socializing imperatives of a minimalist citizenship curriculum in favour of a more robust maximalist conception of citizenship where '. . . education is concerned with empowerment, with developing pupils' ability to take control and exercise responsibility over their own lives' (p. 91). 'This conception of citizenship education', they contend, 'is concerned equally with content and with learning processes . . .' (p. 91). In this brief discussion of student behaviour and school discipline, I commence from Buck and Inman's theorizing of citizenship education as a key to students' personal and social development, to argue for educational policy and curriculum which provides students with the opportunity to be engaged in an 'apprenticeship in democracy' (Knight, 1985).

Theorizing and responding to disruptive behaviour in schools and classrooms is currently entrapped within a behaviourist paradigm which is reductionist and in tension with stated aims for personal and social development education within schools. Consideration of recent educational policy making in the UK and Australia (Slee, 1995; Knight and Pearl, in press) exposes missed opportunities to acknowledge and construct bridges between the form, quality and processes of learning and student behaviour and school discipline. Engaging students in the educational project of an apprenticeship in democracy moves beyond the behaviourist quick-fixes and the mania for retribution that distorts current approaches to discipline in schools.

Notwithstanding apparently sympathetic declarations within the Elton Report (DES, 1989), the National Commission on Education (1993) and the Ofsted 'Discussion Paper on Spiritual, Moral, Social and Cultural Development' (1994) the pursuit of citizenship and personal and social development education as an educational aim for schools and their communities, has been compromised by the Conservative education policy discourse of the National Curriculum, education markets, choice and 'raising standards' through published examination performance league tables. The emerging educational manifesto of the Blair Labour government provides little room for us to be sanguine. Educational politics, as they have been played out in the UK, have obstructed the development of citizenship education and reduced aspirations for disciplined schooling to a quest for student compliance and behavioural control.

Written in three sections, this chapter will:

- identify a number of tensions in the politics of education which undermine 'maximalist' thinking and prevent educational understandings of and responses to student disruption in schools;
- consider the implications of different understandings or theories of school discipline and argue for an educational approach to discipline which transcends the seductive behaviourist quick-fixes offered by entrepreneurs and gurus;
- report on a student action research project to suggest ways of pursuing disciplined schooling which is achieved not through fixing or excluding problem students, but by consideration of the potential of curriculum, methods of teaching and learning, and school organizational procedures and processes for engaging students in the goals of learning.

I urge readers not to lapse into frustration born of the fact that this chapter raises more questions than it answers. Central to the problematic condition of schooling in the UK at the present is the proliferation of rapid and superficial resolutions (e.g. Barber, 1996; Mandelson and Liddle, 1996; Reynolds and Farrell, 1996) for complex social and educational problems. My aim in this chapter, therefore, is to call for a more careful theorizing of *discipline* and its relationship to educational goals which articulate with a sustainable future.

Discourses of control: disciplining education

The impacts of the Education Reform Act (1988), and its sequels in the UK and elsewhere[1], have been devastating for educators concerned with a dynamic curriculum which engages all students and articulates with the future. As Ball observes, the National Curriculum, born in the political incubus of a crude form of cultural restorationism, is a 'curriculum of the dead' — '. . . intended to put "real" knowledge back into school and to discipline teachers' (Ball, 1994, p. 33). This form of curriculum development has been backward-looking and adheres to the conservative political agenda for a return to the good society populated by an obedient and passive community.

> . . . the starting point is the deconstruction of the comprehensive, modernist curriculum and then its replacement with a political but depoliticized, authoritative curriculum of tradition. This employs what I have called elsewhere 'the discourse of derision' . . . Simple polarities are deployed within this discourse, based upon the certainties of 'good' and 'evil', the sacred and profane, and sanity and lunacy. . . . The language, style and tone of moral outrage leave no grounds for professional judgement in these areas. There is no doubt, no compromise, no relativism. **This is curricular fundamentalism** . . . (Ball, 1994, p. 39, author's emphasis)

The professional role of the teacher as an educator is reduced (Apple, 1996; Dale, 1996). Teachers become couriers; schools merely National Curriculum franchises to be monitored and checked off by the quality controllers — the sub-contracted Ofsted inspectors. As conduits for, rather than developers of, curriculum, teachers have a restricted capacity to respond to the particular needs of students and their communities. Teachers are dissuaded from those forms of innovative teaching (Mehan et al., 1997) and learning that encourage greater student envelopment in the goals and processes of schooling. This is exacerbated by the tradition-bound culture of the curriculum which lacks connection to the world and cultures of an increasing number of students (Knight, 1988).

The marketization of schooling linked to the publishing of performance league tables in the UK has had deleterious effects upon particular groups of students. Adhering to Hayek's affirmation that unrestricted market competition and an unobtrusive state is the fairest distributive mechanism, Conservative education policy ironically has established the preconditions for market competition in schools in order to raise standards and provide choice and diversity.

> Inequality is undoubtedly more readily borne, and affects the dignity of the person much less, if it is determined by impersonal forces, than when it is due to design. In a competitive society it is no slight to a person, no offence to his dignity, to be told by any particular firm that it has no need for his (sic) services . . . (Hayek, 1944, p. 79)

As has been variously observed this is extremely paradoxical as the state is highly visible and intrusive in its manipulation of school policy through an amalgam of offices of state, statutory authorities, quangos and think tanks. Moreover, choice is a chimera for all but the favoured class of choosers (Gerwirtz et al., 1995; Whitty, 1997) and the pressure of the National Curriculum and performance tables has acted to narrow the curriculum on offer. This is sustained by a pervasive discourse which casts schools as *good* or *bad* according to their performance in the production of meritorious test scores. Good schools are heavily subscribed, others battle to improve the performance of and defend, those who remain against the public vilification of their work through media commentaries on their inspection reports.

Effectively the student population is perceived in relation to its potential as performance indicators. The process does not operate according to a benign liberal notion of rewarding talent. It is classist, disablist and racist (Troyna, 1993; Slee, 1995; Gewirtz et al., 1995; Gillborn and Gipps, 1996). Students with so called special educational needs (Gold et al., 1993; Barton and Landman, 1993; Clark et al., 1997; Slee, 1997) are regarded with great reluctance; they are lead in the academic saddle-bags. Less than *docile bodies* (Foucault, 1979) are also excluded from the achieving school (Gillborn and Gipps, 1996; Sewell, 1997).

The inspectoral model in the UK demands a highly fragmented curriculum, divided into separate subject groups with further divisions into performance requirements at Key Stages. Links for cross curricular goals such as personal and social development may be expressed in text, but do not always transfer to the classroom as teachers struggle to guarantee student mastery of subject requirements for imminent tests and inspection rounds. The obsession with measurement and comparison has been intensified by the growing political influence of the 'effective schools research'. In its present form, proponents such as Reynolds (1995) exhort schools to become 'high reliability organizations' akin to flight control operations, surgical theatres and nuclear power plants. While I agree that we ought to be able to expect effectiveness and levels of efficiency in school operations, this kind of analogy is appallingly reductionist.

The reductionist imperative finds its clearest expression in the work of Reynolds and Farrell (1996). They suggest, on the basis of an international school effectiveness research project, which has numerous methodological flaws and epistemological limitations (Hamilton, in press; Brown, in press), that children's learning outcomes and the national economic performance in the UK could be improved by adopting whole class instruction methods, similar to those in tiger economy countries such as Taiwan. Having grabbed the political imagination (not an oxymoron is it?), particularly that of the fledgling Labour government which has set up an office of school effectiveness, this research genre and its demand for a return to Taylorism in the classroom endorses the overall culture of 'hurried empiricism' (Lyotard, 1984, p. 52) or performativity (Lyotard, 1984; Ball, 1996; Yeatman, 1994). The pressure on schools is to yield crude comparable measures of achievement which occlude a vision for the future and progress towards a social development curriculum.

Add to this the increasing politicization of discipline and control in schools and one can appreciate the pressure on schools to find quick remedies for what represent problems underscored by a constellation of educational and social issues. The national demonizing of a Nottinghamshire student; the tragic killing of Phillip Lawrence — a London headteacher — as he attempted to defend one of his students outside the school gates; the closure of the Ridings School in October of 1996 and attribution of its problems to 60 severely disruptive students; the racialization of school exclusions (Gillborn, 1996; Sewell, 1997); the rapid proliferation of off-site pupil referral units; the press for home-school contracts and the mooted introduction of large fines for the parents of truanting students, all serve to reinforce the notion of a crisis in schools which demands quick and tough responses. This has its parallel in Australia where events at a school camp off the coast of Queensland escalated into the general panic about law and order as the parties sought to outbid each other to convince the electorate that they were going to be tougher on disruptive students. The more careful drafting of educational responses to disruption and the quest for students' personal and social development through a planned curriculum was forfeited to the politics of control.

This political climate, with its emphases on the measurement of performance, the reduction of the goals of learning to discrete elements for national and international comparison, the reinforcement of a punitive school culture to enforce compliance and passivity, and the exclusion of high risk pupils, colludes with the behaviour management gurus and traditional special educational practitioners to prevent a careful theorizing of the nature of the tensions in schools and to promote snake-oil solutions. The remainder of this chapter will provide a more considered educational theory of discipline to suggest other options for educators to facilitate personal and social development learning that limits the reliance on an overt technology of control.

Discipline or control? Language and meaning

Conceptual slippage and reductionism undermine the discussion of school discipline (Slee, 1988). Discipline has become, in its most common usage, a synonym for control and punishment. Behaviourist psychology following B.F. Skinner's pigeon-led propagation of a 'science of behaviour' (1968, 1972) and Carl Roger's humanist psychology (1969) provide the intellectual pedigree for much of what is passed off as discipline theory in education. These traditions have proven convenient to the task of governance and control in schools. School authorities across North America (Freiberg, in press), the UK and Australia (Slee, 1995) draw from these conceptual models as they are seen to provide the theoretical rationale and the practical machinery for student compliance as a necessary precondition for learning. This has very little to do with education. On the contrary, this behaviourist paradigm provides the discourse of and technologies for control.

The behaviourist expunges social context from the equation of trouble in schools. Disruptive events are explained in terms of individual problem students. Individual student problems are then ascribed to pathological defects within their physiological, cognitive or emotional make-up. Political and social relations articulated through the forms of educational provision collapse into a 'spurious biology' or 'set of biological metaphors' (Bernstein, 1996, p. 11). Where the diagnostic gaze fails to locate causes within the child, family pathologies are examined for defects. This particular form of explaining disruption supports the bureaucratic imperative of schools and shields the professional interest of teachers. There is no pressure to interrogate curriculum, pedagogy or school organization from these diagnostic probes.

An educational theory of discipline is entirely consistent with, and becomes part of, the goals of a personal and social development curriculum. Discipline, as an educational concept, should demonstrate connection between the pedagogical and curriculum goals and the processes of student governance (Knight, 1988; Pearl, 1988; Crittenden, 1991). An educational theory of discipline accounts for the cognitive development and the social context of young people as part of the educational project (Vygotsky, 1962, 1978). Disciplinary theory and techniques which are merely a euphemism for behaviour modification, compromise the educational role of the school in enabling students to determine socially responsible behaviour. Extrinsic behaviour modification is not conducive to the considered development of student behaviour, it fosters submission and subversion (Dewey, 1916).

Some time ago John Locke (1693) warned 'tutors' of the capacity of the control mechanisms they employed to '. . . create a disliking to that which it is the tutor's business to create a liking to'. Since that time a number of educational theorists have urged for greater consistency between discipline and the aims of education (Dewey, 1916; Stenhouse, 1971; Wilson, 1971; Crittenden, 1991). Dewey (1916, p. 129) establishes this point in his treatise on democracy and education:

> A person who is trained to consider his (sic) actions, to undertake them deliberately, is in so far forth disciplined. Add to this ability a power to endure in an intelligently chosen course in face of distraction, confusion, and difficulty, and you have the essence of discipline . . . Discipline is positive. To cow the spirit, to subdue inclination, to compel obedience, to mortify the flesh, to make a subordinate perform an uncongenial task — these things are not disciplinary according to the development of the power to recognise what one is about and to persistence in accomplishment.

Discipline, it would seem, is not subjection to the will of authority; it is an educational exchange. Schooling ought to be thought of not as the training of circus animals (Wilson, 1971; Smith, 1985), but as providing the environment in which young people learn to think about their behaviour, its consequences and the range of alternatives. The disciplinary framework must cohere with the educational aims and the pedagogy adopted to achieve those aims. Connection between the learner, what they are doing, how they are doing it, and where it is leading them is fundamental to the development of an educational orderliness (Slee, 1995, p. 28). This line of thinking is not an indulgence in ivory tower semantics. As Kurt Lewin is credited with saying there is nothing as practical as good theory, and by implication good practice is informed by a robust theoretical foundation. My argument is that an educational theory provides more, rather than fewer, options for teachers when confronted by the problem of disruption. Rather than having to rely on the authoritarianism of their behaviourist methods or their prowess as counsellors or corridor confidantes, they can draw upon the skills and knowledge in which they have been educated. Let me explain this further.

Connection between the learner and the curriculum presses us to consider the contexts, prior knowledge and skills of the student and to interrogate the relevance of the curriculum schools offer. If, as Ball suggests, the present offering is a 'curriculum of the dead' which fails to engage other than the 'sponsored' students we will have to rely on external control mechanisms to keep 'marginal' students to the task (Polk, 1984). If our preferred teaching methods fail to reach out to students to encourage learning, rather than reaffirm *their* failure, we amplify the potential for disaffection and resistance. If the students realize that what they are doing in school has no bearing on where they will end up after school, that schooling offers a ticket to nowhere, then our behaviour controls will have to be extremely severe to shore up this institutional/social failure.

Schools have always produced failure and disaffection. In times passed the unskilled labour market, segregated special education and the requirements for domestic (female) labour in the home colluded with a narrow curriculum to conceal the failure of schools. Failure wasn't a problem for the schools, it was written off, by sleight of hand, as the defects of individual students. These 'underachieving' students had somewhere else to go; the shop floor, the factory, the mine, the farm. Moreover, each of these places offered payment with which students could negotiate a legitimate, independent life. Presently the market pushes youth to have purchase on an identity forged through the composites of music, clothing, body decoration. This pressure coincides with a period when we are extending their dependency. Crisis in the labour market has exposed this failure of schools for an increasing number of young people. They remain at school not because of their attachment to the goals and experience of learning — there is nowhere else to go. The state extends retention in schools to keep the youth problem off the streets and in the school where it belongs! Simply put, the conditions exist for creating a powerful cocktail of disaffection and disruption in schools which demands greater analysis and more comprehensive responses than those advanced through the behaviourist paradigm.

Let us leave this epistemic discussion by lastly considering the relationships between learning, authority and democracy. What culture of authority do we seek for our schools? Do we seek the restoration of authoritarian educational and organizational cultures? Do we prefer to educate teachers to be authoritarian or authoritative? What is the relationship between democratic process, the exercise of authority and the educational exchange?

Education for participation in civil society requires an appropriate democratic apprenticeship.

> To become expert in democratic citizenship the student must observe leadership that is consistent with democratic principles. Only when seen in action does all of the training the student receives come together. Only then is it real. Cynicism is bred when a student sees a teacher preach one thing and practice something distinctly different.
>
> Democratic principles are confusing. A great many sins are committed in the name of democracy. As with nothing else, democracy has become a game of the name.

> Educators who prate about it really do not know whereof they speak. And whatever they mean by democracy does not conform to any acceptable standard. (Pearl, 1972, p. 147)

Spencer observed as much in the public school houses of his England and registered his anxiety for the shape of future governments recruiting from those schooled in authoritarianism.

> . . . the culture of our public schools, by accustoming our boys to a despotic form of government and an intercourse regulated by brute force, tends to fit them for a lower state of society . . . this barbarizing influence becomes a hindrance to national progress. (Spencer, 1910, p. 134)

This is not to argue against limits. Democracy is not *laissez-faire*. It is convention-ridden and cumbersome. It is respectful of due process and affords legitimate status to dissent. The fact that dissent is not legitimate and no proper fora are provided in many schools drives it underground and forces its expression in anti-social behaviour. In their Melbourne-based (Australia) research, Lewis, Lovegrove and Burman (1991) found that students expect rules, they simply seek a role in their determination and fair application. Moreover, Knight and Lewis (1993) found that in a large cohort of Australian primary and secondary schools teachers become less democratic with students as they move from primary to secondary school. Hirschi's (1969) work on delinquency demonstrates that young people will attach themselves to society and accept the moral authority of rules when they are engaged in the making of rules.

Behaviourism adheres to a narrow form of learning where the teacher is the active agent in the selection and transmission of 'worthwhile knowledge' and the student the passive recipient. Friere (1972) described this form of teaching and learning as the banking system of education. Teachers, as bankers, take charge of students' affairs — including their behaviour — never relinquishing control. Students are not equipped to make decisions.

Such a model has limited utility in a society that aspires to the production of independent problem-solvers to be able to participate in a more complex set of social and productive relations. Working with dynamic technologies is better achieved through constructivist rather than rote learning approaches (Richardson, 1997). Democratic citizenship demands the ability to interrogate problems, to weigh up sets of issues, articulate and defend a position, compromise and to determine a course of mutually beneficial action. There exists no more relevant area of learning for democratic participation than school governance. Students have the opportunity to debate the necessity of a social contract; its form and procedures, to respond to reasonable challenges to it and practice obligations of community membership. The progress of student action groups and school councils in Victoria, Australia in the 1980s provides testimony to the educational and social gains accrued through removing the false dichotomy between the academic and social development curriculum (Holdsworth, 1988; Knight, 1988).

Bringing students in from the cold

While this discussion has deliberately emphasized the importance of careful theorizing as the practical first step in establishing the indivisibility of the personal and social development curriculum, the academic curriculum and the framework for school discipline, it is important to connect this with a strategy for change. Elsewhere, I have argued for the importance of strategic planning and action in the pursuit of a more disciplined schooling (Slee, 1991, 1995). In the first instance there exists a need to respond to teachers' calls for the development of classroom management skills. This is quite appropriate so long as it is stressed that this exercise must focus upon the role of curriculum, approaches to teaching and learning and school organization and ethos as part of the management strategy. The methods derived must complement the school's educational mission.

Given our earlier discussion of the political economy of discipline in schools, planning for change demands that we consider ways of responding to the need to change those aspects of education policy which intensify competition between schools and students and thereby force more students to assume marginal identities and career tracks. For so long as we subscribe to league tables and narrow testing regimes to provide the evidence base for evaluating standards in schooling, we condemn ourselves to narrowing the potential for increasing numbers of young people. We condemn ourselves, and those students, to more frequent exclusions, to expanding provision of pupil referral units and segregated special educational needs facilities, and to a dual system of schooling of 'haves' and 'have nots'.

It remains a stark irony that many of our approaches to the resolution of discipline problems continue to push marginal students further to the fringes of school life and beyond. There is a wealth of research evidence to demonstrate the folly of the over-reliance on suspension and exclusion (Wu et al., 1982; Slee, 1995; Edwards, 1996), to demonstrate the exponential growth and costs of off-site educational provision for disruptive students for limited benefit beyond teacher and student respite (HMI, 1978; Mongon, 1988), to alert us to the deflective nature of epidemics such as Attention Deficit Disorder (ADHD) (Slee, 1995). All of these approaches take disaffected students and push them further to the fringes of school life. The capacity for personal and social development to be located within the educational project of the school is denied.

Some time ago John Furlong (1991) contended that there needed to be a reconsideration of student resistance through the application of psychological and sociological analytical frames. His was a call to consider the utility of a sociology of emotion where students' perceptions of schools' infliction of hidden injuries upon students be established as a first step in restoring students to the educational enterprise. The structures of schooling and of the disarticulation between school and the labour market needed to be examined to change the experience of school for students, and in turn, for teachers.

Add to this the growing body of work with students to establish their perceptions of schools and how they might be improved to enhance students' opportunities and the quality of life for all within the organization, and we have an excellent point from which to embark. By way of conclusion, let me provide an example of a project, now quite dated, where students were encouraged to investigate the educational needs of 13–15 year olds as a basis for school reform.

A group of 15 Year 11 students were invited to form a research team to research the educational needs of 13–15 year olds in inner-city Melbourne. They attended a series of workshops at Melbourne University to discuss the problems of students and schooling for the 13–15 phase and to become familiar with a range of research methods useful to their task. After developing and testing a survey questionnaire the students then administered it in three neighbourhood secondary schools. They had 240 responses, a 100 per cent response rate. Back in their classroom, the students collated, analyzed and documented their data. In the course of discussing the data, the students also suggested that the research should be extended to interrogate those young people who were not in school as their perceptions would be most relevant to improving the experience of schooling for those most at risk of schools' failure.

During the project a group of teacher education students were invited to observe and evaluate the progress of the project. They filmed the research team and interviewed them to determine the value of the exercise for the researchers. It is vital to note that the team's work was assessed as part of their school curriculum (it counted) and that the evaluation work was counted as part of the course work for the teacher education students.

The main findings can be summarized in three areas:

- curriculum
- teaching and learning
- school organization

Curriculum

Not surprisingly the student data attested to the critical importance of maths and English and sought a range of supports for learning in these areas. The major finding of the team in relation to curriculum was that learning outcomes improve to the extent that teachers are able to establish clear links between the lesson and where it is leading in terms of post-school options. Curriculum also becomes more purposeful when connected to the world of the student. Purpose, relevance, and meaningfulness were recurrent terms in the data.

Teaching and learning

Students experience a limited repertoire of teaching and learning methods in their schooling according to the data. This contributes to boredom, disengagement and disruption. More particularly, the research suggested the deleterious impact of restricted and restrictive pedagogy. When asked for explanation, teachers tend to repeat themselves, only slower and louder! The assumption is that students learn through the same approach and that the rate of progress varies. The student data reconfirms our belief that different people require different approaches to learning to secure understanding. This challenges the very heart of current education policy in the UK.

School organization

In the workshop discussions of this section of the research students referred to this as the happiness factors. Students were not calling for the dismantling of schools as we know them. Nor were they interested in anarchic organizations. They believed in the necessity of rules, but sought greater levels of participation in rulemaking and the provisions for protecting rights of reply when students believed they had been unfairly treated. Girls' responses were interesting in that although they believed that they got as good a deal from schooling as boys, they consistently registered more negative responses to the happiness questions.

Interviews with young people who had left or were prematurely forced out of school yielded useful information. They argued that methods of discipline forced them to 'up the ante' in their resistance. Attempts at remediation in school tended to be humiliating and stigmatizing, inclining students towards disengagement. Where students stayed at home to look after siblings, they were punished upon their return to school for what ought to be construed as responsible behaviour. Some of the young people interviewed suggested that the provision of child-care facilities and greater flexibility in school organization and support structures would have enabled them to continue at school.

The data provides a strong base of insider views for school reform conducive to disciplined schooling. It is important to observe other outcomes from the research. First, students described as disruptive were part of this research and showed no such inclination throughout the project. In fact, students were extremely diligent because they had agreed to present their results to the senior executive officers of the Victorian Ministry of Education and to the State Board of Education. These students who were in a non-academic track were used to lowered expectations at school, but demonstrated they could improve the quality and outcomes of their work in a changed curriculum and work environment; through a different approach to teaching and learning. These students participated in INSET sessions for teachers following the publication of their research.

The lessons from this project support the aims and themes of this text. Personal and social development cannot be detached from the academic curriculum. Moreover a system of schooling that disregards the centrality of personal and social development education in the construction of its curriculum runs the risk of becoming a troubling and troubled school for students and teachers alike. Student behaviour is connected to the behaviour of teachers and education policy-makers. In other words if the pedagogy, curriculum and organization of the school support student engagement, the scaffolding of learning on prior competences, purposeful, relevant and diverse learning experiences that lead to viable post-school options, schools will have to rely less on extrinsic control mechanisms that generate further resistance. It would seem that this represents a call for schools to consider the quality of the education rather than their position on the league table; a call to beware of 'statistics behaving badly' (Kellner, 1997).

A postscript on assessment

Assessing personal and social development is highly normative, even more so when making judgments about school discipline and student behaviour. Educational psychologists have generated an extensive battery of measurement instruments and schedules for charting students' behavioural development. The major aim of this measurement activity has been to diagnose behavioural disorders. Clearly the behaviour of some students signifies conduct disorder or perhaps even pathological dysfunction. Unfortunately, this variation upon the medical model of diagnosis and treatment has dominated thinking about school discipline.

The preceding discussion, in this chapter, encourages us to think of student behaviour as more than a question of student pathology. School discipline is influenced by a range of factors. These factors are both internal and external to the school. Curriculum, pedagogy and school organization individually and collectively critically influence students' and teachers' behaviour. Assessing student behaviour is reflected by data such as truancy rates, exclusion rates, disruptive incidents in the classroom and so the list goes on. However, a much more complete evaluation of student behaviour and school discipline must consider a broader data-base to ask questions about the relationship between school and classroom processes and levels of student attachment and commitment as precursors to student behaviour. Simply put, evaluating student development reflects the level of development of the school as a suitable organization to host teaching and learning for a range of different students.

Note

1 For a lucid discussion of the regressive impact of neo-right education policies in North America see Apple, 1996 and Rose, 1995, and in Australia see Lingard and Porter, 1996 and Taylor, Rizvi, Lingard and Henry, 1997.

References

Apple, M. (1996) *Cultural Politics and Education*, Buckingham: Open University Press.
Ball, S.J. (1994) *Education Reform: A critical and post-structural approach*, Buckingham: Open University Press.

BALL, S. (September 1996) Performativity and Fragmentation in 'Postmodern Schooling'. Paper presented to Postmodernity and Fragmentation of Welfare Conference, University of Teeside.

BARBER, M. (1996) *The Learning Game*, London: Victor Gollancz.

BARTON, L. and LANDMAN, M. (1993) 'The politics of integration: Observations on the Warnock Report', in SLEE, R. (ed.) *Is There a Desk with My Name on it? The Politics of Integration*, London: Falmer Press.

BERNSTEIN, B. (1996) *Pedagogy, Symbolic Control and Identity: Theory, Research, Critique*, London: Taylor & Francis.

BROWN, M. (1988) 'The Tyranny of the International Horse Race', in SLEE, R., WEINER, G. and TOMLINSON, S. (ed.) *School Effectiveness for Whom?*, London: Falmer Press.

BUCK, M. and INMAN, S. (1995) 'Citizenship education', in INMAN, S. and BUCK, M. (eds) *Adding Value? Schools' Responsibility for Pupils' Personal Development*, Stoke-on-Trent: Trentham Books.

CLARK, C., DYSON, A., MILLWARD, A. and SKIDMORE, D. (1997) *New Directions in Special Needs*, London: Cassell.

CRITTENDEN, B. (1991) 'Three approaches to classroom discipline: philosophical perspectives', in LOVEGROVE, M.N. and LEWIS, R. (eds) *Classroom Discipline*, Melbourne: Longman Cheshire.

DALE, R. (1996) *Markets and Education*, Buckingham: Open University Press.

DEWEY, J. (1916) *Democracy and Education*, New York: The Free Press.

DES (1989) Committee of Enquiry into Discipline in Schools: report of the London Committee of Enquiry, London: HMSO.

EDWARDS, B. (1996) 'Suspension in Victorian secondary schools', unpublished Med dissertation, Bundoora, La Trobe University.

FOUCAULT, M. (1979) *The History of Sexuality*, London: Allen Lane.

FREIBERG, H.J. (ed.) (in press) *Beyond Behaviorism: Changing the Classroom Management Paradigm*, New York: Allyn & Bacon.

FRIERE, P. (1972) *Pedagogy of the Oppressed*, New York: Herder and Herder.

FURLONG, J. (1991) 'Disaffected pupils: Reconstructing the sociological perspective', *British Journal of Sociology of Education*, **12**, 3, pp. 293–307.

GEWIRTZ, S., BALL, S.J. and BOWE, R. (1995) *Markets, Choice and Equity in Education*, Buckingham: Open University Press.

GILLBORN, D. (1995) *Racism and Antiracism in Real Schools, Theory, Policy, Practice*, Buckingham: Open University Press.

GILLBORN, D. and GIPPS, C. (1996) *Recent Research on the Achievements of Ethnic Minority Pupils*, London: Office For Standards in Education.

GOLD, A., BOWE, R. and BALL, S.J. (1993) 'Special educational needs in a new context: micropolitics, money and "Education for All"', in SLEE, R. (ed.) *Is There a Desk with My Name on it? The Politics of Integration*, London: Falmer Press.

HAMILTON, D. (1988) 'The Idols of the Market Place' in SLEE, R., WEINER, G. and TOMLINSON, S. (ed.) *School Effectiveness For Whom?*, London: Falmer Press.

HAYEK, F.A. (1944) *The Road to Serfdom*, London: Routledge.

HER MAJESTY'S INSPECTORATE [HMI] (1978) *Behaviour Units: A Survey of Special Units for Students with Behavioural Problems*, London: HMSO.

HIRSCHI, T. (1969) *Causes of Delinquency*, Berkeley CA: University of California Press.

HOLDSWORTH, R. (1988) 'Student participation projects in Australia: An anecdotal history', in SLEE, R. (ed.) *Discipline and Schools: A Curriculum Perspective*, Melbourne: Macmillan.

KELLNER, P. (1997) 'Statistics behaving badly in the classroom', *The Observer*, London, Sunday, August 24.

KNIGHT, T. (1985) 'An apprenticeship in democracy', *The Australian Teacher*, **11**, pp. 5–7.

KNIGHT, T. (1988) 'Student discipline as a curriculum concern', in SLEE, R. (ed.) *Discipline and Schools: A Curriculum Perspective*, Melbourne: Macmillan.

KNIGHT, T. and LEWIS, R. (1993) 'Resisting the vanishing moral point: systemic solutions to school discipline', Research Seminar Presentation, King's College, University of London, June.

KNIGHT, T. and PEARL, A. (in press) *Democratic Schooling: Theory to Guide Educational Practice*, NJ: Hampton Press.

LEWIS, R., LOVEGROVE, M.N. and BURMAN, E. (1991) 'Teachers' perceptions of ideal classroom disciplinary practices', in LOVEGROVE, M.N. and LEWIS, R. (eds) *Classroom Discipline*, Melbourne: Longman Cheshire.

LINGARD, B. and PORTER, P. (1997) *A National Approach to Schooling in Australia? Essays on the Development of National Policies in Schools Education*, Canberra: The Australian College of Education.

LOCKE, J. (1693) *Some Thoughts Concerning Education*, (F.W. GARFORTH edition, 1964), London: Heinemann.

LYOTARD, F. (1984) *The Postmodern Condition: A Report on Knowledge*, Minneapolis: University of Minnesota Press.

MANDELSON, P. and LIDDLE, R. (1996) *The Blair Revolution: Can New Labour Deliver?*, London: Faber & Faber.

MCGOUGHLIN, T. (1992) 'Citizenship, diversity and education: a philosophical perspective', *Journal of Moral Education*, **21**, 3.

MONGON, D. (1988) 'Behaviour units, "maladjustment" and student control', in SLEE, R. (ed.) *Discipline and Schools: A Curriculum Perspective*, Melbourne: Macmillan.

NATIONAL COMMISSION ON EDUCATION (1993) *Learning to Succeed*, London: Heinemann.

OFFICE FOR STANDARDS IN EDUCATION (1994) *Spiritual, Moral, Social and Cultural Development*, London: Ofsted.

PEARL, A. (1972) *The Atrocity of Education*, New York: The Free Press.

PEARL, A. (1988) 'The requirements of a democratic education', in SLEE, R. (ed.) *Discipline and Schools: A Curriculum Perspective*, Melbourne: Macmillan.

POLK, K. (1984) 'The new marginal youth', *Crime and Delinquency*, **30**, pp. 462–480.

REYNOLDS, D. (1995) 'Using school effectiveness knowledge for children with special needs — the problems and possibilities', in CLARK, C., DYSON, A. and MILLWARD, A. (eds) *Towards Inclusive Schools?* London: David Fulton Publishers.

REYNOLDS, D. and FARRELL, S. (1996) *Worlds Apart? A Review of International Surveys of Educational Achievement Involving England*, London: Office for Standards in Education.

RICHARDSON, V. (1977) 'Constructivist teaching and teacher education: theory and practice', in RICHARDSON, V. (ed.) *Constructivist Teacher Education: Building a World of New Understanding*, London: Falmer Press.

ROGERS, C. (1969) *Freedom to Learn*, Columbus: Merrill.

ROSE, M. (1995) *Possible Lives*, New York: Penguin Books.

SEWELL, T. (1997) *Black Masculinities and Schooling: How Black Boys Survive Modern Schooling*, Stoke-on-Trent: Trentham Books.

SKINNER, B.F. (1968) *The Technology of Teaching*, New York: Appleton Century Crofts.

SKINNER, B.F. (1972) *Beyond Freedom and Dignity*, London: Jonathan Cape.

SLEE, R. (ed.) (1991) *Discipline in Australian Public Education: From Policy to Practice*, Hawthorn: Australian Council for Educational Research.

SLEE, R. (1995) *Changing Theories and Practices of Discipline*, London: Falmer Press.

SMITH, R. (1985) *Freedom and Discipline*, London: George Allen and Unwin.

SPENCER, H. (1910) *Education: Intellectual, Moral and Physical*, London: Williams and Northgate.

STENHOUSE, L. (1971) *Culture and Education*, London: Nelson.

TAYLOR, S., RIZVI, F., LINGARD, B. and HENRY, M. (1997) *Educational Policy and the Politics of Change*, London: Routledge.

TROYNA, B. (1993) *Racism and Education: Research Perspectives*, Buckingham: Open University Press.

VYGOTSKY, L.V. (1962) *Thought and Language*, Cambridge MA: Massachusetts Institute of Technology Press.

VYGOTSKY, L.V. (1978) *Mind in Society: The Development of Higher Psychological Processes*, Cambridge MA: Harvard University Press.

WHITTY, G. (1997) 'Social theory and education policy: the legacy of Karl Mannheim, *British Journal of Sociology of Education*, **18**, 2, pp. 149–163.

WILSON, P.S. (1971) *Interest and Discipline in Education*, London: Routledge and Kegan Paul.

WU, S., PINK, W.T., CRAIN, R.L. and MOLES, O. (1982) 'Student suspension: a critical reappraisal', *The Urban Review*, **14**, pp. 245–303.

YEATMAN, A. (1994) *Postmodern Revisionings of the Political*, New York: Routledge.

Chapter 6

A Curriculum Framework for Personal and Social Development: A National Project

Alma Harris

Abstract

This chapter explores the practicalities and possibilities of a whole school approach to personal and social development. It describes the development and evaluation of the 'Pathways towards Adult and Working Life Project' which provides a curriculum framework for personal and social development from Key Stage 1 to Key Stage 4. The chapter considers issues of assessing personal and social development and concludes by suggesting that more sophisticated assessment procedures are required to capture the breadth and complexity of PSD learning.

Introduction

Prior to the arrival of the Education Reform Act in 1988, personal and social development (PSD) received wide and substantial political support in a range of official government publications (HMI, 1983; 1986). A large number of LEAs registered their formal support for PSD by publishing their own individual policy statements and guidelines on the area (Pring, 1987). In many respects, this plethora of policy statements and guidelines at both national and local levels simply reflected the diverse array of practice concerning PSD in secondary schools at the time.

Despite a growing measure of support for PSD prior to 1988, it has not fared well since the Education Reform Act. The prevailing climate of pressure upon teachers and schools has resulted in the marginalization of important dimensions of the curriculum. The standardization of both the curriculum and the inspection process has promulgated the view that the subject-based curriculum is of paramount importance. Government legislation and financial support has served to reinforce this view of the academic, subject-based curriculum. As a result, many areas of curriculum activity which do not fall neatly into the boundaries of the National Curriculum have lost support and position. Such areas have included careers, business education links and a wide range of extra-curricular activities which all make a contribution to PSD in some way.

Yet, if one considers Section 1 of the 1988 Education Reform Act there are overarching responsibilities of the school curriculum to:

- promote the spiritual, moral, cultural and physical development of pupils;
- prepare pupils for the opportunities and responsibilities of adult life.

Clearly, this points towards personal and social development (PSD) as much of the teaching and learning in this area aims to develop the knowledge, understanding and attitudes of young people concerning themselves and the world around them. However, the factors which lead to enhanced learning in PSD demand a much broader scope of teaching and learning activity than the National Curriculum currently provides. The unanswered question seems to be 'how do schools provide the learning experiences necessary for the development of the whole pupil?'. This inevitably leads to some scrutiny of the current curriculum provision for PSD.

Current curriculum locations

To organize and implement the teaching of PSD for most schools has proved to be remarkably difficult. Schools tend to have highly idiosyncratic responses to PSD and in many schools this position is entrenched. Where schools take the view that PSD is important, it still requires considerable planning and monitoring, both at the level of the whole school and by individual subject departments. Also, given that a priori, there is little evidence to suggest that such an undertaking would improve performance in either the league tables for SATs tests, or GCSE, there is little incentive for schools to pursue this course of action. However it remains clear from the research findings concerning school effectiveness, that schools with positive social outcomes tend to place a premium on developing the whole child (Reynolds, 1992). These are schools which recognize that pupils' academic and social success is ultimately grounded in the quality of the classroom relationship. In short, such schools plan the teaching and learning for academic and social learning outcomes.

The effective teaching of PSD involves choices about implementation, about particular ways it should be catered for, or presented within the school. There are currently two obvious curriculum locations for the explicit taught provision for personal and social development (PSD) within schools. There is PSE as delivered through the pastoral care system and discrete curriculum locations in which PSE is taught by specialists. Both approaches have have proved far from ideal in teaching PSD in a coordinated and effective way. It has been argued for example, that pastoral care structures are largely ill equipped to coordinate and provide PSD throughout the school (Watkins, 1986). Others have suggested that the pastoral care system is not best placed to manage, coordinate and deliver PSD (Hargreaves et al., 1988).

One typical way in which schools have made specific provision for pupils' personal and social development is outside the mainstream curriculum, in extracurricular activity. Traditionally, this has been one response to the difficulties of successfully delivering PSD within the curriculum. Consequently, school clubs, teams and societies provide pupils with the opportunity to engage in social interaction and to refine social skills. Sometimes, the personal and social qualities that participation in extra-curricular activity encourages are planned and intended. More often, however, the personal and social elements of extra-curricular activities are unplanned and no PSD learning outcomes are specified.

The explicit teaching of PSE within the curriculum and the implicit teaching of PSE outside the curriculum may contribute little to pupils' personal and social development, particularly if they remain separate from each other. Alternatively, both make an important contribution if they are part of a whole school approach to PSD. It could be argued also that subject areas have much to offer a whole school approach to personal and social development. Consequently, to confine PSD to discrete parts of the curriculum is to risk fragmentation, omission and possible duplication.

There are a number of problems with the current curriculum provision of PSD. The first problem relates to the fact that one of the most managerially attractive options for tackling PSD is to make some kind of separate, or additional provision for it, in addition to the school's existing curricular and organizational arrangements. A taught course, the PSE programme, extra-curricular or cross curricular activities all ensure that PSD occurs with the least amount of disruption, or challenge, to what the school is already doing. Separate provision of PSD rather than a coordinated whole school approach will inevitably place it on the margins of school life and at the tail end of staff and pupils' priorities.

A second problem relates to coordination of the learning within PSD. Coherence would seem to be imperative between the different parts of young people's educational and human experience which comprise PSD. So, too is orderly, key stage by key stage progression in the learning that pupils undertake in this sphere. Effective coordination within PSD is vital to offset fragmentation and duplication in learning and ensure coherence and continuity in education. However, there would appear to be an absence of coherence, continuity and progression within existing PSD provision in schools because of the absence of a whole school approach.

A third problem relates to consistency and coordination of PSD within schools. This extends far beyond the bringing together of different bits of PSE provision, or different parts of the curriculum, to the core of the teaching process itself. For PSD, initiatives are unlikely to meet with any great or lasting success if what they teach and what they encourage is contradicted by what a pupil learns, understands and experiences in the remainder of their school life. One of the most important goals of any PSD programme must be to try and secure some consistency in the personal and social qualities, skills and understandings that they are being encouraged to develop across the entire range of their school experience. This is only really possible via whole school planning and coordinated delivery of PSD.

Finally, with a subject curriculum so tightly bound up in specifying learning outcomes, it is clear that by comparison the PSD provision in schools appears rather vague and unstructured. The net result of this situation has been to lower the prestige of PSD in comparison with subject teaching. This affects the enthusiasm with which all teachers pursue it in their classrooms and include the development of the whole child as part of subject teaching. Without a clearly defined 'subject type' discourse it seems most likely that teaching PSD will continue to be undermined and steadily marginalized within the National Curriculum. This leads one to the position of arguing for a well defined whole school PSD framework to complement rather than compete with the National Curriculum.

'Pathways Toward Adult and Working Life'

PSD is an area of such all encompassing relevance to life and the development of young people that high expectations for its success call for high levels of involvement from all teaching staff. Repeatedly, it has been shown that the coherence and effectiveness of any particular aspect of PSD teaching in schools depends on the wider support for and commitment to the subject throughout the school as a whole. It is this whole school approach to PSD that the 'Pathways Toward Adult and Working Life' project endorses.

The 'Pathways' project arose from concern that the existing curriculum provided little scope for enhancing the development of knowledge, attitudes, understanding and behaviours concerned with personal and social development. The demise of the cross curricular themes had led to much insecurity about the future of education-industry links and young people's understanding the world of work. Industrialists and educationalists who were committed to preparing young people for the world of work by developing the knowledge, skills and attitudes necessary for making informed choices saw little in the curriculum for work-related learning opportunities and skill development. Consequently, the Pathways project was funded by prominent industrialists and developed with teachers for teachers as a means of providing a whole school approach to work-related learning and the other important dimensions which comprised PSD (LENTA, 1996).

The 'Pathways Toward Adult Life Project' was deliberately designed to facilitate whole school planning of pupil learning in the specific areas of personal and social development. As a curriculum framework its intentions were to supplement and enhance the existing National Curriculum by encompassing those learning experiences which most effectively contributed to the preparation of young people for adult life. These learning experiences were intended for all pupils irrespective of age, or ability, as the Pathways' Framework operates from Key stage 1 to Key stage 4.

The resulting Pathways' Framework has two main purposes. Firstly, it is a curriculum framework which maps much of the knowledge and many of the PSD skills required to prepare young people for adult and working life. Based upon clearly defined learner outcomes, the Framework is intended as a curriculum template for those areas of the curriculum associated with preparation for adult and working life. Secondly, the Framework is intended as a management tool for school effectiveness insofar as it provides the basis for restructuring the curriculum for improved teaching and learning purposes within the areas of Personal and Social Development (PSD), including Careers Education and Guidance (CEG).

The 'Pathways' initiative is a curriculum approach which is chiefly concerned with preparing young people for adult and working life in its broadest, social sense. Its aim is to move away from a narrow interpretation of preparation for adult life which simply provided those values and skills that enabled young people to slot into the world of work. The Pathways Project is mainly concerned with qualities of independent judgment, resistance to pressure, personal strength and critical appraisal rather than narrow technical skills, or vocational competences. In addition, the project recognizes that political education is an important aspect of preparation for working life. In this respect, it is premised upon enabling young people to internalize those values which are essential to the maintenance of the democratic form of life and to contribute constructively to those social institutions and communities which affect their welfare and well being.

The Pathways Project

The Pathways Project includes: a whole school PSD framework from which individualized learning programmes can be negotiated, thus permitting individualized schemes while maintaining standards, quality and currency.

A profile recording the results of a variety of kinds of assessment and a process of profiling which involves the learner in developing skills of self-assessment and requires the active engagement of teachers.

Participative and resource based learning methods which can adapt to a variety of learning needs within the same group and which make use of the community and business as a resource.

Overall, the Framework is intended to be a curriculum model for PSD which incorporates coherence, continuity and progression (Harris, 1996), with defined areas of knowledge required to prepare young people for adult and working life. Previous projects of this kind deliberately resisted defining learner outcomes in this way despite an acknowledgment that this would inevitably raise the status of PSD and work-related activities (Jamieson, 1991; Jamieson and Harris, 1992). In this respect, the Pathways' Framework is learner outcome-led and prescriptive in terms of curriculum structure rather than pedagogy and content.

Pathways in practice

The 'Pathways' curriculum model has been extensively piloted over a two year period with primary and secondary schools in the three authorities of Cheshire,

Figure 6.1: Improving pupil achievement in PSD

Specified learning outcomes which are made explicit to pupils
Linkages between learning outcomes for pupils i.e. there is some form of content mapping for pupils
Providing a coherent language for learning
Valuing and recording experience and achievement
Systematic review and evaluation of both process and content.

Figure 6.2: Improving pupil performance through PSD

Enabling the learner to draw upon previous experience to understand and evaluate the present i.e. it is learning which is reflective and experiential
Providing a consistent model of learning
Focusing on clear learner outcomes
Encouraging the learner to be autonomous and self-reliant.

Doncaster and Lewisham. The evaluation of the pilot project has demonstrated the potential of the Framework to be a catalyst for curriculum restructuring and development (Harris, 1997). The majority of schools in the pilot have used the Framework as a means of school development planning and a vehicle for school improvement. The evaluation has provided evidence of increased pupil attainment in a range of personal and social skills and in other areas of PSD.

The Framework deliberately moves away from dividing PSD knowledge, skills and attitudes into artificially discrete areas, even though such a division can prove useful in terms of assessment and planning. Instead, the framework attempts to offer a more coherent approach to PSD provision. Progression has been carefully structured within the Framework to enable schools in both the primary and secondary sectors to be working towards the same set of learning outcomes. It is no accident that the Framework reflects those features of teaching and learning which are associated with improved pupil achievement. These features are summarized in Figure 6.1.

Similarly, in terms of learning, a number of consistent features which lead to improved pupil performance are incorporated in the Framework. These are shown in Figure 6.2.

Pathways is not intended to be an alternative curriculum but has been designed to reinforce key skills, knowledge and abilities within personal and social development.

There are three basic components, or sections within the Pathways Framework which are interrelated. The first section focuses on the self, the second on the self and others and the third focuses upon self in the world of work and the wider community. These sections are not mutually exclusive but overlap to reinforce Framework learning outcomes from different perspectives and contexts.

Self — personal development and personal skills

The first section focuses upon Self — Personal Development and Personal Skills. In this section it is anticipated that learners will understand the importance of respecting themselves and others and of looking after themselves. Also the section aims to ensure that learners will come to know their own strengths and current limitations and will be able to plan to improve their personal effectiveness, meet their needs and manage personal resources. The learner outcomes in this section are as follows:

1.1 Learners know their own strengths and current limitations
1.2 Learners can develop skills of self-evaluation and planning to meet personal development needs
1.3 Learners can identify their own learning needs, can seek resources and can plan learning opportunities
1.4 Learners understand the importance of managing personal resources
1.5 Learners understand the importance of having a personal and moral code
1.6 Learners understand the importance of respecting themselves and others

This section focuses upon individual growth and development. It is intended to resource young people with the skills needed for personal autonomy as a learner in areas such as decision making, information finding and self-evaluation. The focus of this section is upon self-analysis and improvement. Linked to this is setting criteria for assessing personal effectiveness so that learners can plan ahead using their own criteria. Similarly, the identification of personal learning needs is important to ensure that learners can use the resources at their disposal and can plan learning opportunities for themselves.

A central part of this section emphasizes that learners can approach tasks independently and effectively. The aim of this is to ensure that learners gradually take more and more responsibility for their own learning. It is envisaged that this skill will be developed and practised in a wide variety of curriculum and learning contexts. In addition to managing their own learning, the section also includes the personal management of resources. Overall, it is anticipated that this section will deal with issues of morality and personal codes of conduct. Linked to this is overall personal responsibility and, in particular, understanding the importance of looking after themselves. The learning contexts for this set of learning outcomes could be very varied and would obviously lend itself to PSD related activities and experiences.

Self and others

The second section focuses upon Self and Others — opportunities, choices, rights and responsibilities. In this section it is hoped that learners move away from considerations of self to appreciate their roles in the family, at school and in the community. They will be able to work with others and understand the implications of living in a pluralistic society. They should be aware of the importance of tradition, rules and laws, and know about political systems and their adult responsibilities and rights. This section also focuses upon the importance of pupils respecting themselves and others. This overall aim of the section is to develop personal qualities which include tolerance and respect. In particular the emphasis is upon learners demonstrating respect towards other beliefs and cultures. It is foreseeable that this can be taught through many different curriculum contexts and would encompass discussions of spirituality and the development of a personal moral code.

The second section builds upon the first by focusing upon knowledge and understanding of opportunities, choices, rights and responsibilities. The learning outcomes in the second section are as follows:

- 2.1 Learners can form appropriate relationships in different contexts
- 2.2 Learners can work collaboratively and appropriately with others
- 2.3 Learners are aware of how external influences affect their role as responsible citizens
- 2.4 Learners know about political systems and about their adult responsibilities and rights
- 2.5 Learners can seek out information and help from a variety of careers education and guidance agencies
- 2.6 Learners know that there will be changes in working patterns and career opportunities in the future
- 2.7 Learners can record information about choices and opportunities

An important component of this proactive stance is the ability of learners to form appropriate relationships in various situations. This section begins by focusing upon the roles and responsibilities of individuals at home and school. It encompasses the meaning of friendship and loyalty and emphasizes how individual actions have consequences for other people in the context of school, work and the wider community. It progresses to a general appreciation of the role of the family, religion, culture and society in maintaining social stability and influencing social change.

The importance of shared working and group work is continually emphasized by employers but it is a skill that requires constant practice and refinement. Learners will work together in groups, listen to others, share with others in a learning context as an important dimension of this learning outcome. Working with people from other cultures is emphasized as well as understanding how prejudice and discrimination affect relationships at home, at school, at work and in the wider community. It is anticipated at post-14, learners will show that they can accept responsibility for their own choices and decisions and can explain their choices and decisions to others including adults.

Self in the world of work

The third section focuses upon Self in the World of Work and the Wider Community. It is designed to enable learners to understand the changing nature of work, as well as how to seek and record information from guidance agencies. This section is concerned with the process of wealth creation and challenges young people to consider environmental issues concerned with valuing the natural world. The learner outcomes included in this section are as follows:

3.1 Learners understand the implications of living in a diverse society
3.2 Learners know about the scope and range of different organizations
3.3 Learners know and understand the process of wealth creation
3.4 Learners know how services are provided in different sectors of society
3.5 Learners value the natural world
3.6 Learners know about and can investigate the interrelationship between the economy and the environment

This section is intended to enable learners to explore the relationship between the economy and the environment. It is a further extension on section two as it takes the learner into contexts away from home and the immediate community. There is evidently much scope in this section for the use of business and industry as a context for exploring issues concerning choice and environmental cost.

In planning the teaching against the learner outcomes, schools in the project used a planning sheet with seven columns. Two examples of completed sheets appear as appendixes to illustrate the planning process and the types of learning pupils became engaged in as part of the project. Appendix 1 is an example of primary school planning to address learner outcome 3.6. This school used a quarry as a focus for learning about the world of work. The evidence of pupil learning which was collected as part of this topic included written work, drawings, video evidence, self-assessment, models on display and feedback from adults.

Appendix 2 focuses upon a learner outcomes 1.1 and 1.2 from section one of the framework. In this case, the secondary school is focusing upon specific subject areas such as art and English to provide some opportunities to demonstrate this learner outcome. In addition, there is some recognition that the work based programmes and the awards evening have a major role to play in PSD of this kind. This planning sheet shows that the school has a range of curriculum based assessment mechanisms which include self-assessment, peer-assessment, individual tutorials, PSE lessons, action planning, careers interviews and the achievement programme. However, the assessment issues relating to Pathways were not without some problems. This issue will be returned to later in the chapter.

The Pathways framework is deliberately designed to facilitate whole school delivery of personal and social education. By definition it aims to ensure continuity, coherence and progression between the key stages. Moreover, as a curriculum framework which bridges all key stages it is premised upon progression between the primary and secondary school phases. The framework attempts to ensure progression for all the Pathway learner outcomes by providing a detailed descriptor for each outcome at each key stage. These descriptors largely reflect what pupils should know, understand and be able to do at each key stage in the Framework. For example for the first learner outcome which is:

Learners know their own strengths and current limitations

the key stage descriptors are as follows:

KS 1 Learners are aware of what they are good at from external feedback and can say what they would like to be good at in the future.
KS 2 Learners can assess their own strengths and current limitations and describe their plans for future self-development to others.
KS 3 Learners can assess strengths and weaknesses independently.
KS 4 Learners can assess their strengths and current limitations independently. They can use feedback and critical appraisal in a formative and constructive way. They can identify personal development needs and seek appropriate information to help meet personal needs.

These key stage descriptors follow a similar pattern of *awareness*, *articulation analysis* and *application* at each successive key stage. The descriptors deliberately move from the concrete to the abstract, from simple to complex ideas. While the content and focus of individual descriptors vary within the framework, collectively they offer a coherent learning programme for each key stage and phase.

An important dimension of the Pathways evaluation was progression and continuity. Much time was spent obtaining the views of teachers and pupils concerning the appropriateness of individual key stage descriptors. This feedback subsequently directed much of the re-structuring and re-working of the final Pathways Framework.

Evaluating Pathways

The Pathways' evaluation involved a longitudinal study of two cohorts of students (Years 6 and 10) in both Pathway and non-Pathway schools. All the Pathway schools were involved in the evaluation and in each of the three LEAs there were both secondary and primary 'control' schools. In both Pathways and control schools 20 per cent of the appropriate year group (i.e. Year 6 or 10) were randomly selected for involvement in the data-collection process over the two year period. A wide range of data was collected throughout the pilot phase. Qualitative data was collected via interviews with teachers and pupils to ascertain the impact of the Framework on teaching and learning processes. In addition, HMI and Ofsted conducted independent surveys of the 'Pathway' schools and the schools themselves collected in-depth case-study evidence. Quantitative data which focused specifically on PSD learning outcomes was collected by means of specially designed student questionnaires (see Appendix 3). The questionnaire data was independently analyzed at the NFER.

The administration of the questionnaires at the outset of the project provided some 'base-line' evidence. This data showed that at the start of the project the Pathways schools and the control schools were relatively homogeneous and that no major differences existed between pupils in either group of schools in repect of those areas identified in the questionnaire. In terms of self-knowledge, making choices and understanding the world of work, both groups of pupils demonstrated little difference at the start of the project. This analysis was important because it enabled subsequent comparisons to be made between Pathways and non-Pathways students and schools.

The evaluation of the Project focused upon how the framework was being used in schools and its subsequent impact upon pupil learning in PSD and showed that the majority of schools in the pilot project used the framework as a basis for planning PSD across the curriculum. The Framework had been written into whole school developmental and action plans through the identification of specific PSD targets, tasks, timescales, responsibilities, resource implications and review procedures. Several of the Pathways schools introduced curriculum entitlements for PSD which specified the learning outcomes for all pupils, outlining what learning outcomes pupils can expect within the context of PSD. The evaluation also found that the incorporation of the Framework into whole school development planning had both a practical and a symbolic purpose within the Pathways schools. In practical terms, teachers expressed the view that the framework had enabled them to be sure about their particular contribution to PSD. In symbolic terms, they felt that it had raised the profile and status of the subject within the curriculum. It is notable that in several of the pilot schools the framework is viewed as a mechanism for curriculum planning and development.

The evaluation discovered that the schools in the pilot phase of the study made particular efforts to promote Pathways' learner outcomes within the mainstream curriculum. In these schools the Pathways' learner outcomes were well known to pupils, teachers and parents. Every effort was made by these schools to make learner outcomes explicit for pupils and to reinforce the importance of these skills throughout the curriculum. In this respect a variety of strategies have been used by the schools to assist implementation. These include:

- making Pathways' learner outcomes the foundation of the PSD programme;
- linking the Pathways' learner outcomes explicitly to the National Record of Achievement; and

- asking students to record Pathways skill development as part of work-experience debriefing and other forms of experiential learning.

It would appear that the interpretation of Pathways' learner outcomes has impacted upon teaching and learning processes in the schools in the pilot study in four main ways:

1. establishing substantial consensus about what constitutes Pathways' learner outcomes between pupils, teachers, and employers;
2. reinforcing learner outcomes in everyday classroom practice and ensuring progression between the key stages;
3. evaluating the individual personal and social development of pupils more effectively; and
4. establishing the basis for a dialogue about personal and social development between teachers from different phases.

One important issue which did arise in a number of the schools in the pilot study concerned the importance of progression and continuity which the framework provided. For both primary and secondary schools the existence of a common framework has enabled teachers to plan together and to ensure that duplication of effort was avoided and that the potential for PSD which built upon previous learning was maximized.

Assessment, recording and accreditation

One of the main ways of making Pathways' learner outcomes explicit to pupils has been through the school's formal assessment and accreditation procedures. A number of the pilot schools used their merit and reward schemes as important mechanisms in making Pathways' learner outcomes both highly visible and valuable to the pupils. This was particularly important in the primary school where the learner outcomes could not be recorded or assessed more formally. However, in one LEA the learner outcomes were incorporated into a Primary Learning Record under other areas for development.

In terms of more formal accreditation mechanisms, the secondary schools selected various ways in which achievement in Pathways' learner outcomes were recorded. In several Pathways schools formal accreditation schemes were already in place that were subsequently selected to reflect work-related learning. These schemes have included the ASDAN scheme and the Youth Award Scheme. It was generally felt by the teachers in the Pathways Project that formal accreditation for Pathways was crucially important in raising pupils' motivation for PSD. This clearly relates to the issue of valuing learning that can be easily measured and assessed more than learning which is less accessible to formal accreditation or assessment. In all the pilot schools, the Record of Achievement was used to record and accredit pupil achievement in the Pathways learner outcomes. It was noticeable that in these schools the Record of Achievement was highly valued and that pupils placed a high degree of importance upon the Pathways learner outcomes because they were explicitly stated within the ROA. A consistent feature of those schools which demonstrated high rates of success with the project was the fact that a direct linkage was made between learning and the recording of achievement in this area. Teachers generally shared the view that such assessment and recording mechanisms were very important because they highlighted and reinforced the importance of PSD to pupils (Harris, 1997).

The Pathways schools also used action planning extensively and exclusively as a means of recording achievement in PSD. Most of these action planning initiatives resulted in the production of a National Record of Achievement which incorporated and made explicit the Pathways learning outcomes. The details of the action planning process in each school reflected the Pathways framework in content and process. One very important element in making this process work was ensuring that young people had enough information on which to base their judgments. For example, such information could refer to their present position against Pathways learner outcomes as well as what they need to do next to improve. Pilot schools were very good at giving young people feedback on their current performance, *and* in facilitating experiences where young people could develop certain skills further.

In one school for example, all subject staff periodically rated their pupils on five Pathways related outcomes with others in the class, all on a five point scale. These assessments were then passed to the form tutors and the pupils and formed part of the action planning discussion. In another pilot school the PSD provision contained self-assessment exercises centred around Pathways' learner outcomes which were completed at various stages. The results of these contributed to action planning discussions. Most of the pilot schools ensured that young people completed some form of vocational preferences exercise, for example, JIG CAL or Jobwise which also formed data that was useful for Pathways skill recording and personal action planning.

In Pathways' schools young people were encouraged to undertake experiences which were felt to be useful within the context of PSD and action planning. At its most modest this was little more than pupils returning to school with evidence that they had taken part in some event or organization, for example membership of the Girl Guides or a local band. At its best young people filed feedback on performance from a wide range of different activities in their action planning base files. Sometimes action planning itself resulted in young people seeking out experiences in order to further one of their Pathway learner goals. The pilot schools used the Pathway learner outcomes as automatic targets for their pupils. Where this was carefully explained, where targets were realistic, and where young people could see the real benefits in achieving the targets, there was evidence in the evaluation that this approach worked very effectively (Harris, 1997). In the pilot schools action planning was viewed by pupils as a central way of devising personal development targets.

Pupil evaluation

From the quantitative and qualitative evidence collected over two years there was evidence of differences between the two cohorts of pupils i.e. Pathways and the control groups. Differences were most acute within the area of personal, or self-knowledge. This area largely comprised statements concerning personal skill and social development. The quantitative data analysis showed that for this factor the differences between Pathways and non-Pathways schools 'were appreciable with evidence of Pathways schools leading to higher scores on these items' (Harris, 1997).

From the qualitative data comparisons between round one and round four of the data collection revealed that pupils in the Pathways schools were more confident about personal knowledge than pupils in the control schools. The interview data similarly revealed that the Pathways pupils were more able to analyze their own skills and abilities than their counterparts in the control schools. The following range of comments are examples of those made by pupils and illustrate the differences between pupils in the Pathways and control groups.

> *I think I know my own good and bad points. We do a lot of looking at that in action planning on that so you go over it again and again. (Pupil 3 Pathways)*

> *Yes, I think I know myself pretty well. I mean you have to know what you're good at or you could go for the wrong A levels. I am good at communication but not so good at practical things really, so I'm going to do journalism. (Pupil 5 Pathways)*

> *The Pathway Targets help me to know how well I'm doing. They help me think about myself rather than about science, maths or geography. (Pupil 8 Pathways)*

> *This school tries to make you list your strengths and weaknesses but most people only write down the good things. I mean there's no point in writing down what you're bad at. (Pupil 3 Control School)*

> *I don't think I really know what I'm good at. You need other people to tell you. We have Records of Achievement but I've no idea what to put into the file. (Pupil 5 Control School)*

> *I think you need some guidelines, or goals to help you develop personally, all the PSE lessons are very different with no common thread, it's very confusing and we are all really bored in those lessons. (Pupil 6 Control School)*

> *All the teachers help you with your Pathways targets, I mean we are all working in the same direction, same targets and goals. It helps to know where you are then you can plan where you need to go next. (Pupil 11 Pathways School)*

The quantitative and qualitative evaluation showed that the Pathways Project had a positive effect upon pupils' development of self-knowledge. Furthermore, the quantitative evidence suggested that pupils in the Pathways schools were showing improvement over time in self-knowledge and that this was at a greater pace than pupils in the control schools.

In summary, the Pathways evaluation evidence showed that several differences were in evidence between the Pathways and non-Pathways pupil cohorts. In the Pathways schools pupils were much more confident about career guidance and planning than their non-Pathways counterparts. The evaluation evidence showed that the Pathways pupils were more able to access career information/seeking help and guidance within the school than the pupils in the control schools. Similarly, Pathways pupils demonstrated far greater confidence about their knowledge of self and personal skills than the control school pupils. All this points to the importance of a having a PSD curriculum structure, or framework within schools. Also, it reinforces the importance of clear assessment practices and procedures which capture pupils' learning in personal and social development.

Without shared PSD targets and an effective way of recording pupil progress in this area, it would appear that the possibilities for effective PSD within schools becomes severely reduced. However, this is not to discount the difficulties associated with implementing an effective PSD curriculum which is appropriately assessed. The evaluation evidence showed that teachers had most difficulty in completing the evidence column of the planning sheet. In the primary schools this difficulty was less marked but in the secondary schools the provision of evidence concerning pupil learning against the learning outcomes proved problematic. A number of reasons for this difficulty can be posited. Firstly, that teachers in the secondary sector are more subject focused and are less experienced in assessing personal skills, knowledge and abilities as part of their subject teaching. Secondly, that the assessment procedures and practices within schools are not appropriate for recording PSD because in most cases they focus narrowly upon knowledge attainment rather than personal development. Finally, as noted earlier, the current pressure upon schools to raise standards and to raise achievement militates against schools placing resources, effort and emphasis upon PSD assessment.

Conclusion

In educating young people we cannot predict with certainty the skills and the knowledge they will need. Nor can we draw upon a shared tradition of values to meet the many problems that young people will face in their personal and social lives. Therefore, we cannot, in preparing them for such a future, rely upon our traditional authority in teaching with confidence as to how they must deal with specific problems. First, we are not clear what these problems will be. Second, part of the present moral and social climate is a distrust of authority, especially in the realms of values. Third, without an agreed tradition of values it is not easy to see how one can promote with confidence one particular set of values rather than another.

The solution therefore, must lie in a deeper concern for the whole person — a respect for pupils or students as people, enabling them to articulate and to refine their feelings to achieve self-esteem and sense of personal worth, to develop the capacity to reflect upon experience and to accept seriously the values and attitudes that they bring to school and college. The Pathways Project is premised upon the development of the whole person and offers schools the opportunity to approach this challenge in a structured way. For many schools this approach might be overly prescriptive, or too demanding on the existing curriculum. However, there is a growing research and development base concerning PSD which shows that without clearly defined targets and robust assessment procedures this important dimension of pupils' development will be lost in the pursuit of subject-based imperatives. Consequently, while the Pathways Project is not the only solution to the curriculum conundrum facing PSD, it does offer an opportunity to ensure that PSD is taken seriously within the curriculum and that pupil progress in personal and social development is effectively monitored, recorded and assessed.

References

HARGREAVES, A. et al., (1988) *Personal and Social Education: Choices and Challenges*, Oxford: Joshua Associates Press.

HARRIS, A. (1996) *Pathways Evaluation: Interim Report*, London: LeNTA.

HARRIS, A. (1997) *Pathways Evaluation: Final Report*, London: LeNTA.

HMI (1983) *Learning Out of Doors*, London: HMSO.

HMI (1986) *Health Education 5–16*, London: HMSO.

JAMIESON, I.M. (1991) 'School work and real work: Economic and industrial understanding in the curriculum', *The Curriculum Journal*, **2**, 1.

JAMIESON, I.M. and HARRIS, A. (1992) 'Evaluating economic awareness, Part 1: Management and organisation issues', *Economic Awareness*, **4**, 1.

LENTA (1996) *Pathways Toward Adult and Working Life: Project Overview*, London: London Enterprise Agency.

PRING, R. (1984) 'Personal and Social Education in the Curricula: concepts and content', London: Hodder Stoughton.

PRING, R. (1987) 'Implications of the changing values and ethical standards of society', in THACKER et al. (eds) *Personal Social and Moral Education*, London: NFER–Nelson.

REYNOLDS, D. (1992) 'School effectiveness and school improvement: an updated review of the British literature', in REYNOLDS, D. and CUTTANCE, P. (eds) *School Effectiveness: Research, Policy and Practice*, London and New York: Cassell.

WATKINS, C. (1986) 'Does pastoral care = personal and social education?', *Pastoral Care in Education*, **3**, 3.

WHITTY, G.J., AGGLETON, P.J. and ROWE, G. (1992) *Cross Curricular Work in Secondary School: A Summary of Results of a Survey carried out in 1992'*, London: Institute of Education, (mimeo).

Appendix 1 — Planning for learner outcome 3.6

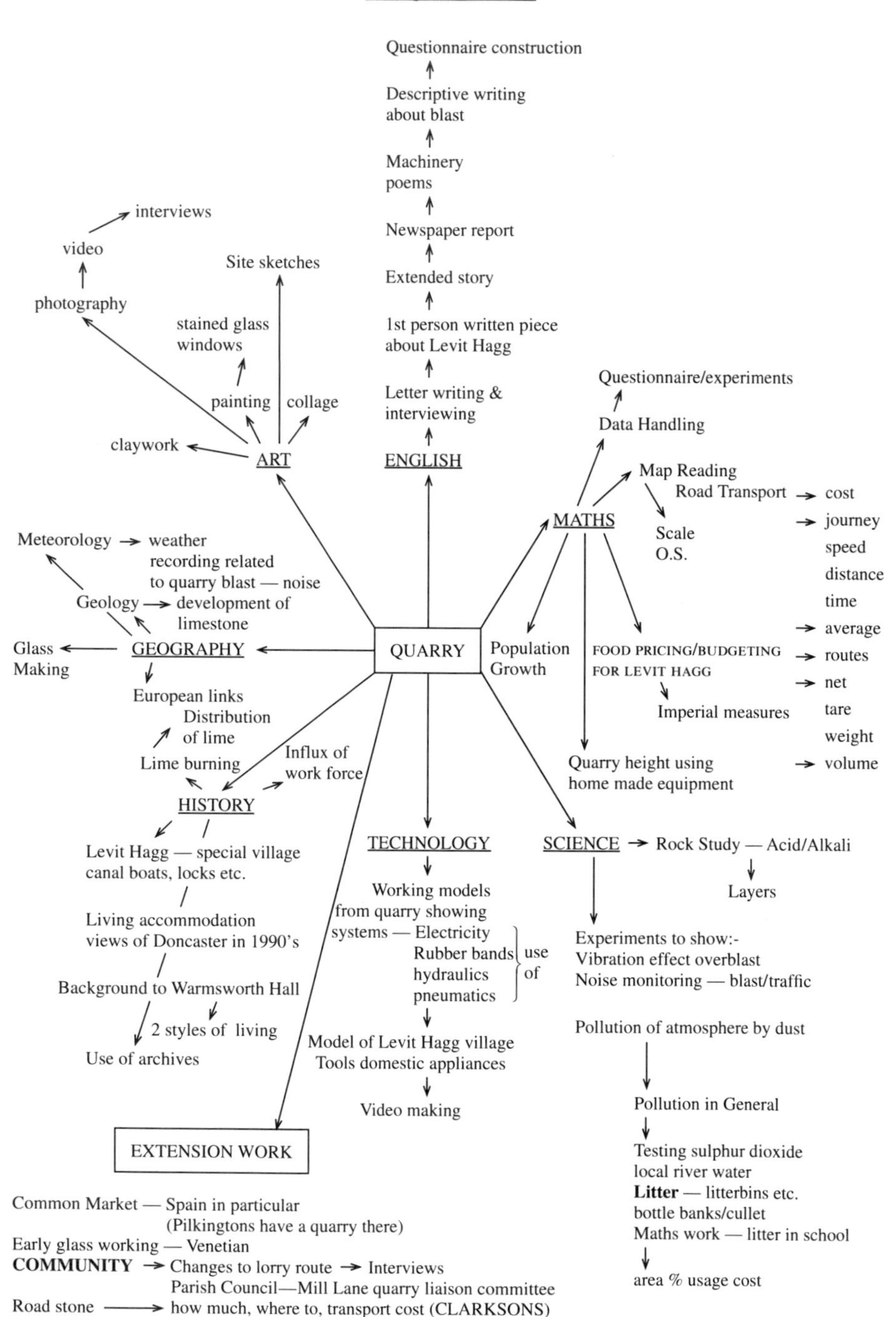

Appendix 1 — continued

Planning for learner outcome 3.6

Student Outcomes	Evidence of Achievement	Existing school practices	Proposed school practices	Partners' existing work	Proposed Partners' Plans	Anticipated benefits for Partners
KS1 Learners can record what they have learned about the world of work on one medium e.g. a poster.	Pictures Written work Models	Topic work based on ourselves & home & people we need.		To visit and let children 1st hand what work is about.		
KS2 Learners can record what they have learned about the world of work in a variety of ways using different media e.g. video, drama, creative writing.	Video Display work Ind. topic folders Self ass. topic document Models on display Feed back from Moat House & Quarry i.e. they come into school.	Making Video Quarry blast Written work Data handling Computer graphs Poetry about machines etc. Drama.	Menu — easily read. Design area for children | user friendly food creative ↓ new concept for children dining	Quarry visit Quarry make specific arr. for children to be present at heart of cliff face.	Criteria necessary for menu to be put into practice & criteria for new area for children dining.	
KS3 Learners can record what they have learned about the world of work and can draw out general principles concerning the world of work e.g. health and safety, pay, hours of work.						
KS4 Learners can draw general principles from what they have learned about the world of work as a basis for personal development future planning.						

Appendix 2 — Planning for learner outcomes 1.1 and 1.2

1. Learner outcomes	2. Evidence that Student Outcomes have been achieved
1. KNOWLEDGE AND UNDERSTANDING OF DEVELOPING SELF AND PERSONAL SKILLS	
1.1 Learners know their strengths and current limitations	
KS1 They are aware of what they are good at from external feedback and can articulate what they would like to be good at in the future.	
KS2 They can assess their strengths and some of their current limitations and describe their plans for future self-development to others, ie I'd like to be good at, I'd like to be better at.	
KS3 They can assess strengths and current limitations independently, can record this in an appropriate way and use this information as the basis for on going personal development planning.	Students can demonstrate that they are able to assess strengths and weaknesses accurately
KS4 They can assess their strengths and current limitations independently. They can use feedback and critical appraisal in a formative and constructive way. They can identify personal development needs and seek appropriate information and help to meet personal needs.	Students can demonstrate that they are able to assess strengths and weaknesses accurately and can plan personal development needs on the basis of this assessment
1.2 Learners understand the importance of respecting themselves and others	
KS1 They can recognize the range of emotions they feel and others express.	
KS2 They can understand that individual responses to events will vary and respect other people's emotions and feelings.	Students can demonstrate that they are able to give and receive praise and encouragement to boost their confidence
KS3 They are able to give and receive praise and encouragement in order to promote self esteem and self confidence.	

Appendix 2 — continued

3. Existing School Practices dedicated to assisting learners achieve the Outcomes	4. School plans to assist learners inc management and monitoring issues.	5. Details of Partners' existing work with the School	6. Partners' plans for working with School to assist learners inc Management issues	7. Anticipated benefits to Partners, a commentary
Year 8 art-self evaluation after each project aimed at identifying skills and areas for development Termly review in English Plan work programmes based on skills required Use of day books, merit awards, awards evening	Detailed pastoral log to be kept by student from year 7–11 Revise present pastoral system. Should head of year and form tutor move with tutor group? Monitor and revise day book	Careers officers mainly years 9–11 Speakers into assemblies Business and industrial tutors who assist with year 11 Record of Achievement.		

Appendix 3

PATHWAYS TO WORKING LIFE PROJECT

PUPIL QUESTIONNAIRE

We are interested in your skills and abilities and your future plans. We are also interested in what you are learning at school about the world of work. We would be grateful if you could complete this questionnaire. In most cases this requires you to write in numbers or to draw circles around numbers to indicate your replies.

Your answers will be strictly confidential to the project. Please think carefully about your answers to the questions. The success of the project largely depends upon the answers which you and other pupils give. Thank you for your help.

Please complete

Name ....

School ....

Year Group ....

For Project purposes only:

Pupil No ....

School No ....

Date ....

Data Collection No ....

NB This record will be kept for project purposes only and will remain confidential.

SECTION ONE

There are two sections to the questionnaire. Please complete both sections.

In this first section please circle the number which best represents the extent of your feeling to the question. Remember there are no right answers, we are only interested in your opinions and views. For example, if you felt that you are fairly successful at school your response to question 1 might look as follows:

So far, how successful do you feel you have been in your school work?	very successful	1 2 ③ 4 5 6 7	not very successful

QUESTIONS

So far, how successful do you feel you have been in your school work?	very successful	1 2 3 4 5 6 7	not very successful
How well do you think you know your own strengths?	very well	1 2 3 4 5 6 7	not very well
How well do you think you know your own limitations?	very well	1 2 3 4 5 6 7	not very well
How well do you think you know your own skills and abilities?	very well	1 2 3 4 5 6 7	not very well
How important do you feel it is to respect yourself and others?	very important	1 2 3 4 5 6 7	not important
How important do you feel it is to respect other cultures?	very important	1 2 3 4 5 6 7	not important
How easy is it for you to write down what you want for the future?	very easy	1 2 3 4 5 6 7	not at all easy
How clear are you about how you might record personal goals and plans?	very clear	1 2 3 4 5 6 7	not very clear
How easy is it to identify future goals for yourself?	very easy	1 2 3 4 5 6 7	not very easy
How much do you think that making a record of your personal goals and plans will help you in the *near future* (this academic year)?	very much	1 2 3 4 5 6 7	not at all
How often do you expect to look at or consult your personal action plan or record of personal goals?	about once a month	1 2 3 4 5 6 7	about once a year
How likely are you to continue using an action plan or record of personal goals in the future?	very likely to	1 2 3 4 5 6 7	not very likely to
How likely is it for you to work on your own in school?	very likely to	1 2 3 4 5 6 7	not very likely to

How important do you feel it is to be able to work with others?	very important	1 2 3 4 5 6 7	not important
How clear are you about which career you might follow when you leave school or college?	very clear	1 2 3 4 5 6 7	not at all clear
How well do you think what you are learning at present suits your future career plans?	very well	1 2 3 4 5 6 7	not very well
How clear are you about how to get information to help you plan what you might do in the future?	very clear	1 2 3 4 5 6 7	not at all clear
How clear are you about who is available at school, to help you plan your future?	very clear	1 2 3 4 5 6 7	not at all clear
How easy is it for you to discuss your future plans with your careers teacher?	very easy	1 2 3 4 5 6 7	not at all easy
How easy is it for you to discuss your future with someone from the careers service?	very easy	1 2 3 4 5 6 7	not at all easy
How much help do people from the careers service give you about your future choices?	as much as I need	1 2 3 4 5 6 7	not enough
How well do you think people from the careers service know what is suitable for you?	very well	1 2 3 4 5 6 7	not at all well
How well do you think you know which work skills you need to develop in the future?	very well	1 2 3 4 5 6 7	not very well
Overall, how useful do you think your school work is for your future career?	very useful	1 2 3 4 5 6 7	not at all useful
How keen are you to do well in your future career?	very keen	1 2 3 4 5 6 7	not that keen
How clear are you about the skills you will need to do well in your future career?	very clear	1 2 3 4 5 6 7	not that clear

SECTION TWO

A: Work-related activities

1. Please tick those activities from the list below which you experienced in year 9.

Work Experience	....
Work Shadowing	....
Industrial visits	....
Meetings with the Careers Service	....
Individual interviews with the Careers Officer	....
Visits by speakers from various jobs/professions	....
Careers Workshops	....
Mock Interviews	....
Industry-Related Project Work	....
Understanding Industry Courses	....
Mini-Enterprise	....
Business or Industry Conferences	....
Work Simulations or business games	....
Any other (please specify below)	....

2. Which 2 work-related activities did you enjoy the most? Please explain why? What did you learn from each activity?

B: Work

The following questions require you to place the four suggested answers in RANK order ie with 1 being your first preferred answer, 2 being the second, 3 being the third and 4 your least preferred answer to the question. Each of the four places need one of the four numbers and you cannot use the same number twice. For example your response to the first question might be as follows:

B1. A company needs to make a profit to:-

a) Make the owner money	....1....
b) To ensure the work force keep jobs	....3....
c) To enable the company to survive	....2....
d) To invest in new ideas for the future	....4....

QUESTIONS

1. A company needs to make a profit to:-

a) Make the owner money	....
b) To ensure the work force keep jobs	....
c) To enable the company to survive	....
d) To invest in new ideas for the future	....

2. Services are provided in different sectors of society because:-
- a) There are different forms of ownership ....
- b) Some services are more essential than others ....
- c) Some services need to be located in different areas ....
- d) Some services have to be provided free of charge ....

3. There are different types of business because:-
- a) People have different skills and abilities ....
- b) There are varying demands for goods and services ....
- c) Of competition between businesses ....
- d) Of the geographical spread of people ....

4. On discovering theft of company property an employer needs to:-
- a) Sack all staff ....
- b) Tighten the company's security arrangements ....
- c) Discuss the problem with staff ....
- d) Plan a way of catching those responsible ....

5. The best way to ensure that the company doesn't have problems with trade unions is to:-
- a) Persuade the workers not to go on strike ....
- b) Ban the trade unions from operating ....
- c) Pay the work force well ....
- d) Enable all employees to voice their concern to the management on a regular basis ....

6. Better products are made on the production line because:-
- a) all products are of a similar quality ....
- b) It cuts the cost of production ....
- c) The average worker could not be expected to learn how to do everything ....
- d) The product can be produced more quickly than it would be if it were produced by one person from beginning to end ....

7. If a company has so many orders that it cannot supply the goods to the customer, it should:-
- a) Refuse to return the customers telephone calls in case they make a complaint ....
- b) Sack the sales manager ....
- c) Tell the customer the problem and hope they understand ....
- d) Speed up production and make everyone work overtime and try to finish the order on time ....

8. If a company is accused of damaging the environment it should:-
- a) Consider developing alternative technologies and materials ....
- b) Shut down its operation ....
- c) Invest in conservation programmes ....
- d) Try and cover up the damage ....

9. The key to successful selling is:-
  a) Spending a lot of money on advertising ....
  b) Carefully planning how best to sell your product or service ....
  c) Giving high bonuses for sales to the sales staff ....
  d) Charging less for your product(s) or service(s) than your competitors ....

10. It is important for the company to keep accurate financial records because:-
  a) It helps plan production ....
  b) It would be difficult to prepare a statement of tax without the information ....
  c) It prevents the company selling products at a loss ....
  d) It helps to prevent theft from the company ....

C: UNDERSTANDING WORK

Finally, we would like you to consider how much school has helped you to understand the following? Please ring the appropriate number.

	Very Helpful	**Helpful**	**Not Helpful**	**Useless**
	1	**2**	**3**	**4**
The world of work	1	2	3	4
How business and industry work	1	2	3	4
Human relationships	1	2	3	4
The economy and wealth creation	1	2	3	4
The relationship between the economy and the environment	1	2	3	4
Different kinds of work	1	2	3	4
Deciding on a career	1	2	3	4
Different kinds of job opportunities	1	2	3	4
Opportunities open to you in FL & HE	1	2	3	4
Different qualifications	1	2	3	4

What other areas would you include in this list as very important but not really dealt with at school?

Thank you for your co-operation.

Chapter 7

Value Development in the Early Years: Approaches Through Story

Miles Tandy

Abstract

This chapter examines the rationale and practicalities of approaching values education in the early years through story. It begins with a discussion of the case for including story and story telling as part of an overall approach. There then follow two case studies, one from a first school and one from a nursery, which give an account of what such an approach might look like in practice. The final section considers issues of assessment, relating them to recent national developments.

Introduction — Why story?

I once took my family to have lunch with some old friends. The talk around the table flowed noisily as we all caught up with each others' news. My son, who was seven at the time, had been waiting to make his own contribution. After several unsuccessful attempts, he spotted a brief lull in the conversation. 'This is the story,' he began in a clear, confident voice. 'This is the story of the time I got kicked by a horse.' Everyone present stopped talking, turned to him, and waited to hear the tale. As he spoke, and held his audience's attention, I was reminded of *The Palm of the Hand*:

> Nobody, but nobody was paying attention. Her arguments were sound, her ideas compelling, her phrasings striking. But her speech was falling on stony ground. No one was taking any interest. She paused. 'Once upon a time,' she said, starting again. Suddenly everyone was quiet, everyone was listening.
>
> 'Once upon a time, the Prime Minister of India went for a walk with a swallow and an eel.' She had them all now, she knew, in the palm of her hand. (Wood and Richardson, 1992, p. 3)

This brief tale encapsulates the innate power of narrative to engage and hold human attention: whenever I read it to teachers, particularly those who work in the early years, it is greeted with smiles of recognition. Many early years classrooms give a very high profile to story: teachers read and tell stories; children are encouraged to share the stories of their own experiences; they 'make' stories through their play and they are encouraged to read and write stories as their literacy develops.

Barbara Hardy (1977) regards narrative as a 'primary act of mind' and suggests that it is the essential means by which human beings organize memory. It is through story that we structure, store and retrieve experiences. Go into any staff room on the first morning back after a holiday and you will find it full of people 'storying' as they relate experiences and their consequences to one another: the eventful holiday; the broken washing machine; the sick relative — all these experiences will be organized and re-told in a narrative form. This same 'storying' behaviour is likely to continue in classrooms as children relate their own experiences either semi-formally, for example through 'circle time', or informally in the course of their conversations with each other. As we become more experienced with this kind of informal storytelling, we learn how to 'edit' our experiences for that which is most relevant and to structure them in ways which will hold the attention of the listener. As 'editors' of our own stories, we also learn to recognize those aspects of our daily experiences which are most significant, which will interest others and perhaps pass on something useful, entertaining or enlightening.

Our desire to hear and tell stories derives not only from their capacity to entertain and amuse, but also from a sense that they contain something important about the world and the ways in which we and others live in it. Indeed, for moral philosopher Alisdair MacIntyre, stories play a central role in our personal, social and moral development:

> It is through hearing stories about wicked stepmothers, lost children, good but misguided kings, wolves that suckle twin boys, youngest sons who receive no inheritance but must make their own way in the world and oldest sons who waste their inheritance on riotous living and go into exile to live with the swine, that children learn or mislearn both what a child and what a parent is, what the cast of characters may be in the drama into which they have been born and what the ways of the world are. Deprive children of stories and you leave them unscripted, anxious stutterers in their actions as in their words. (MacIntyre, 1981, p. 201)

If MacIntyre's bold assertion holds true, then the act of storytelling in the early years classroom assumes far greater significance than a pleasant activity with which to round off the day, or a vehicle for developing children's literacy: storytelling is seen as fundamental to children's personal and social development; their sense of who they are and how they should live. MacIntyre argues that our very conception of self is in the form of a narrative and that it is only from our understandings of our own narrative and those with which it connects that we are able to act morally:

> I can only answer the question 'What am I to do?' if I can answer the prior question 'Of what stories do I find myself a part?' (MacIntyre, 1981, p. 201)

The idea that stories can provide a framework within which human actions and their consequences can be held and examined is far from new. From the time of

Aesop (and probably well before) there have been tales which have sought to teach the young, to give them warnings, to offer 'morals' by which they might live. Many teachers will be familiar with well-worn books of stories, often brought out for school assemblies, which aim to teach the perils of lying, the wrongs of stealing or the virtues of true friendship and kindness to others. More recently, the Citizenship Foundation has also sought to exploit the potential of story to raise and explore issues for developing 'social and moral responsibility for primary schools' (Rowe and Newton, 1994). It is interesting to note that, given the level of public debate and sense of crisis referred to in Chapter 1, these materials were sponsored by the Home Office — as former Secretary of State, Michael Howard writes in the foreword to Rowe and Newton:

> A society needs responsible citizens who can understand the purpose of law and respect the rights of others. Such attitudes of respect must be nurtured and encouraged by all those with whom young people come into contact.

The materials, which seek to make their own contribution to the development of such 'responsible citizens', rely heavily on stories to exemplify, raise and explore matters of friendship, rules, property and power, respecting differences, and community and environment.

For Bruno Bettleheim, stories, in particular fairy tales, have a power which goes well beyond the didactic (Bettleheim, 1976): he sees a much deeper psychological function through which we take and develop symbols from within the stories we hear. Tales in which good triumphs over evil become symbolically transformed into part of our subconscious view of the world and our place within it. We each find our own particular meanings and significance within the tales we are told. Though Bettleheim's view of the function and importance of stories is different from MacIntyre's, both would support a view that there is far more to storytelling than 'teaching right from wrong'.

Storytelling, though each of the listeners might make her or his particular and private interpretation of the tale, is essentially a very public and social activity. As such it can be viewed as a very public manifestation of the values and experiences which any group or culture regards as important. Whether the storyteller relates an anecdote about a complaint in a shop, or tells an epic tale of the creation of the world, they do so very deliberately and share their story in the belief that it holds something of value.

The social anthropologist Clifford Geertz defines culture as: 'The ensemble of stories we tell ourselves about ourselves' (Geertz, 1973, p. 8). Such a bold definition needs to embrace a broad understanding of what constitutes a story. For Geertz, stories are told far beyond the bounds of 'once upon a time': he would regard all of our cultural life from the television news to the soap opera to the evening at the theatre as 'stories we tell ourselves about ourselves'. Children growing up in late twentieth century Britain live in a culture which teems with stories: some told through the television or other media; others told at school; others told locally through their families and other cultural groups to which they belong.

The application of this broader definition of 'story' to the culture of a school might lead us to regard all sorts of aspects of education as the telling of stories about school, the world outside, and the ways we should live in each. School uniform, the way we walk into assembly, how the food is served at lunchtime, all these features of daily school life might be seen to tell particular tales about how the world is, how it works and how we should all behave in it. Much of the groaning mountain of school documentation could also be viewed in this way: brochures, policies and curriculum plans each tell their own particular tale of how things are or how we would like them to be.

In an increasingly 'global' culture, the extraordinary diversity of the stories we tell ourselves about ourselves makes it difficult not only for children, but for any of us, to find a clear and coherent set of values and principles by which we might live. So diverse are the stories told and the values they embody that teachers often feel a particular sense of unease about adhering to and promoting any particular set. Schools, and the individual teachers within them, struggle daily with the tension which cultural theorist Fred Inglis identifies:

> The individualizing of values which is the inevitable product of a global culture made up of dozens of maps of local knowledge means that none of the old structures of morality and the education they fathered can hold. . . . In these circumstances, a moral education composed of relatively secure precepts and maxims will not serve. (Inglis, 1993, p. 212)

He goes on to conclude that:

> the stories we tell ourselves about ourselves are not just a help to moral education; they comprise the only moral education which can gain purchase on the modern world. (ibid., p. 214)

Yet during an inspection by the Office for Standards in Education (Ofsted) a primary or nursery school is publicly judged on the extent to which it: '. . . teaches the principles which distinguish right from wrong' (OFSTED, 1995, p. 82). There is a clear expectation that, whatever the difficulties and tensions inherent in such an endeavour might be, schools should set out and exemplify a clear set of values which can provide the basis for a moral framework within which children might live.

If, as Inglis suggests, 'the stories we tell ourselves about ourselves' are to form the basis of a moral education, then what kind of practice might enable the telling and hearing of stories, with the broad definition of the term 'story' which I have suggested, to lie at the heart of values education, yet still allow teachers to give a clear account of how they are fulfilling the onerous responsibilities placed upon them?

The two case studies which follow are examples of practice which seeks to take account of the very complex nature of the issues at the heart of values education, yet recognizes that, provided the contexts are made relevant for them, children may begin to explore complex and sophisticated ideas from a very early age. Each of them starts from what might be called the 'palm of the hand principle' — the recognition of the power of narrative to engage and hold attention — but they go on to attempt an exploration of the extent to which young children can understand and articulate the complex matters of value which lie at the heart of the stories we tell ourselves about ourselves.

Case study 1 — Filling the storyteller's chest

This work took place with a Year 1 (five and six year old) class in a primary school situated in the southern part of Leamington Spa. The school takes children from a wide variety of backgrounds and has a long tradition of close involvement with its community. The class teacher and I worked in partnership to devise, teach and review the project which was designed to encompass the following learning objectives:

- learning about aspects of the past through stories from different periods and cultures;
- the construction of a story — having a beginning, middle and end;
- the different sorts of story we tell — funny, traditional, frightening, mystery etc. and their purposes;
- telling stories, both real and imagined, exploring and clarifying ideas;
- learning how stories can be shared in a variety of ways — in song, in dance, in drama, in pictures and in the written and spoken word.

Some of these learning objectives are taken directly from the National Curriculum programmes of study and are identified in the school's long-term curriculum planning, others were specifically identified by us through our interest in the extent to which they are applicable to children of this age.

In order to begin to meet these objectives, the class were to be engaged in a wide range of storytelling and story-making, drawing on stories from a variety of origins and in a number of forms. We felt it was important to find a way of linking the stories and activities in some way so that the work had coherence, particularly from the point of view of the children who were engaged in it. There was an extent to which the work needed a 'story' of its own to link the various parts and to provide a sense of continuity, so a context for the work was developed by using the idea of a storyteller who had lost all his stories — the children's job was to help him find them.

My first visit to the class was intended to set the context for future work. I introduced the idea of a land where a storyteller lived — everyone in the land liked to go to hear his stories. Through a short piece of drama work, the children were invited to be the people of the land where the storyteller lived. We used the classroom carpet to represent a 'special place' where the people of the land would gather to hear stories. We also developed a small ritual whereby the people sat and signalled their readiness to listen. All this initial preparation work was intended to build a context within which the children could explore the business of stories and storytelling at a slight distance from their immediate experience, allowing them to view the work with something of the perspective of an outsider.

A 'rag coat', which I had borrowed from a local school who have a Morris dancing side, was used to signify the role of the storyteller. In role as the storyteller, I told the story of the *China Dog* (Barton, 1986) who wanted to go to school: this is a story which encourages the children to join in with a 'chorus' — the choice of story is not particularly significant in itself, but I was anxious to get the children as actively involved as possible and the inclusion of points at which the children could join in the telling was very useful. At the end of the story, the teller asks the children if they want to hear another. He then goes to a large wooden chest which, he tells them, is used to keep all his old stories and ideas for new ones. When he gets to the chest it is empty — the stories have all gone. When presented with the problem of the empty chest, it is perhaps not surprising that the children immediately volunteered to help fill the chest with new stories. Initially they offered a number of written (published) stories from around the classroom, but through discussion in role, the storyteller explained that some of the things in the chest had just been to remind him of a particular story, a story that he could then remember and tell in the same way as he had told the story of the *China Dog*. Did they have any stories they could tell? The children were then encouraged to put the storyteller's coat on themselves, to sit in the storyteller's chair, and to share with the rest of the class any stories that they knew. They visibly enjoyed the power that the coat gave them and were encouraged to respect it as listeners — if someone was wearing the coat and telling their tale, the rest of us would try hard to listen. Still in role as the storyteller, I expressed gratitude for what they had done so far, but asked if they could help further between now and my next visit.

From this first visit the children agreed to:

- gather stories to fill the chest;
- sort the stories into groups;
- think about where the stories came from, how we knew them and why they might be told.

Although the children had greatly enjoyed the experience of being told and telling stories themselves, most of their initial ideas for contributions to the storyteller's chest centred on the idea that a story was something that was contained within the pages of a book. We were not surprised by this: most of the contexts in which children hear the word 'story' refer to it in the written form. But once they were encouraged to extend their idea of a story, they identified that they listened to tapes, watched videos, sang 'story songs' and told stories through movement. One child brought in her puppet show — the puppets were then kept in the story chest to remind us that stories could also take this form. We were also able to take advantage of the school's tradition of community involvement as a number of parents came in and told stories to the class.

The children began to develop the idea, which the 'storyteller' had originally suggested, that symbols could be kept in the chest to represent certain stories. Gradually, they began to add such items as shells, leaves and teddies, each of which symbolized or reminded them of a particular story. These stories were then told to the rest of the class. The children also developed the idea that a story could be, as one child beautifully put it, 'a bit of your life'. In this way, anecdotes and family stories about themselves, the things they had done and the things that had happened to them, could all be valued and added to the chest of stories. Many were able to find and bring stories of themselves when they were younger: family tales of minor injuries and mishaps, of getting lost or making everyone laugh. By bringing these ordinary stories of daily life and adding them to the growing ensemble in the chest, we not only gave the stories a certain status, but opened up a discussion about why certain 'bits of our lives' are remembered while others seem forgotten.

As the number of stories we had gathered grew, it became clear that it was necessary to find some way of classifying them so that they were not all kept in the same box. What ways could be found of classifying and sorting them? After some discussion, the children came up with the following categories:

- scary stories;
- funny stories;
- traditional stories;
- teaching stories;
- ghost stories;
- love stories.

The inclusion of the category 'teaching stories' gives a fascinating insight into the children's understanding of what some adults may be up to: whether the messages of certain stories had got home or not, they certainly understood what had been attempted.

Some children were quite definite about the categories to which certain stories belonged and could classify them quickly and easily. Others however, began to tease at the idea that many stories contained elements of more than one category and could not easily be classified into any particular one: the complexities of the ways in which many stories are constructed were beginning to become apparent. The discussion also opened up debate about traditional stories — stories that everyone seemed to know, but no-one quite knew their origins. The classification of the stories, though it developed quite naturally out of the problem that the chest was starting to get over-full, provided a means by which children could be encouraged to begin to think more deeply about the meanings and values of the stories they had heard and told. Though on the surface a fairly simple and conventional 'sorting' activity, the task is actually very complex and demanding and the conclusion of some children that certain stories defy classification was an indication of their growing awareness of the complexities involved. Through their discussions and their experiences of listening to 'told stories', the children were introduced to the idea that many stories had been passed down through generations by word of mouth. They also began to realize that told stories might change in the telling. As the discussion about told stories developed, it led to the idea that many 'traditional' stories were intended to tell the listeners something about the differences between right and wrong and to offer some guidance to the listener about how they might live.

One parent came and told the class the story of Mira, a rebellious and emancipated Indian princess who went to live among the poor. She remembered this story from her own childhood, she said, and it had been told and passed on by the poorest people. This story was then compared with the stories of Sita as told by the rich and powerful (Jaffrey, 1985): the children were encouraged to think about the similarities and differences in the stories and the reasons why the rich and powerful might have told one and the poor the other.

The children had spent some time exploring the idea that people tell different stories for different reasons. This led to discussion about the suitability of certain stories for particular audiences. They were asked, for instance, whether a story such as the *Three Little Pigs* would be suitable for the children in the nursery — most were in no doubt that it was too violent and would give such young children sleepless nights. Consideration of the suitability of a story for another audience encouraged deeper reflection about content and meanings, but also allowed children to pass comment at something more of a distance: it is perhaps easier to say, 'I think this story is unsuitable for a three year old in the nursery' than it is to admit 'I am frightened by this story'.

The last story I told was a Native American creation story, *Brave Muskrat*. This tells of how the world was created by the courage and sacrifice of Muskrat who was prepared to make one last attempt to get the mud from the bottom of the sea which the Creator needed to start the world. At the end of the telling, one of my questions to the children was 'Is this story true?'. They were in no doubt that it was not. 'Why then,' I asked, 'would anyone tell it?' One child answered, 'The people who told it told it because they believed it. And it was their believement'. The use of the word 'believement' gives some insight into the child's struggle with a difficult idea: that the story held a particular cultural significance for the people who originally told it. In the discussion that followed, the children were quite clear that we could share and enjoy the story, even if we didn't share the 'believement'.

This project had attempted to bring the practice of telling and hearing stories into the classroom in a way that enabled the children to begin an exploration of the significance and meaning of some of 'the stories we tell ourselves about ourselves'. There was never an expectation that they would engage in some abstract cognitive discussion about symbol, metaphor or meanings. The intention was more to provide a way of valuing the act of storytelling and to develop a deeper appreciation of the huge range of stories humans tell themselves about themselves. By turning the classroom into a place where stories are naturally shared and valued, we begin to develop what might be called a 'storying culture' where we tell our own stories and listen to those of others. If, as I have already suggested, stories embody values and render them tangible and accessible, then opportunities such as these to examine and explore them will begin a process whereby young children can more easily recognize and discuss the values in their own and others' lives.

Case study 2 — Living with the Egyptians

This work took place in a nursery school in Nuneaton. Through its action plan, the school had identified a need for staff development on ways in which the spiritual, moral, social and cultural aspects of the curriculum could be built into their work.

The school had already developed its own practice whereby children were 'absorbed' in a theme or topic over a number of weeks. They had decided that during the summer term they would explore the theme of Ancient Egypt. As part of the work I was asked to spend a day with them as a storyteller.

In planning the work, we were anxious that values and beliefs should be openly and naturally explored, just as the children might explore the tactile qualities of clay or the passages of the 'pyramid' which had been created around the climbing frame — yet these children were only three- and four-years-old. We agreed that during each of the sessions, morning and afternoon, I would tell three stories. Each was told as if by an Egyptian storyteller as part of the planned range of experiences for the children on that particular day.

The first story was developed from Pat Hutchins' *Don't Forget the Bacon* (Hutchins, 1976). I told the tale of a boy called Asif who was sent by his mother to buy things from the market: the items described in the original story were substituted for produce that might have appeared in an Egyptian market and 'don't forget the bacon' became 'don't forget the garlic'. The story was told using what storyteller Marion Oughton calls 'active storytelling' (Oughton, 1988) in which children are encouraged to take part in and form the direction of the story as it unfolds. The most significant impact of the story was seen in the following weeks in the children's play. The market which had been set up outside became the focal point for much of their activity as the original story was taken, played with, and developed further. As their own stories grew, they gave clear indications of the ways in which they were relating the story to their own experience: one child commented, 'I don't go to the market on my own . . . I just sleep at Pauline's . . . Mum says "be good!"'. Many children expressed concern that the boy in the story had been sent to the market alone, making a clear and unprompted connection between the story and their perceptions of the dangers in their own lives.

The second story was adapted from *A Name for a Cat* (Gersie, 1992, p. 48). In our version, *The Pharaoh's Cat*, each of the Pharaoh's courtiers tries to outdo the others by thinking of a more powerful name for the cat. The absurdity of the tale lies in the eventual naming of the cat 'Mouse'. In our telling it was Asif who, in an echo of *The Emperor's New Clothes*, pointed out the silliness of the name to the Pharaoh's messenger. During the telling of this story the child who came to play the Pharaoh was distracted by another who was not paying attention. The Pharaoh ordered the child to be still and threatened to put her in gaol if she didn't (such punishment had been threatened in the story for anyone who couldn't remember the cat's new name). The threat was unsuccessful so some sweets were offered as a bribe, then a drink, and only with the offer of drinks and sweets did the child settle. Issues of power and influence and how they are exercised lie at the heart of this story, and such was this child's understanding of this that there was an almost immediate translation into her own playing of the role.

The third story was told as the last part of the story of Asif's day. He went to bed when his mother told him, but was so filled with excitement from the day's events that he could not sleep. Eventually he grew afraid of the dark and imagined monsters lurking in every corner. To comfort him, and to help him to be unafraid of the dark, his mother led him outside and told him of *The River in the Sky*. This is based on the idea from Egyptian mythology that the Milky Way is a river which crosses the sky and along which Re, the sun god, will sail his boat Sektet (Philip, 1995, p. 16). As long as Asif can see the river, his mother tells him, he need have no fear of the dark for he knows that Re will sail again in the morning. The story is not only significant because of what it says about the beliefs of others about how the world came to be, but because of the way it is told to offer comfort to a young child who cannot sleep. Even if children find the 'big' story hard to understand, they can almost certainly identify with the experience of being unable to sleep and afraid of the dark.

The staff reported that all three stories had significant impacts on the children's subsequent play. As they became absorbed in their imagined world of Ancient Egypt, the stories they had been told and the values which they embraced, became part of that world and their play within it. The staff never intended that the children should learn facts about Ancient Egypt; rather that they should create an imagined world in which the children could become fully immersed. By bringing in the storyteller, that imagined world also allowed for the beginnings of exploration of values and attitudes: through the stories their world became a place where matters of fairness, safety, power, fear and hope could all form a natural part of their play experiences. Staff commented that through their play the children explored the stories at considerable length, changing and modifying them through negotiation with each other, and talking comfortably and openly with adults about what happened in their own versions of the stories and why.

Assessment — recognizing the values?

Both case studies attempt to show how understandings of human values and the capacity to articulate them can begin in the early years. In neither case have the personal and social aspects of the curriculum been added on as an afterthought: they are the central concern of both. Both examples make deliberate use of imagined worlds in which the children are encouraged to engage and 'live' as fully as possible. In the nursery, the children were absorbed into the world of Ancient Egypt; in the first school, they became part of the world of the storyteller. In both cases, opportunities are given to children to move out from their daily experiences to other worlds of other possibilities. The central principle is that from the vantage points of these imagined worlds children gain insights into their own world and the ways in which they and others live in it. By encouraging children to explore human values within these worlds, we offer them some distance from their own daily concerns and free them to talk more openly about human behaviour without any sense that their own actions and attitudes are judged or criticized.

If we are to give a full account of the learning that takes place in work such as this, then we need to develop means by which children can be enabled and encouraged to articulate their own learning. Any approach that is adopted however, needs to take account of the inherent ambiguity in the 'meanings' of particular stories and preserve the distance they offer from children's immediate experience.

In his work on the use of religious story in the primary school, Merlin Price (1985) developed strategies for questioning and discussing stories with children which provide some helpful pointers as to how we might gain clearer insights into what and how children are learning. Rather than asking children to abstract ideas and meanings from the stories they hear and tell, Price suggests an approach to questioning which makes 'human sense' to the child (Donaldson, 1978). Questions such as 'What is this story about?' are likely to elicit little more than a straightforward re-telling, but questions such as 'If I told this story to the children in the nursery, what do you think they would learn from it?' are likely to encourage a much deeper response. When the children I worked with were asked about some of the stories they had heard and told, this line of questioning opened up very thoughtful discussion, for instance about the rights and wrongs of telling a story like *The Three Little Pigs* to 3- and 4-year-olds. Such questioning encourages children to think about a story and the values it embodies in considerable depth, yet offers a way of articulating their response which does not require them to express complex ideas in abstract forms. By asking questions such as 'What do you think . . . (a particular character) learned from what happened in the story?' we keep our questioning, and allow children to make their own responses, *within* the imagined world of the story.

If we can develop the kind of 'storying culture' to which I referred in the first case study, opportunities to hear, think and talk about human behaviour and values arise in a wide variety of contexts. If such a culture is nurtured then discussion of values can become a natural and accepted part of everyday classroom discourse. Assessment of the personal and social development which takes place within such a culture needs to focus on the child's growing ability to talk about the stories they hear and tell and their capacity to reflect upon and respond to the kinds of questions Price identifies.

Such responses can be clearly related to some of the expectations set out in the School Curriculum and Assessment Authority's *Desirable Outcomes for Children's Learning* (SCAA, 1996). The first set of outcomes which SCAA identify refer to children's personal and social development. These outcomes focus on 'children learning how to work, play and co-operate with others and function in a group beyond the family' (SCAA, 1996, p. 2). The outcomes include statements such as the one below.

> Children are sensitive to the needs and feelings of others and show respect for people of other cultures and beliefs. They take turns and share fairly. They express their feelings and behave in appropriate ways, developing an understanding of what is right, what is wrong and why. They treat living things, property and their environment with care and concern. They respond to relevant cultural and religious events and show a range of feelings such as wonder, joy or sorrow, in response to their experiences of the world.

The child's comment in the first case study about the 'believement' of another people is as clear evidence as one might ever hope to get of his 'respect for people of other cultures and beliefs' and the comment gives a clear insight that such respect is developing. It is unlikely that we would wish to to record such an outcome as having been finally and completely achieved, but the child's comment is worth recording as evidence that he is developing in this direction. Storytelling is one of the 'cultural events', albeit on a small scale, that we can offer regularly in the early years classroom and, as I hope I have shown, it offers an abundance of opportunities for children to experience and explore 'feelings such as wonder, joy and sorrow'.

Though the desirable outcomes for personal and social development make no explicit reference to storytelling, those for language and literacy do:

> In small and large groups, children listen attentively and talk about their experiences. They use a growing vocabulary with increasing fluency to express thoughts and convey meaning to the listener. They listen and respond to stories, songs, nursery rhymes and poems. They make up their own stories and take part in role play with confidence. (SCAA, 1996, p. 3)

Both case studies are attempts to show how opportunities to develop these outcomes can be planned and structured. The approaches outlined allow the teacher, by bringing the class together, to share in many of the children's stories, to listen to and observe their responses, and to plan inputs to deepen and challenge their understandings.

SCAA's final set of desirable outcomes refer to the creative development of the child. Again, specific reference is made to stories:

> Through art, music, dance, stories and imaginative play, they show an increasing ability to use their imagination, to listen and observe. (SCAA, 1996, p. 4)

Telling stories to children, listening to the responses they make, and listening to the stories they make and tell each other, offers important insights into the development of their capacity to listen and observe *and* the development of their imaginative responses. It is through active engagement with the imagined worlds which stories create that children are able to begin to reflect not only on human actions, but on the consequences of such actions.

Any attempt to define and classify the outcomes we expect from children's learning experiences will necessarily lead to the creation of artificial boundaries between them; there is clearly a good deal of overlap between the outcomes to which I have referred. Listening to children make and tell stories and reflecting on the responses they make to the stories we tell them will offer valuable insights into the development of the outcomes which SCAA identify. In three out of the six headings under which SCAA identify desirable outcomes for children's early learning there are clear connections with story and storytelling. If the 'storying culture' can be created and sustained in the early years classroom, the teacher is offered regular and structured insights into children's development.

Conclusion

The use of storytelling can only form part of an overall approach to values education in the early years: children's personal and social development will be affected by many other factors and experiences in their lives in school and outside. It would also be naive in the extreme to expect that these approaches to values education will have an immediate impact on children's attitudes and behaviour. Telling a story one week cannot be expected to improve playground behaviour the next. But the 'canon of the world's stories' (Inglis, 1993, p. 213) is an important means by which we help a child to clarify and develop its sense of values. Though the canon is made up of a dazzling and sometimes frightening array of tales, an early introduction to and exploration of some of the world's stories might at least lay down some markers from which children can begin to take their moral bearings.

Acknowledgments

Thanks are due to Alison Stringer, Deputy Headteacher, and the children of Clapham Terrace Community Primary School, Leamington Spa. Also to Shirley Bracegirdle, Headteacher, and the staff and children of Camp Hill Nursery School, Nuneaton.

References

BARTON, B. (1986) *Tell me another*, Ontario: Pembroke Publishers.

BETTLEHEIM, B. (1976) *The Uses of Enchantment: The Meaning and Importance of Fairy Tales*, Harmondsworth: Penguin.

DONALDSON, M. (1978) *Children's Minds*, London: Fontana.

GEERTZ, C. (1973) *The Interpretation of Cultures*, London: Hutchinson.

GERSIE, A. (1992) *Earthtales: Storytelling in Times of Change*, Woodbridge, Suffolk: Green Print.

HARDY, B. (1977) 'Towards a poetics of fiction: an approach through narrative' in MEEK, M., WARLOW, A. and BARTON, G. (eds) *The Cool Web. The Pattern of Children's Reading*, London: Bodley Head (pp. 12–23).

HUTCHINS, P. (1976) *Don't Forget the Bacon*, London: The Bodley Head.

INGLIS, F. (1993) *Cultural Studies*, Oxford: Blackwell.

JAFFREY, M. (1985) *Seasons of Splendour: Tales, Myths and Legends of India*, Harmondsworth: Puffin Books.

MACINTYRE, A. (1981) *After Virtue: A Study in Moral Theory*, London: Duckworth.

OFFICE FOR STANDARDS IN EDUCATION (1995) *Guidance on the Inspection of Nursery and Primary Schools*, London: HMSO.

OUGHTON, M. (1988) 'Active Storytelling' in WEIR, LIZ (ed.) *Telling the Tale: A Storytelling Guide*, The Library Association Youth Libraries Group.

PHILIP, N. (1995) *The Illustrated Book of Myths: Tales and Legends of the World*, London: Dorling Kindersley.

PRICE, M. (1985) 'Religious story in the primary school', *Resource: A Journal for the Teachers of Moral and Religious Education*, **7**, 3 (Summer, 1985).

ROWE, D. and N.J. (1994) *You, Me, Us! Social and Moral Responsibility for Primary Schools*, Citizenship Foundation.

WOOD, A. and RICHARDSON, R. (1992) *Inside Stories: Wisdom and Hope for Changing Worlds*, Stoke on Trent: Trentham Books.

Chapter 8

Conferencing: Structured Talk and PSD in the Secondary School[1]

Helena Burke

Abstract

This chapter explores the contribution which pupil/teacher conferencing can make both to pupils' personal and social development and to teachers' assessment of that development. I am using conferencing to mean a formal and planned one-to-one session between teacher and pupil. The aim is to provide an opportunity for the pupil to reflect upon their own learning and development facilitated by the teacher.[1]

This chapter describes and evaluates a piece of action research completed in an inner London secondary school in 1997. The aim was to evaluate the usefulness of such conferencing both as part of the planned provision for and the assessment of pupils' personal and social development.

My journey to engaging in this research has been quite a long one. From my earliest experiences as a teacher I have believed that pupils' personal and social development is at the heart of their school experience. More recently I have come to realize that, despite the fact that it has been discussed by educationalists and society at large since the 1944 Act, it is still an area requiring further practical development. Part of the reason for believing we need to improve provision for young peoples' personal and social development (PSD) comes from my own experience as a teacher in inner London, where I worked in the same school and with the same tutor group for five years. I knew those 32 young men and women as well as most teachers can hope. I had a commitment to their development as young people who had a lot to offer to our future society and who could become valued members of that society. During the five years I had met most of their families or carers and knew some of them very well. Yet school still failed a significant number of them. One young woman, J, didn't attend for two weeks at the beginning of one term. I called home a few times but got no reply. Within another week she had been withdrawn from school, with the support of her social worker and moved to an off-site centre. I never found out what J had experienced that prompted the drastic move and it is highly possible that it was nothing to do with school itself. However, the chances are that I did not have time to talk to her when she needed it or that J did not perceive school as a place where she could talk about her personal experiences.

A young man, R, was also failed by school but in a different way. He had some learning difficulties but worked hard and was popular with staff and pupils. He did get into bother but of a very harmless nature. This began to shift in Year 9 and he was threatened with permanent exclusion many times, with myself and others arguing for him to be given 'one more chance'. He was eventually excluded and we had in effect done little to stop this. The extra chance meant little on its own, further support strategies needed to be put in place. At one time this could have been done through collaboration with a school counsellor or other support services but such facilities were already cut by the time R needed them.

However, it was not just the children who were failed by school that moved me to consider PSD further. A third student, O, had a successful experience of school in many ways. She was a quiet, shy young woman who hated being the centre of attention. She completed all her work on time to the best of her ability and achieved good grades at GCSE and went on to study 'A' Levels. I knew her as well as many teachers in the school; well enough to know she had a great sense of humour and had an outgoing lively side to her which she showed in her small group of close friends. However, I question how much school enabled her to develop her confidence, to be able to express herself in larger groups, to realize her full potential. O was successful in many ways and will no doubt develop her self-confidence as she grows into adult life. Nevertheless, I would assert that school could and should have made a greater contribution to the process if we were to fully realize our responsibilities for pupils' personal and social development.

The school in which I was working had a strong reputation for PSD. It had an effective personal and social education (PSE) programme which was planned and taught by a group of committed, interested and skilled teachers. This programme was beginning to be integrated with the pastoral time which form tutors spent with their groups in order to provide coherent provision. It drew on the strengths of different teachers and acknowledged the different relationship which form tutors and PSE teachers may have with pupils. The pastoral care system was also strong, with many committed form tutors and heads of year who had a genuine interest in the young people. They took time to listen to them, spent time after school with them and in many cases were involved in school journeys for whole year groups. That isn't to suggest that the existing provision for PSD could not have been further developed or that all elements ran smoothly. Rather, my purpose is to show that the school had some good systems in place and some strong and positive relationships. However, as the experience of the pupils I have mentioned will testify, this was somehow not enough. One explanation is that the systems didn't facilitate sufficient focus on the individual. I spent a lot of time thinking of how we could have done more for this group of young people but in effect I think it was about learning to do some things differently. In retrospect, it seems to me that the young people needed to perceive school as a place where their personal and social development was central. They needed to feel that time was provided in a structured and formal way alongside the less formal supportive environment which many teachers provide already. It seems that conferencing would be one way of giving them this time to explore their own PSD.

Providing a context for conferencing: The personal and social development of pupils

In order to examine the appropriateness of conferencing, to explore the role which it could play in relation to other aspects of provision, it was necessary for me to reassess my understanding of PSD. Experience has shown that PSD is not something which can be added to a long list of subjects to study in school, although the 'add on' nature of the cross curricular themes and dimensions (1990) may have indicated that this was a possibility (see Whitty, Rowe and Aggleton, 1994). Rather, the totality of pupils' experience in school, everything which occurs in classrooms, assemblies, playgrounds and corridors contributes to pupils' personal and social development. Furthermore, the interaction between the school life and 'outside' life of the young person also needs to be taken into account in planning for PSD. To say this is not new. What has changed more recently is the expectation that such provision will be more planned and explicit. One of the key documents which requires schools to reflect further on PSD provision is the OFSTED Inspection Framework (OFSTED, 1995) with its specific sections focusing on attitudes, behaviour and personal development and spiritual, moral, social and cultural development. In addition, further guidance has come from the OFSTED discussion paper on spiritual, moral, social and cultural development published in 1994 (OFSTED, 1994) and the work of the Forum for Values in Education (SCAA, 1996). Such documentation has served to raise the profile of PSD once more and identify it as a key element of school experience. However, it is still seen by some schools (and inspectors) as an addition, something to be considered *after* the work on academic attainment.

Provision for PSD varies but it is clearly not enough to say it permeates all of the schools' work. The structure of secondary schools encourages an approach which focuses on attainment via the subject-based curriculum and which makes a more holistic approach hard to achieve. However, if we see PSD as permeating *all* of the schools' work how can it not be linked with academic achievement? Rather than taking time away from issues of academic achievement I would argue that good provision for PSD supports it. One area in which this close link between personal and social development and intellectual development has long been recognized is that of literacy. As Plackett tells us;

> There is considerable evidence to show that a child's development as a reader is influenced by his or her sense of personal and cultural identity. (Plackett in Inman and Buck, 1995)

This view is supported in much of the School Effectiveness work where a number of the criteria of effective schools link to elements of school life central to PSD. The work of Rutter (1980) identifies that;

> Providing opportunities for children to take responsibility and to participate in the running of their school lives appeared to be conducive to favourable outcomes. (Rutter, 1980 in Reynolds and Cuttance, 1992)

More recently this was supported by the National Association of Headteachers. Their model for reshaping the National Curriculum suggests a core of teaching about values that would be compulsory in every school and would be the starting point for the curriculum rather than an afterthought (see Carkel, The Guardian, June 3 1997).

As I have indicated above, once we recognize this central importance of PSD we need to address it in a more rigorous manner than many of us have in the past. This means looking carefully at provision and outcome, and it means taking on issues of assessment of outcomes. As has been outlined in Chapter 1, we cannot claim that PSD is central to pupils' experience and fail to set up structures to assess pupil outcomes and monitor practice in the light of these outcomes. It is in an attempt to look more carefully both at provision and outcome that I felt the need to look more closely at the potential role of conferencing.

Conferencing: Definitions and aims

Conferencing has been more common to the primary sector than secondary, although many secondary teachers will have been involved in one-to-one work with pupils. Much of the pioneering work in this area was done through the Primary Language Record (1988) produced by The Centre for Language in Primary Education (CLPE). More recently this has been developed into The Primary Learning Record (PLR) which provides a framework for teachers to analyse children's learning (Hester, 1993). A key part of this framework focuses on conferencing with both the child and her or his carer (see Figure 8.1). CLPE sees the conference as a one-to-one opportunity for the child to reflect with the teacher upon their experiences as a learner. It should build upon existing dialogue between the pupil and the teacher, encouraging the child to play an increasingly active role in their own development. CLPE suggests that;

> It provides a framework for planning, for observing, for recording progress and for making assessments. (Hester et al., 1993)

One aim of the PLR is to enable children's progress to be mapped across the curriculum, looking at the relationship between different learning areas. However, in the secondary context I am proposing a specific focus on PSD. This may well draw from across a range of subject areas but would not involve all teachers. However, many of the areas for discussion raised by CLPE would seem to be highly pertinent in a conference which was taking an overview of the child's personal and social development. In addition to the experience of the PLR I have drawn on the development of other one-to-one work in secondary schools. Much of this has come under the title of 'mentoring' and has had academic attainment as its primary focus. In many cases it provides positive opportunities for young people to reflect upon their achievements and to engage in action planning. Mentoring is

Figure 8.1: Primary Learning Record (PLR)

Primary Learning Record

Teachers should bear in mind LEA policies on Equal Opportunities (e.g. race, gender and class) and on special educational needs in completing each section of the record.

School | Year Group [1] | School Year

Name Ad. | DoB | Summer born child ☐

☑ Boy ☐ Girl

Languages understood | Languages read

Languages spoken | Languages written

Details of any aspects of hearing, vision, coordination or other special needs affecting the child's learning. Give the source and the date of this information.

Names of staff involved with child's learning development.
Class teacher
& support teachers

Part A To be completed during the Autumn Term

A1 Record of discussion between child's parent(s) and class teacher

Ad. is very practical — he enjoys helping everyone at home & likes the responsibility of jobs like cleaning out the animals etc. He enjoys making things from junk. The television is rarely on — he asks for nature programmes to be taped & then enjoys watching them. He is very much into animals/nature. The home is full of pets. He asks lots of questions & has a good memory for recalling the answers. His interest in books/magazines etc. has grown since he's been at school & Mum is able to take a lead from the PACT form comments. He loves the Monster's Tea Party & Maths Fun. He does some writing activities with his Nanny. He is keen to get a computer — he enjoys playing on his Uncle's one. He is seeing numbers around him a lot more. He also suggests counting — at one time he counted 1–10 but missing out 5 — this seems better now. He asks what the time is & plays with a clock puzzle. He sings known carols — enjoys playing 'percussion'.

Signed Parent(s) .... Teacher .... Date ....

A2 Record of conference with child

"I like helping Daddy — I take the tools up the ladder for him & I don't fall down. I do the hoovering — it's a vax — you can clean anything with it like the drains & do the spills. I got Cindy, Carn, Sheba, the snake, the birds, the rats (he counted on his hands). Daddy gives the little rats to the piranha — it eats it. Daddy makes fishing baits too — with cat food & he puts in colours — red, Daddy is going to take me fishing sometime. I've got Norbury Nan and next door Nan. When I went from school I went shopping with Daddy. I can reach my books on the sideboard — Noddy did hit someone — I copy the books in Nanny's house. I do some stamps with my stamping set. I've got letters. I can count 1, 2, 3, 4, 6, 7, 8, 9, 10, 11, 12, 13.

Signed Child AD. .... Teacher Class teacher.... Date ....

Ad. Year 1 — boy *Languages*: English

This is Part A of Ad.'s Record. Parts B and C appear in each of the following sections. Both the Parent discussion and the Child conference reveal Ad.'s intense curiosity about the natural world. They also show the different roles that the adults in his life play in supporting his learning at home and at school.

Reproduced with kind permission from Hilary Hester, Sue Ellis and Myra Barrs: *Guide to the Primary Learning Record* (Centre for Language in Primary Education, 1993) teacher intensive work but has enormous potential and could be further exploited with more rigorous and focused use. It was from the possibilities of combining the primary and present secondary approaches that I began to explore using conferencing as part of pupils' personal and social development.

There is a need here to distinguish conferencing from other one-to-one work with pupils. It should not be confused with counselling although it may have some overlap. The role of counselling is to support pupils with problems they may be experiencing in their personal lives. The role of conferencing is one much more focused within the direct responsibilities of schools; to contribute to and assess identified learning outcomes. It is true that some pupils may use the opportunity of the conference to seek help with specific problems and issues. Our role as teachers here is to offer support and identify appropriate routes for dealing with such issues in the same way as we do when pupils approach us with problems in a whole range of settings within school life. Furthermore, whilst conferencing is not the same as counselling it may require many of the same skills. This has consequences for professional development in supporting teachers willing and able to take up this aspect of PSD provision.

The potential of the conference for PSD is twofold. It can contribute to the provision for personal and social development and offer a forum in which pupils could provide evidence enabling teachers, parents and pupils themselves, to assess aspects of pupils' PSD. There is also a third benefit. Through reflection on the outcomes of conferences teachers can evaluate existing provision for PSD, both for the class and for the individual child. This seemed just the sort of opportunity which could have benefited J, R and O in having a more positive experience of school.

Provision for PSD

The process of conferencing, alongside other provision for PSD, provides opportunities for pupils to develop a number of specific learning outcomes. (I will explore these in greater depth later in this chapter.) These relate to the unique opportunity for the young person to reflect upon themselves, their own interests and achievements in partnership with the teacher. The best practice of many subjects in the secondary school curriculum encourages pupils to evaluate their work. However, secondary schools' structure rarely allows for one-to-one support from a teacher and where such support is provided it is usually located in relation to the specific subject area. I believe conferencing also has a valuable contribution to make in developing young people's self esteem. As all who work with children and young people know, 'special' attention from an adult is a highly valued commodity. When this attention is focused positively on the young person's views and needs it can make a great contribution to their sense of self worth and as I have indicated previously, both of these elements of PSD impact upon the likely academic achievement of the young person.

Assessing PSD

The second purpose of conferencing which I have identified, that of assessment, is much more problematic. If we argue for PSD's centrality to the experience of schooling we cannot leave it to chance. We would be rightly horrified if it were suggested that development in English or maths was not assessed regularly with records kept and clear targets set. However, in the past it has been frequently accepted that PSD is somehow not suitable for assessment.

To assess PSD is essential but, as indicated in Chapter 1, such assessment is not straightforward. There are a number of issues to consider here; can and should all aspects of PSD be assessed? What constitutes evidence of personal and social development? What forms of progression can we expect within PSD? How can we record assessment? While the procedures for assessing knowledge and skills within PSD will need to be worked through, most teachers would agree that such areas can be assessed and monitored (see Chapter 10).

There is much less agreement when we turn to the issue of attitudes. Some would argue that it is inappropriate to talk of assessing attitudes because we would in reality be assessing the degree to which a given pupil's attitudes coincided with our own. Such teachers would suggest that there is such a great diversity of attitudes that the degree of subjectivity involved in identifying the 'right' attitudes and then assessing pupils against these criteria would lean towards indoctrination. This suggests a degree of relativism which is not present in our schools or society. Most schools identify their values via their aims or mission statement. These values are then promoted in a range of ways throughout the school, they are reflected in the curriculum, the rewards and sanctions procedures and assemblies. Staff actively encourage pupils to develop attitudes which uphold these values and make judgments expressed through day-to-day interactions and reports. For example, 'X works well with others, is open to new ideas and shares her views', 'Y does not take responsibility for her own actions'. While there is clearly diversity of values in society, there are some values which most schools expect pupils to demonstrate in their actions. Both SCAA (1996) and OFSTED (1995) have attempted to make some of these attitudes more explicit. We need to develop this further in school to be more open in planning and assessment of these attitudes. We need to ensure that we have a sound evidence base for judgments and share our understandings with pupils and parents.

The issue of evidence in this field is also complex. In relation to some desirable outcomes it is clear that both the evidence and assessments are fairly straightforward. For example, if a pupil is regularly attentive and produces carefully completed work we can fairly safely conclude that this pupil has a willingness to listen and takes pride in their work. In this case we have both sound evidence and are able to make confident assessment conclusions. However, for other aspects it may prove much more complex. What are we to make of contradictory evidence? Take the example of a pupil who is involved in a number of fights at school. We could conclude the pupil to be unable to sustain effective relationships with others, yet discussion with his parents reveals him as a boy who relates to his younger brother in a responsible and caring manner. Or we could consider a pupil who is unwilling to discuss the reasons for an outburst against another pupil. Here we could conclude that we have evidence of an inability to reflect upon one's own actions. In actuality it may be more to do with the pupil retaining some privacy, feeling too angry to talk, or a range of other reasons associated with the particular context of that incident. In both of these cases we need to treat the evidence carefully and be aware that any judgments made must be tentative and formative. We need to ensure that we do not make hasty summative assessments of pupils. Rather we should use such information to plan opportunities for these young people to demonstrate or develop identified learning outcomes, in a range of contexts and situations. I believe that conferencing could well provide one such situation.

I feel clear that *aspects* of PSD must be assessed, but it may be that other aspects are not amenable to assessment. Spiritual development may be one such aspect. We are also faced with the problem that aspects of personal and social development are not linear. As adults we regress and progress in different aspects of our personal and social development throughout our lives. Our willingness to listen to the ideas of others, our capacity to reflect upon our own experiences and our level of self-esteem will shift. However, the complex nature of personal and social development does not prevent us from planning opportunities for progression. We can provide for progression whilst acknowledging that other factors will influence development at given times for given pupils.

Finally, we need to consider carefully the way in which we can record assessment of PSD. Chapter 1 has raised issues of ownership of such records — later in this chapter I shall go on to look at ownership in relation to conferencing records.

Informing Our Planning

The third benefit, that of providing teachers with information on future planning needs brings me back to the issues which interested me in conferencing initially. Through structured and planned time with individual pupils we can learn more about both the future curriculum needs and possibly more importantly, the individual needs of pupils. It can also add to the all too few opportunities to discover what young people think they need from their school and teachers in order to succeed. It could provide opportunities for teachers to engage with young people in exploring these perceived needs, where appropriate challenging them and enabling students to have a more active role in their future development. Very many good and committed teachers discover this through the numerous informal exchanges which occur every day in school. This alone cannot provide the structured security which many young people need if they are to perceive school as concerned with who they are and what is important to them.

Conferencing: Action research

The research project

Having worked for some years as a teacher, I am presently employed as a lecturer in Education. My current role impacted upon the form which my research took. Clearly there were some benefits which came from my being 'an outsider researcher', the greatest of which was time to spend on one-to-one work with the young women involved in this project, but there were also negatives which resulted from the artificiality of being a visitor to the school. It meant that I had no previous relationship with the young women I worked with, nor was I able to make the conference 'part of an ongoing dialogue'. It also meant that for the purposes of the research I saw the young women more frequently over a shorter period of time than would be desirable or practical in a normal school situation. Acknowledging these restrictions, I will go on to give the details of the action research and to identify what I believe it has to offer to schools. The conferencing took place in an inner London girls' school over a period of three months. It was not the original intention that the work be done only with girls but well-established contacts with this school made it a useful location for the research. I met with eight young women once a month for 30 minutes each time. The young women were chosen in collaboration with the head of PSE, a teacher developing practice in this area who was very familiar with the group from which the pupils were selected. We worked within a loose framework that all should be pupils who would benefit from the research themselves for a range of reasons. Some were pupils who were under-achieving or having difficulties with school life, others were quieter, more withdrawn pupils who were less likely to demand attention in a class situation. Finally, some were very able pupils who could potentially be further stretched through the conferencing. The pupils were drawn from across the secondary age range from Years 8 to 11.

I followed the CLPE model in deciding how to record the conference (Figure 8.1) and an agreed written record was completed by myself during the conference (Figure 8.2). This meant that the young women could decide what they wanted to be recorded and we could agree that the record was an accurate one. While video or audio taping could have provided me with more detailed data for the purposes of research, I decided to reject these methods for two reasons. Firstly I felt they could have a stifling affect on the pupil, creating a greater level of self-consciousness, but more importantly I felt there was an issue of ownership. The written record allowed the pupil to take part in deciding what they wanted to be recorded. The importance of this became clearer as I actually undertook the conferences. A number of the pupils took the opportunity to discuss important details of their personal lives that would be highly inappropriate to keep as part of a teacher's record-keeping of pupils' development. Records of achievement in PSD need to be used for many of the same purposes as other record-keeping, including sharing information between staff. The young people concerned need therefore to be empowered to make decisions as to what information about them will be used for such public purposes. The agreed written record meant that we could keep an account of the outcomes of

Figure 8.2: Record of conference (1)

Record of Conference

Name of Student L

Date 27. 2. 97 **Session Number** 2

Student's own beliefs, values and attitudes:

L describes 'culture' as her background & 'how the people around you behave'. She describes music, dance and family as important to Jamaican people. Having respect for your family is important — being helpful not taking advantage. Not putting yourself in situations where people won't respect you — letting people walk over you, degrading yourself. Different cultures express this in different ways.
Examples of how her opinions affect her behaviour are: self confidence allows her not to be pressurized by others — still being able to speak your point of view. Your religion means that you will intervene if somebody is doing something wrong — being nasty to someone else.
Able to apply this to the situation in Bosnia — to articulate her views.
Also talks about when she knows she's done something wrong, how she reflects and remembers it and tries to avoid it.
Very clear that she mostly lives by her views.

Self reflection on achievement and target setting:

L has handed in all h/w on the in the last 3 weeks
Does it seem useful, a good idea for pupils to have time with teachers?
If there are there are problems she speaks to Ms — You think some pupils like to keep things more private 'you don't want teachers to know you too well' — 'you have to be how they expect you to be' — 'a bit like having your mother work with you', — about being different in different places — being 'free-er'
Less confident & low self-esteem would be helped by someone to talk to & get more confidence & help.
'The school is right for me, for the time being.'
'The teachers helps — esp drama, soe, pse.'

the conference without including the personal experiences that sometimes were the context of the young women's discussions.

The pupils were also given a further sheet to add to later. This was an optional opportunity for them to add to the discussion either through private reflection or discussions with friends, parents or guardians (Figure 8.3). In this way the pupils built up a file which formed a record of the conferences and which we could refer back to in later sessions. In addition I completed a teacher commentary following each session (Figure 8.4), which allowed me to stand back from the conference and consider what I had learnt about the young person's development and what I would need to offer in a future session. For teachers working in school it would also be the point at which to consider future provision for PSD in the range of other settings outside of the conference. These reflections were also shared with the young people in the following session.

Learning outcomes

An essential element in setting up the conferencing project was clarity of purpose. As stated earlier it seemed there were three possible benefits from conferencing:

1. To enhance the provision for personal and social development;
2. To provide a forum in which pupils could provide evidence for the assessment of aspects of their personal and social development;
3. To provide teachers with information in order to monitor present provision and plan for future provision, both for the class and for the individual child.

The third was to be achieved primarily through reflecting on what pupils said during conferences. The first two required me to identify which learning outcomes could be provided for and assessed through conferences. In constructing this list I drew on a number of sources, in particular the previous work of Buck and Inman (1992, 1993, 1995) and the guidance given through the OFSTED Inspection Handbook (1995). Figure 8.5 is by no means an exhaustive one. It could certainly be adapted or added to if one wished to shift the focus of the conference to complement other provision for PSD existing in a particular school. The conference should only be seen as *part* of provision for these learning outcomes. The list is divided into broad areas of knowledge, skills and attitudes though it is clear that these overlap considerably. For example, some of the outcomes identified as skills would clearly require particular attitudes or dispositions if they are to be sustained. A pupil would only be able to demonstrate the ability to give account of their own beliefs if they had developed a degree of self-awareness.

Not all of these areas could be both developed and assessed through conferencing but many overlap. Often the opportunity provided for assessment, also provides an opportunity for the pupil to further develop the area in question. This is the case here as it is often in other settings in school.

Figure 8.3: Record of conference (2)

Record of Conference

Name of Student K —

Date 30. 1. 97 **Session Number** 1

Student's own beliefs, values and attitudes:
We talked a little about abortion and K — explained her views. She gave an interesting example of her getting in a discussion with her friends about this. Her friends had become very heated and K — decided to come away from the argument because she didn't want to upset anyone.

Self reflection on achievement and target setting:
K — says she is particularly good at and enjoys PE. She has always enjoyed sport. She enjoys being fit and representing the school. She loves being picked for teams especially when she wins. Winning makes her feel giddy and she talks about it a lot. Her mum is always pleased for her and watches her play. K — plays netball and swims for the borough. She wants to work in sports and carry on with her netball. She doesn't really like contact sports. She's also good at Maths and Science and enjoys them because its like tackling problems. She's interested in anatomy because it links with PE.
K — is not so good at cooking & likes CDT better. She also thinks that she is not good at oral work and tries to get out of presentations because it makes her nervous in a way that doing sport in public doesn't. Her target is to start talking more in class.
From now for the next 4 weeks she will try to volunteer to answer a question in class twice a day!

Figure 8.4: Teacher commentary following conferencing sessions

Teacher Commentary

Name of Student C ——

Date 1. 4. 97 **Session Number** 1

C —— demonstrated a strong ability to reflect upon herself, showing she could be both positive and critical. She demonstrated high self esteem in relationship to others, particularly her peers. She enjoys and recognises her achievements — she is proud of those things which she does well. She was also able to identify the characteristics of a situation in which she can learn well.
For the next meeting:
Devise some opportunities for C —— to discuss her beliefs and feelings in relation to broader settings than her friendship group. Also discuss the link between her beliefs and her action in relation to her school work.

Date ______ **Session Number** ______

Figure 8.5: Learning outcomes potentially developed and assessed through conferencing

Learning Outcomes Potentially Developed and Assessed Through Conferencing

Knowledge:
- An understanding of their own beliefs
- An understanding of themselves in relation to personal, local, national and global issues

Skills:
- An ability to give account of their own beliefs
- An ability to articulate their own values

Attitudes:
- High self esteem and a positive self image
- Confidence and assertiveness
- An ability to reflect upon their own learning and to plan for the future
- Self awareness and an ability to state their own views
- An ability to make moral decisions based on reason
- Having attitudes which promote consistency between belief and action
- An ability to make a personal response to questions about the purpose of life
- Having values in relation to themselves at different levels (local, national, global)
- Valuing their own and other cultures

Figure 8.6: Framework of questions for initial conference

Pupils were invited to talk about:
An area of achievement or enjoyment in or out of school
(*Developing self-esteem, a positive self-image, confidence and assertiveness*)
An area that they felt needed development and ways in which this could happen
(*Self-awareness*)
Changes which they would want to make in their school life
(*Ability to reflect upon own learning and plan for the future*)
Issues that they held strong opinions on (suggestions were made here by the teacher to open discussion, local issues, international issues, moral issues)
(*An understanding of their own beliefs, ability to give account of own beliefs and articulate their own values*)
Why they held those opinions and how they would react toward those who might disagree because of a different value system
(*An understanding of their own beliefs, ability to give account of own beliefs and articulate their own values, valuing other cultures and views*)
How such opinions might affect their actions
(*An ability to make moral decisions based on reason, having attitudes which promote consistency between belief and action*)
Something that they were proud of in their own background or culture
(*Valuing their own and other cultures*)

The learning outcomes should not be regarded as fixed but rather they should adapt and develop in line with a number of factors in school;

- The age of the pupils as they progress through the school;
- The other provision offered in the school; and
- The progression or regression of individual pupils.

The kinds of questions which pupils would be asked would need to relate closely to the three factors identified above. Using this information schools could plan more precisely the learning outcomes desired through each conference. The short time of my project allowed some of this to occur in relation to the age and development of individual pupils. In order to focus the conference I established a framework of suggested question areas related to these outcomes (Figure 8.6).

One or two of these were loosely used in the first conference with each pupil. They were adapted and refocused on the basis of the teacher commentary as I was able to identify the needs and plan for individual pupils. The nature of the questions asked and the evidence that one might expect varied according to age range and development of the given pupil. For example, in identifying issues on which pupils held strong opinions I made different suggestions to pupils of different ages. A Year 8 pupil discussed the way in which 'The Spice Girls' dress. She felt that their clothes were disrespectful and disagreed strongly with some of her friends on this matter. She described a discussion she had had with her friends about dressing up as the band and although they had decided they would do this she had refused. This to me provided evidence that this young woman could give account of her own views and articulate her values at a level appropriate to a 12-year-old. However, the context was quite different for one Year 11 pupil who expressed in some detail her objections to violence in school and TV. At this stage of her development the young woman was much more able to generalize and to see herself and others in relation to national and global issues. It was essential that I continuously checked the questions back against purpose, in order to ensure that the conference was focused on appropriate areas. Each of the initial questions linked to the learning outcomes in Figure 8.5.

Findings from the research

In order to analyse the action research conferencing project I will return to the aims which I originally hoped could be achieved through the contribution of conferencing to PSD. These were:

1. to enhance the provision for personal and social development;
2. to provide a forum in which pupils could provide evidence for assessment of aspects of their personal and social development; and
3. to provide teachers with information in order to monitor present provision and plan for future provision, both for the class and for the individual child.

Clearly the action research occurred with a small group of young people over a limited period of time. The findings are therefore illustrative of the issues concerned with conferencing. This project, alongside the extensive work done by others, particularly in the primary sector, would support the case for further research and development of conferencing.

1. To offer part of the provision for personal and social development

The particular aspects of PSD which I aimed to enhance provision for through conferencing fell into three groups.

Firstly there were those concerned with self esteem and confidence;

- high self esteem and a positive self image;
- confidence and assertiveness.

Secondly; those related to pupils' ability to reflect upon their own learning and planning for the future;

- An ability to reflect upon their own learning and to plan for the future

Finally, those related to pupils' self awareness.

- An understanding of their own beliefs
- An understanding of themselves on different levels

- An ability to give account of their own beliefs
- An ability to articulate their own values
- Self awareness and an ability to state their own views

To begin with the first. There were some indicators that the very fact of an adult spending 30 minutes in school with an individual pupil gave them a sense of their own value. Other pupils asked if they could also join the group and some of the friends of the pupils involved asked if they could also come along. Some particularly important points were raised by some of the young women involved when they were asked at the final session if they felt conferencing within school would be useful. T said

> It all depends who you are, some people are too shy just to go up and talk to teachers. I think its important to have time, otherwise you keep it inside. It shows someone thinks about you and notices you. Some teachers don't notice you.

K stressed the importance of pupils having someone who listened to them;

> It is important to have someone to talk to about your life, if you don't it can build up too much stress.

R drew attention to a mentoring system present in the school to help pupils achieve grades A–C. She said she felt everyone needed something like this, some pupils coped well without extra time but it all depended on 'How well you're coping with different situations'.

In looking at opportunities for pupils to reflect upon their own achievements in learning and to plan for future learning, I was impressed. The young women had considerable ability to assess their areas of strength and areas needing development. In her first session (with her friend), D informed me that

> I am very good at communicating, in drama and in writing and other people find it easy to talk to me. I enjoy being the centre of attention!

What was possibly more impressive was the same young woman's ability to identify an area in which she did not shine and to suggest why. D told me that she wasn't very good at geography. The process of conferencing allowed me to pursue this further. On further questioning D was able to identify the link between her attainment and her approach to the work. Because she didn't feel her marks would be as high as in other subjects she gave up a bit as she really liked to do very well or not try at all. The conference had provided an opportunity for D to reflect upon her reasons and to make some plans for the future. D suggested that what she needed to do was 'Do my homework better and on time and listen more'. She also agreed to keep a record of how she felt she was doing in the subject. D decided to focus on her geography work to investigate just how good a grade she could get.

Another pupil, C felt

> Maths is my best subject, it's easy to learn and I listen more. It's important for when I'm older and leave school because I want to be an accountant. I get a lot of things right and I'm in the top group.

On the other hand she felt she was not good at English and disliked reading 'It's my worst subject, I don't like it and I don't think I'm any good at it'.

Again the conference provided a context to pursue this with the individual pupil. We discussed the idea that some people enjoyed reading to relax and looked at what she did. In this way she described her usual evening at home and explained that she didn't like to read at home because the television was on and it was always more interesting. She told me what programmes she liked and we came up with the suggestion of finding some books on the same topics. She then told me she might read if she took the book to her room. C and I set a target of reading for one hour each week and telling me the story of what she had read when we next met.

Finally, T discussed her considerable achievements in sport, playing a range of sports competitively both in and outside school.

> I enjoy being fit and being picked for teams. I especially enjoy winning, it makes me feel giddy and I talk about it a lot. My mum is pleased and comes and watches me play.

However, she also identified what she felt had been a problem for her since primary school, a lack of confidence in talking out in class. Our discussion allowed her to consider why talking out in class made her feel uncomfortable when being watched at sporting events did not.

> In sports I'm usually not on my own and in class I might not get it right, sometimes everyone knows more stuff.

It seemed a key issue was success. T set herself a target to offer answers in class when she felt sure of success rather than waiting for the teacher to pick her to answer.

These are all very small examples, but what seemed key to me was that these pupils had themselves engaged in critical self-reflection on their learning and identified achievable goals for the future. The conference seemed to provide an opportunity for the teacher to enable the individual pupil to investigate their motivations in more depth than the day-to-day organization of school often allows. Both the pupils and I were looking forward to discussing these plans at the next meeting.

It turned out that T had managed to answer a few questions in classes, though not as many as she had hoped.

> It felt okay in Maths. I had to do mental arithmetic and the teacher wrote my answer on the board. I wasn't nervous, I knew everyone. Science was a bit strange, it's a new higher group and I've just done stuff that's more simple.

C told me about the first two chapters of her book and what she thought of reading it 'I *quite* enjoyed it. I read upstairs instead of watching tele and my cousin made fun of me'. When I asked how this made her feel she said 'Funny, I didn't feel like reading anymore but I think I'll finish it.' She suggested that one place she might keep reading was on the bus coming to school and I asked whether she would like to have someone check this with her. C felt she could best do this herself

> I'm good at checking up on myself and doing homework even when the teacher doesn't fuss about it.

D had a triumphant story of an excellent grade in her geography test announced to her mother at parents' evening.

I am not suggesting that one conference will help all pupils' fulfil their potential. Clearly there were pupils who did less well with their goals. S had decided to try to improve her attitude towards maths and her relationship with her teacher. Rather than achieving more she had been moved class for further disruptive behaviour. What is important here is that all of the pupils concerned had been given an opportunity to take more control over their own learning. They knew there was a guaranteed reference point to return to with the outcome. I, like many other teachers tried to provide this for my form where I could but without a formal structure it was too often left to chance. In this case conferencing could contribute to the planned provision that this element of PSD requires and deserves. As one pupil put it:

> It would be helpful to have this because someone can give you more idea of your targets. People would behave better if they knew more what they needed to do.

The final area of provision I was aiming to achieve through these conferences related to a wider sense of pupils' self awareness:

- An understanding of their own beliefs;
- An understanding of themselves on different levels;
- An ability to give account of their own beliefs;
- An ability to articulate their own values; and
- Self-awareness and an ability to state their own views.

I began a second conference with R by asking her situation in maths. However, I had also identified a need to provide an opportunity for her to develop self-awareness if she was to identify ways of avoiding confrontation with adults. Thus part of the teacher commentary after the first session read:

> Need to pick up on issues of understanding herself on different levels and developing further her self-awareness about how she can choose to act in different ways.

Thus the discussion as to how she *had* behaved in the maths lesson moved on to how she *could* behave. She reflected on her ability to behave in the ways that she and her mother would want her to and that this sometimes meant she behaved in different ways in different settings:

> I can be polite when I want to be, some people behave in the same way all the time, I know how to be different with different people. I've learnt for myself to speak with respect to people I don't know from how I want to be treated. She (mum) would always want me to respect — I can be feisty so she has her doubts when I'm in trouble, it might be my fault.

She also was able to reflect on who she was in relation to her own culture given the opportunity:

> I'm both Caribbean and British. If I'd have lived in the Caribbean some things would be different, discipline, clothes, but some would be the same, young things.

Another young woman K, also demonstrated that this provided her with an opportunity to reflect upon how she sees herself on different levels:

> I'm Indian, I've been brought up the same as I would be in India. When I go to India the only people I feel different from are Hindu not other people from my religion.

There were many other examples of these young women demonstrating their ability to reflect on who they were, how they should behave and how they saw themselves in relation to others. In this way conferencing felt like a quality contribution to provision for the development of these skills and attitudes. The framework of questions which I had begun with was developed according to the individual pupils' needs and demonstrated abilities. This facilitated an opportunity for the young women to develop the identified skills and attitudes in greater depth than in whole class work.

2. To provide a forum in which pupils could provide evidence enabling us to assess aspects of their personal and social development

I have indicated earlier some of the difficulties associated with assessment of this area. However, I feel the information gathered through the conferences illustrates that valuable evidence can be gained through this process. Progression can be recorded, some of the examples that I have quoted in the previous section provide some of this assessment evidence. Teacher commentaries written following the sessions with R and K quoted above referenced their ability to value their own culture and to understand themselves in relation to national and global issues. Other examples indicated areas that may need development for pupils. D talked about believing in equality for all people

> If you mean big unfair situations, like Stephen Lawrence, that makes me feel the same as unfairness against me. It makes me angry.[2]

But when asked further about her behaviour in that area she described occasions when she and her friends had made fun of a lesbian couple who lived nearby. This was an interesting example of the complexities involved in looking at consistency between our beliefs and our actions. Did this demonstrate that D had not developed attitudes that showed consistency between belief and action? It was clear in D's tone that she could see the contradiction here and she also responded to my questioning look. 'I know . . . it isn't right, is it?'

My judgment was that D was able to be self-critical here. She was reflecting well on the inconsistency between her beliefs and actions. What followed was a discussion as to other ways of behaving and the planning for future opportunities to explore this with D through provision in conferencing and class work.

Similarly, another young woman demonstrated that while she was able to reflect upon her own personal beliefs in a very open way, she was not yet able to look at these in relation to broader implications. Having lived in a children's home for some years she was very clear that she had been very unhappy there and felt badly treated. However, she found it very difficult to answer when I asked her whether she thought children's homes were always unhappy places. This could be taken as evidence of an inability to articulate her own beliefs or to see herself in relation to broader issues. I feel this is a good indicator of the need to be very tentative in making assessment in some of these areas. L's experiences are very personal, this may well not be the right time in her life to consider some of the implications of these experiences. What is important here is to provide appropriate opportunities for reflection not to assess a pupil as unable to do this. The teacher commentary following this session reads

> L is able to describe her own life and background with great frankness. However, she is less willing (or able)? to talk about how it felt. I need to provide less personal and sensitive contexts for L to demonstrate her abilities here.

This issue was explained very well by S when asked if she felt the conferencing had been useful:

> If there's a problem it's good to be able to speak to someone, but some pupils like to keep things more private, you don't want the teachers to know you too well. If they did you might always have to be how they expect you to be, it would be a bit like having your mother work with you. Its good to be different in different places, being free-er.

For me this serves as an important reminder of the purpose of this work, it is not to become a counsellor for pupils nor to invade their privacy. It is vital that in conferencing we provide a *range* of opportunities for pupils to develop these skills and attitudes and for us to assess them. Some pupils will use it as an opportunity to share information with school as they wish but others must be allowed to explore issues at more distance. The short period of time of this research meant it was difficult to identify progression in a meaningful way. Some small examples have been identified earlier, predominantly in relation to pupils reflecting upon their own learning and planning for the future. The more complex areas in relation to attitudes would need to be monitored over a much longer period of time and with the involvement of a range of key staff. This could be included as part of existing school policies on profiling using them in conjunction with pupils to explore their own progression. The most important lesson learnt in terms of progression in this project relates to planning future opportunities for pupil progression discussed below.

3. To provide teachers with information in order to monitor present provision and plan future provision, both for the class and for the individual child

The conferences provided me with information which could be used in planning curriculum provision, future conferences and identifying needs which may lie outside of the school provision. It became clear that trends in pupils' demonstration of particular skills and attitudes could provide an important monitoring tool for PSD provision, be it whole school, subject specific or PSE curriculum. As an 'outsider' to the school involved in a short term project I could not take full advantage of this but as an ex-PSE coordinator I could certainly see the potential. While all the young women involved demonstrated different needs which could be pursued through future conferences, some trends emerged. Almost all demonstrated examples of their actions being inconsistent with their beliefs. Such information could be fed back to appropriate members of staff to plan further opportunities for exploration of this area within other aspects of the school.

Planning future conferences related to individual pupils' needs was a vital part in ensuring that conferencing fulfilled the role of enhancing provision in relation to individual needs. An example of this can be seen in the teacher commentary below:

> T is very reflective about her own abilities in sport and is able to articulate her feelings really well. She is also able to set targets for development in areas of perceived weaknesses, although they may not be realistic. With support she identified more realistic targets. These will need to be reviewed next time. She is able to articulate situations where she has exchanged views with others, (abortion) and how she handled herself in relation to others who disagreed with her. Next time it will be important to discuss occasions where she may want to stand her ground or be persuaded by others to change her views.

With some of the conferences it became clear that there were needs which could not be met within the expertise of most teachers and that were not curriculum issues. A high number of the young women involved took the opportunity to discuss personal traumas which had occurred in their lives. For some it was clearly an opportunity to discuss something which the everyday business of school did not provide time for and I was merely taking the role of listener. For others there were unresolved issues that it would have been inappropriate for me to attempt to resolve, having insufficient expertise and only a short term contact with the young person concerned. While I stress that in all of these cases the school was already aware of the circumstances, it did raise issues for the conferencing process. First, that conferencing may well provide a support function where young people choose to use it in this way. Second, it is important to recognize that many teachers will not be qualified to deal with some counselling issues which may arise and that these are better referred elsewhere. With one young woman I made a decision to shift the following conference onto issues which were less close to her personal experience. I referred my concerns about her onto the appropriate member of staff. It is vital that a school using conferencing sets in place appropriate professional development and policy guidelines to ensure such issues are handled sensitively.

Future practice

In reflection I feel there are a number of issues that require further exploration. One of the first questions I would want to ask would be how would the experience have been different if the group had included boys. I feel sure that there are young men who would have welcomed the opportunity to discuss issues from a personal basis. However, it may be that some young men and women would benefit more from opportunities to explore issues at a distance. This can be done through use of stimulus materials such as video or case studies where pupils are asked to give opinions as to the actions of fictional characters. It can provide a useful lead in for pupils to discuss their own actions. This would seem to me to be an area requiring further work and exploration. I should also like to look more closely at the issues of record-keeping and monitoring. As I have indicated, the records were written during the conference by myself with the young women's approval. I am aware that the teacher holding the pen is still in a position of power and that many pupils would be reluctant to correct the teacher in writing something. For more accuracy of records it may be that we need to create the time required for the pupil to write or dictate the record themselves. Finally comes the issue of monitoring. Given the limited nature of this piece of action research, little monitoring of the effectiveness of the conferencing by other teachers could be facilitated. Where conferencing is adopted by schools I feel monitoring the effectiveness would be an essential component in ensuring that the work was being undertaken in the best possible way. This would also be vital if it were to be integrated into other provision for PSD. The greatest argument presented against conferencing is lack of time and this is a powerful argument, however, many secondary schools already have mentoring or individual interviews built into the school year. What I am suggesting is a more structured and rigorous approach to such work in order to make the best possible use of such time. This may be work that we cannot afford *not* to do and more teachers engaging in conferencing and monitoring its effects will build a powerful evidence base to support this. As many primary colleagues know, conferencing has an important contribution to make to enriching young peoples' experience of school and as such enabling their personal and social development.

Acknowledgments

I should like to thank the pupils and staff of Sydenham Girls' School for their co-operation and enthusiasm in working on this project.

Notes

1 The term is borrowed from work which has had greater focus in the primary phase but it also has parallels with a range of developing areas in the secondary through mentoring projects.
2 Stephen Lawrence was a black teenager murdered in a racist attack in London in 1993.

References

BUCK, M. and INMAN, S. (1992) *Curriculum Guidance No. 1: Whole School Provision for Personal and Social Development*, Centre for Cross Curricular Initiatives, London: Goldsmiths College.

BUCK, M. and INMAN, S. (1993) *Curriculum Guidance No. 2: Re-affirming Values*, Centre for Cross Curricular Initiatives, London: Goldsmiths College.

CARKEL, J. (1997) '*Power to the Parents*', The Guardian, 3 June 1997.

HESTER, H., ELLIS, S. and BARRS, M. (1993) *Guide to the Primary Learning Record*, Centre for Language in Primary Education. London: CLPE.

NCC (1990) *The Whole Curriculum*, York: National Curriculum Council.

NCC (1990) *Curriculum Guidance 1–6*, York: National Curriculum Council.

OFSTED (1995) *Guidance on the Inspection of Secondary Schools*, London: HMSO.

PLACKETT, E. (1995) 'Reading, identity and personal development' in INMAN, S. and BUCK, M. *Adding Value? Schools Responsibility for Pupils' Personal Development*, Stoke on Trent: Trentham Books.

RUTTER, M. (1980) *Changing Youth in a Changing Society*, Oxford: Nuffield Provincial Hospital Trust.

SCAA (1996) *Consultation on Values in Education and the Community*, London: SCAA.

WHITTY, G., ROWE, G. and AGGLETON, P. (1994) 'Subjects and themes in the secondary school curriculum', *Research Papers in Education*, 9.

Chapter 9

Conferencing in the Primary School: Possibilities and Issues

Pam Slade

Abstract

This chapter explores how child/teacher and parent/teacher conferencing can support children's personal and social development in the primary school. The chapter outlines the processes involved in PSD conferencing, drawing on case study material. The chapter ends with a discussion of some of the issues that arise for children, parents and teachers when using conferencing to promote and assess PSD.

A biographical context

When I was asked to take part in this research on the role of conferencing in relation to children's personal and social development I had feelings of trepidation as well as excitement. I knew that the process of researching and writing would challenge me emotionally and intellectually and would further develop my thinking about PSD and its place in the curriculum. Throughout my career as a teacher I have believed that reflection and analysis of classroom practice are crucial to effective teaching. Putting this process into action research and then writing for a wide audience was a new venture for me, even though I am experienced in writing for children, parents and friends. However, I knew that this process would have a positive effect on my classroom practice and in turn would have a positive effect on some children's education.

My interest in the role of personal and social development and its place in the curriculum stems from my own educational experiences as well as from my early experiences as a beginning teacher. My early schooling was fraught with difficulties and failures. With hindsight and through reflection I have recognized that throughout my education I couldn't learn 'properly' if I didn't feel secure and confident in school. I discovered my friends have had similar problems when they weren't feeling good about themselves during their education.

When I began as an English teacher in a small northern British Colombian town, the question as to whether that I could impart an English curriculum to a class of 15- and 16-year-olds without attending to their attitudes towards themselves as readers and writers, and their attitudes towards themselves in relation to their community, became even more pertinent. I had a class of 35 teenagers who were in what was then called the 'non academic' stream. Many of them had been given the message that they were failures, particularly when it came to reading and writing. I began to realize that the failure was integrally related to the curriculum, both in its content and in the teaching and learning processes. When opportunities did arise to discuss things that were important to them these same teenagers demonstrated a questioning attitude, towards themselves, their families and the wider society. They were intelligent and thoughtful about their own values and personal experiences. When we discussed their attitudes and feelings towards themselves and writing, their writing changed. While technically flawed, it demonstrated sincere interest and involvement in the process of writing that I had not witnessed before. These glimpses of pupils' potential made me aware of how important PSD is to effective learning.

With that in mind, I came to London looking forward to the experience I would gain. Those were the days of the ILEA[1]. It was an exciting and thought provoking time in my education as a teacher. I was aware that young people's achievement in school was fundamentally connected to not only their attitudes about themselves, but also their teachers' attitudes towards them as learners. The notion that our society maintains stereotypical attitudes towards particular groups, and that we as teachers perpetuate these stereotypes was generally accepted and recognized. It seemed to me that the ILEA was attempting to address these issues through a range of policies and practices.

At first I was a supply teacher. I then taught in a school where there was an ethos of scorn towards what the ILEA was doing. As soon as I could I moved to the school I am presently teaching in because it had a reputation for being child-centred and concerned with equality. That was nine years ago (1988). At this school I have been faced with challenges that have supported the development of my knowledge and skills with regard to child-centred education and children's personal and social development.

The school context

The school is an inner London infant school, including a morning and an afternoon nursery class, with up to 240 children. It mainly serves children and families living on a local authority housing estate. The area is socially and economically disadvantaged and many of the children have special needs, some of which are associated

Figure 9.1: Headteacher's statement for OFSTED

> I am mindful that the children who attend our school will be the citizens of the twenty-first century. The aims of the school promote effective spiritual, moral, social and cultural development. We enable children to develop the knowledge, understanding, skills and values to be effective citizens.

with social and economic disadvantage. The majority of children are entitled to free school meals. There are approximately 26 different languages spoken by the families the school serves. The head teacher and deputy-head teacher and other adults who work and have worked in the school consider children's personal and social development as a high priority in the curriculum (see Figure 9.1, Headteacher's statement).

The school's carefully thought out equal opportunities and principles of learning policies, to which most adults who work in the school have contributed, support this statement. The policies are recognized as a framework for the curriculum. The principles of learning policy clearly recognizes that learning is a process that involves not only the academic but also the personal and social, including the emotional development of the child. The governing body is also in agreement and supportive of this approach. The 1996 Ofsted inspection report of the school's main findings opens with the following statement:

> The school effectively provides a secure and caring environment where pupils thrive and are well supported in their personal development. (OFSTED, 1996)

Towards defining PSD

Up until this point I have used the term PSD with little clarification for the reader. I now need to define what I mean by PSD. For me, it involves children's attitudes, values and feelings towards themselves, and others; individually, in the context of their immediate family, local community, and wider society and the world community. It also involves developing skills, and acquiring knowledge and understanding:

- for example, children need to develop skills as to how to resolve conflicts, of how to work with others and how to cooperate (SCAA, 1996);
- they need to acquire knowledge about themselves in relation to their family, their local community as well as the world community;
- they need to acquire knowledge of the range of values and attitudes within their society and how these sometimes come into conflict; and
- they need to learn how to take responsibility for their own actions and how to make moral judgments (Buck and Inman, 1993).

These aspects of a person's education are critical, partly because they affect how well they learn, but also because they affect how they act now and in the future. What is the point of educating people to high levels of skills and knowledge without developing their moral responsibilities and their relationship to all members of society? The current debate with regard to the research into cloning is an interesting example. Scientists can now change how an embryo develops and this change can affect the individual's sex, mental and emotional stability as well as their predisposition to some major illnesses. Some scientists are attempting to prove that an individual's sexual orientation is genetic.

The implications of this sort of research and its 'findings' are obviously frightening and negative if they are used by people who are unthinking, uncaring, feel little or no responsibility towards society and various groups in the society, and have elitist attitudes. It is also frightening to think of scientists and researchers with this knowledge and these skills, harbouring prejudices towards specific groups in our society and indeed in the world. On the other hand, scientific practice shaped by a clear moral and ethical framework has the potential to yield benefits for the wider society.

Therefore, I believe PSD within the school curriculum has a central part to play in preparing young people to be concerned, caring, and questioning citizens. However, effective PSD requires an approach to teaching and learning that explicitly promotes opportunities for children to be personally engaged with their own learning. Within this, dialogue must be central. The dialogue must provide possibilities for children to display their knowledge and understanding, to demonstrate and practise skills and critically reflect on their own values and the values of others. Conferencing can provide one such opportunity for dialogue.

Conferencing

When I use the term conferencing I mean a structured dialogue between two or three people that is explicitly planned by the teacher. Thus it differs from dialogues or conversations that may arise in a whole class discussion or playground situation in that it is planned and structured with intended outcomes in the teacher's mind. The explicitness of the intended outcomes also enables us to use conferencing as a way of assessing pupils' personal and social development. Furthermore, it provides an opportunity for pupils through dialogue, to engage in their own self-assessment. The Centre for Learning in Primary Education (CLPE)[2] has defined the purposes of conferencing. These can be seen in Figure 9.2.

The conferencing process as outlined by CLPE has the potential to promote and capture PSD. However, to ensure that this will happen, we must plan conferences with explicit PSD learning outcomes in mind. An example of such learning outcomes can be seen in Burke (Chapter 8 in this volume) and are reproduced here in Figure 9.3.

Both forms of conferences can help set a basis or a ground on which the child, parent and teacher can work together to support the child's development.

Figure 9.2: Purposes of conferencing

The purposes of the child/teacher conference:

- to establish in a structured way a dialogue between a child and the teacher;
- for the teacher to learn about children's views of themselves as a learner;
- to encourage children to play an increasingly active part in their own learning;
- to listen to the child's views and gain an understanding of its learning experiences in and outside school;
- to use this information to describe the development and learning that is taking place;
- to give positive feedback;
- to find out about any concerns;
- to discuss and help the child to formulate positive strategies to use in their learning; and
- to record decisions arrived at during the conference.

The purposes of the parent/teacher conference:

- encourages a two-way communication between home and school;
- encourages the parent(s) to share their knowledge of the child at home and at school;
- to share their observations, concerns, hopes and expectations; and
- encourages parents to play a role in their child's learning and assessment.

(Adapted with permission from Hilary Hester, Sue Ellis and Myra Barrs: *Guide to the Primary Learning Record*, Centre for Language in Primary Education, 1993).

Figure 9.3: Learning outcomes in PSD

Learning Outcomes Potentially Developed and Assessed Through Conferencing

Knowledge

- An understanding of their own beliefs
- An understanding of themselves in relation to personal, local, national and global issues

Skills

- An ability to give account of their own beliefs
- An ability to articulate their own values

Attitudes

- High self-esteem and a positive self-image
- Confidence and assertiveness
- An ability to reflect upon their own learning and to plan for the future
- Self-awareness and an ability to state their own views
- An ability to make moral decisions based on reason
- Having attitudes which promote consistency between belief and action
- An ability to make a personal response to questions about the purpose of life
- Having values in relation to themselves at different levels (local, national, global)
- Valuing their own and other cultures

Figure 9.4: Examples of questions used in conferencing

Identity and self-knowledge

- What kinds of things do you enjoy doing at school?
- What kinds of things do you like doing at home?
- How would you describe yourself? (shy, outgoing, happy)

Relationships with others

- How do you feel you get on with other children in the class?
- Do you think you are a good friend? Are you independent?
- Do you think you are cooperative and helpful to others?

Themselves as learners

- What are the names of some of your favourite books? Why do you like them?
- Do you enjoy school? What do you especially enjoy/dislike?
- How can I best help you to learn?

Self-confidence

- What are you good at, at school? at home?

Context of this action research

At the beginning of this chapter I suggested that the idea of being engaged in action research and applying it to the role of conferencing within PSD, particularly in relation to assessment, was exciting. However, it was also overwhelming. How would I be able to plan, teach, do the necessary record-keeping, conduct valid research and give the children the necessary attention and stimulus that they require and deserve? How could I meet the requirements of the NC[3] and conduct the inevitable SATs[4] in the summer term? Once I sat down and began to plan what I was going to do I quickly discovered that I was already doing some of the work I would need for this research. During each Autumn term I already conducted child and parent conferences in line with school policy. This time I planned and organized conferences for each child on a termly basis. The presence of a support teacher one day a week enabled me to have a one-to-one conference with each child. While I did have some one-to-one conferences without another adult as support those tended to be shorter, more susceptible to interruption and, in retrospect, were less focused. In conducting this research I have continued to use the CLPE model of conferencing as I would normally do during the Autumn term. However, I broadened my questions to include questions that related to a child's PSD as well as their developing literacy. The questions were grouped around specific areas and these areas were drawn from the PSD outcomes referred to in Figure 9.3. Figure 9.4 shows these areas and examples of questions that I used.

Figure 9.5: Conferencing for PSD

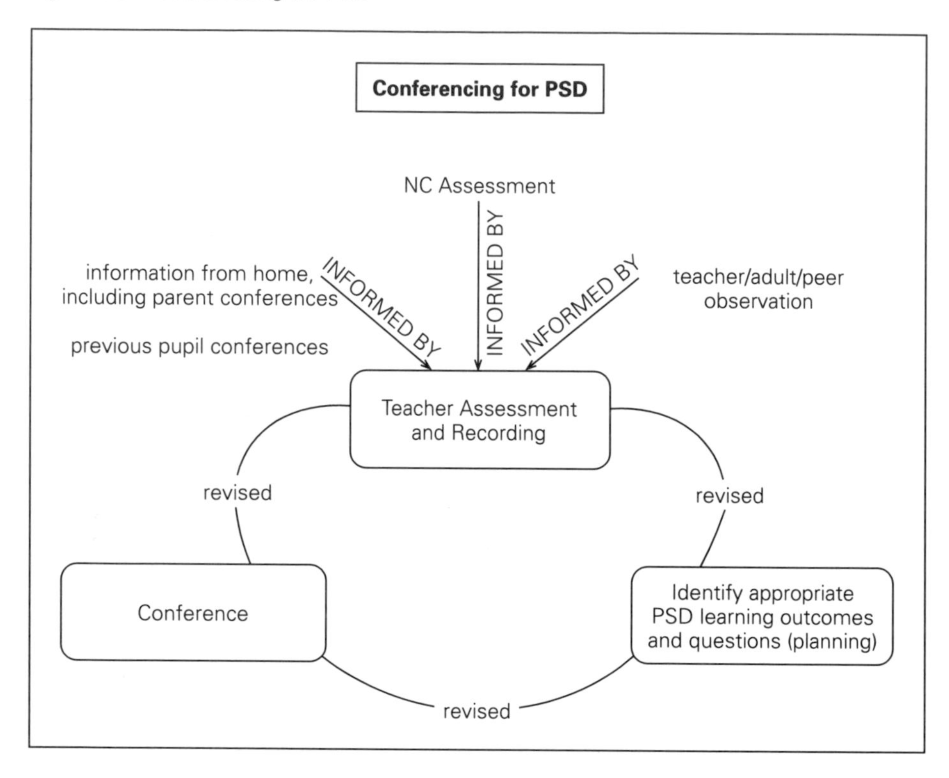

The conferencing process

The conferencing process over three terms can be likened to a one-to-one version of the plan, teach, review cycle. This process in relation to conferencing is described diagrammatically in Figure 9.5.

The diagram clearly demonstrates that conferencing is but one, albeit in my view important, source of provision and evidence for PSD. There is not space here to do justice to the wealth and richness of the data that emerged during the research project. Having conducted three conferences with children over the three terms I was forced to be highly selective in the material chosen. The material selected here best illustrates the processes involved in conferencing for PSD and comes from transcripts for conferences over the three terms with one 7-year-old boy.

My initial assessment of Marvin was positive, though based on limited evidence. In my early notes I described him as;

> a bright, very independent boy. He enjoys having conversations on a one-to-one basis and is generally very personable and articulate. At present he tends to avoid completing tasks initiated by adults and at times will ignore adult suggestions.

My first conference with Marvin was largely concerned with getting to know him better and to hear from him why he found it difficult to stay focused on adult initiated tasks. The questions focused around the following PSD areas:

- relationships with others
- self as a learner

Marvin quickly took control of the conference and made it his space to talk. I didn't interrupt because I thought it would detract from the spontaneity and individuality which was so evident in his talk.

> I like to do drawing and I like to play with my friends. When I come to them they run off and I have to catch them. I like playing with C too, and B and C. When they play with me they always sit on my table at lunch — only sometimes. I'm good at home: when my mum tells me to go to my room I do it. I read my book too. Sometimes I'm not good at school. Sometimes I'm good at school. When I'm not good I wander around the classroom and don't do my work. I sometimes wander around because I don't know where my work is. I listen to a song and don't do my reading. I feel bad because I sometimes have no friends to play with.

The conference confirmed many of my initial judgments about Marvin. However, the conference also raised some issues with respect to his relationships with others; he seemed to have some concerns about his relationships with other children. It was interesting to note that he began talking about 'being good' at school and at home when the question was, 'What do you like doing in school?' Behaviour and school were closely linked. Knowing the family as I do this is consistent with parent/teacher conferences that I had conducted. It was also evident from the conference that he is aware of the behaviour that hinders his learning.

In planning for the second conference therefore, I focused on the same areas but this time attempted to provide opportunities for Marvin to further reflect on his relationships with others and his approach to learning. In doing this, I was indirectly picking up some evidence around other PSD learning outcomes, particularly around self-knowledge. We began the second conference by reading the Autumn conference together. I then picked up on his earlier comments about not always knowing where his work is.

> *Me*: 'What happens to your work when you lose it?'
> *Marvin*: 'Somebody might have took it and is trying to think it's theirs.'
> *Me*: 'Maybe you may lose it because you don't want to finish it?'
> *Marvin*: 'No, I want to do another activity. If my work is gone I just have to do another draft.'

Even though he didn't overtly acknowledge why he was losing his work the conference helped increase his awareness of his behaviour. It allowed our relationship to develop so that it had a stronger element of mutual interest. One of my intended outcomes was for him to take more responsibility for losing his work. I knew that he would find his work if I said that he would have to miss play, but the growth and development towards independence and taking responsibility for one's actions is more effective in my opinion when the child is an active part of the process.

The other area I focused on was relationships with others. I began by asking him if he still felt bad because sometimes he had no friends.

> *Marvin*: 'Sometimes in the playground it's just an accident when I bump into someone.'

This comment was interesting in the context of observations of Marvin. I had observed, as had other adults, that he would often be in his own world and while on the playground would spin about or do cartwheels completely oblivious to others around him. Given this, his notion of 'accidents' made some sense. I pointed out my observations to him and suggested he try to be more aware of others in the playground. He thought he could try to do this.

In the intervening months before the third conference I began to think that Marvin had developed in his relationships with others and in his ability to take responsibility for his work. This assessment was informed by my observations and those of other adults. I decided to test out these assessments in the third conference.

> *Me*: 'Do you remember the conference we had before and we talked about you losing your work and how sometimes you feel bad when you think you don't have friends?'

He indicated that he remembered.

> *Me*: 'You seem to be getting along well now, what's changed?'
>
> *Marvin*: 'Because I'm getting good at school, I don't wander round the place, I just do my work.'
>
> *Me*: 'Do you know why this has changed?'
>
> *Marvin*: 'When I'm at school the rules are don't kick so that's why I behave, I want to follow the rules. At school sometimes I'm very good, sometimes I'm very bad. I don't wander around any more. Wandering around is not following the rules. I'm changing my behaviour.'
>
> *Me*: 'How do you feel about your work now?'
>
> *Marvin*: 'I can draw good and I can write, I can write on the line with guides . . . spellings, sometimes I get them wrong like when I was a kid like when you are in the nursery I'd get my name wrong. I think I've got a good memory for how to spell stuff. . . .'

The conference seemed to demonstrate that some level of development had taken place. His behaviour in the classroom supported this assessment. However, it also revealed some of the complexities of PSD development. Marvin's comments indicated that he perceived himself as having a more positive and responsible approach to his work, described in terms of 'following the rules'. This seems to reveal a somewhat partial understanding of taking responsibility and thus while it was clearly a development for Marvin I would need to push this further in future conferences.

The comments which Marvin made about his peer relation groups were also very revealing. While observations had indicated that he was developing in terms of his relationships with others, the one-to-one dialogue facilitated in the conference suggested that different processes might be occurring. Rather than developing successful relationships based upon cooperation and greater awareness of peers, Marvin seemed to believe that he needed to simply do as he was instructed by other children.

Marvin: 'You know when T and M and me weren't friends I told K. (dinner supervisor) and we came back friends.'
Me: 'What do you do now to be friends?'
Marvin: 'When they tell me to do something I do it.'
Me: 'What do you do?'
Marvin: 'I get their coats, I do it, I follow the rules.'

This clearly identified issues which would need to be pursued in future PSD work with Marvin.

This last conference with him was very informative for several reasons. We had had two conferences already so that he was familiar with the process, there was some trust between the two of us and we had had a positive child/teacher relationship for two years. My final assessment of him on his year end record is as follows:

> Marvin is a bright, articulate and confident child. He responds positively to challenging activities. He can show a mature and sensible approach towards people and school. He is aware of some of his behaviours that can upset and disturb others and is reflective about these behaviours. He is willing to try to change and in some areas has succeeded. However, he needs to develop more awareness as to other people's needs and the fact that he is a part of a community. He needs to develop more self-discipline and not rely on adult supervision for many everyday tasks. We will need to provide opportunities for Marvin to further develop his growing sense of personal responsibility and sustain cooperative social relationships.

Conferencing: some emerging issues

So far I have suggested that conferencing has the potential to be an effective tool to develop, implement and assess PSD in primary schools and have outlined some of the processes involved in doing this. However, during the course of this research project a number of unresolved issues arose. These issues impact upon the capacity of the conferencing process to play an important role in children's PSD.

The attitudes of children and parents

There are a number of issues to do with perceptions of the role and importance of this form of dialogue within the educational process. Perhaps one of the most important of these is the child's view of conferencing. Do children see conferencing as supporting their learning, or are they merely doing what they think they are supposed to do; doing as the teacher says? Are they giving me the answers that they think I want to hear, or that their parents want them/expect them to say? Do they see conferencing as real work, equivalent to that of maths or writing? These issues become even more significant when conferencing focuses on PSD, rather than say literacy or numeracy.

This leads me to another issue; that of parents' attitudes towards teachers and school, and the potential impact of these attitudes on the conferencing process, particularly the teacher/parent conference. Many parents have had negative experiences in school. They may come to the conference with these memories and with feelings of having experienced failure and discrimination at school themselves. I need to be sensitive to the values and experiences that parents bring to the conferencing process. In addition, parents, like children, may feel obliged to give teachers acceptable responses. The perceived status and importance of PSD will also impact on the conferencing process. During the 1980s and 1990s parents have been inundated, through the media in particular, with the notion that schools and teachers are failing their children with regard to teaching them the so-called basics. It makes sense then that some of them maybe wary of a parent/teacher conference in which the focus is on their child's personal and social development rather than on the child's level of achievement in the core subjects. 'My child cannot read, write, spell properly or do sums accurately. So what are you doing about that?' The issue of status is clearly related to the nature of the current curriculum. The NC needs to be delivered and while PSD is built into the curriculum it currently takes a secondary role to maths, literacy, science and the foundation subjects. While, as teachers we know that PSD is at the heart of learning and achievement, including NC attainment, it is not given the status and time that it requires. There is a need for PSD to be at the centre of the taught curriculum and given a higher priority than it has at present. Until and unless this happens we should not be surprised if many parents remain wary of parent/teacher conferences that prioritize PSD.

Teachers personal and professional development

PSD conferencing demands very particular knowledge, skills and attitudes from us as teachers. The conferencing process itself demands knowledge and skills in relation to the setting up and sustaining of one-to-one dialogue with children and with adults. These attributes are not self-evident. Perhaps more importantly, PSD conferencing can and, indeed should, explore values and attitudes that are both complex and personal. This kind of exploration, if it is to be handled sensitively and professionally, demands a level of self-awareness by the teacher. The process of self-reflection for a teacher needs to be continuous and developmental if PSD conferencing is to be an effective tool in classroom practice.

This self-reflection may involve us at times in asking ourselves some of the same questions we ask our children, albeit at a very different level. If teachers are expected to be self-reflective then we will need support in the form of training to develop our skills and knowledge in this area. Issues around teacher's personal and professional development become even more pertinent when children or parents use the conferencing process to discuss areas of personal and family life that may be fraught with difficulty. During the course of my conferencing with children and parents I became aware of some very difficult and distressing family situations, including physical abuse. Once areas such as these are opened up what do we do with the information? What is our responsibility toward the child and parent? Indeed what can we as teachers realistically do to support the individuals concerned? We will need support from outside agencies when parents/carers and/or a child reveal information during a conference that we may find distressing and which we do not have the skills and knowledge, or the remit to resolve.

Conferencing with young children

A third issue relates directly to conferencing with children as young as 6 and 7 years. During the course of my work I became increasingly conscious that working intensively through one-to-one dialogue, difficult enough with adults, had particular problems in relation to young children. Some of the problems were straightforward and obvious; their sometimes limited levels of concentration, their need to work on very concrete examples in order to make sense of some of the more abstract concepts.

The following extract from a conference with a Year 2 girl illustrates the latter point. In this conference, focused around seeing esteem and relationships Sharon uses very concrete 'evidence' from home to demonstrate what she sees as her ability to be a 'good family member'.

Me: 'Are you a good member of your family, Sharon?'

Sharon: 'My dad brought chicken and forgot to buy gravy . . . I reminded him. . . . I said you can't eat chicken without gravy. My mum was going shopping and forgot to buy the cat food and my cat was crying. My mum said why is she crying and I said maybe you forgot to buy the cat food. Another thing, my mum was sweeping the floor, she put the broom down and she forgot so I said you forgot to sweep the floor, she said, thanks for reminding me'.

Other problems were more particular to the conferencing situation. The intensity of the one-to-one dialogue can be overwhelming and uncomfortable, particularly for children so young. I have become aware of the potential intrusiveness of the method and the need for sensitivity on the part of the teacher, a sensitivity that should enable us, where appropriate, to provide closure for the child. The following extract provides an example of a child who is clearly uncomfortable with the decision of the conference.

> I brought up the issue with Naima of her interrupting conversations and she simply would shrug her shoulders and said 'I don't know'. After asking some questions in

different ways I decided she was not ready to either understand or take on why she interrupted so I made a suggestion and was directive. I asked her if she would just try to wait when two people were talking.

Conclusion

I began this chapter by describing my hopes and trepidations for this project. In some measure both of these have been realized. The process of undertaking conferencing for PSD proved to be an important learning experience for me. My conception of PSD shifted and broadened through the course of the project and in retrospect the early conferences reflected more narrow definition, focused largely around children's behaviour. On reflection I was almost unconsciously using the conferences to explore aspects of children's behaviour that were of concern in the classroom and around the school. When I began to broaden my definition and explicitly plan for a wider range of PSD learning outcomes, I obtained information that provided much more of a whole picture of the child's development. For me, the most important reason for undertaking this project was the belief that it would enable me to reflect on and develop my practice. Despite the issues involved in conferencing, the process of working with children in this way has enabled me to make more informed judgments of children's development. This in turn has impacted upon my planning for PSD provision both through future conferences and within whole class provision.

In summation, the experience of this action research has reinforced my thinking that encouraging children to become involved in their learning about themselves and others, to question their behaviour through conferencing, can be effective in supporting them towards becoming questioning, concerned and caring citizens. Furthermore, I found this an effective way for a classroom teacher to be challenged and to revisit some attitudes and beliefs about how and what we all need to learn.

Notes

1 The ILEA (Inner London Education Authority) came into existence in 1965 and was responsible for education in London. In 1981 the ILEA initiated policies and practices aimed at addressing the issue of achievement in relation to a range of inequalities. These included race, gender and to a lesser extent, class, sexuality, and disability. It was abolished under the Education Reform Act, 1988 within considerable controversy. Maclure, S. *A History of Education in London 1870–1990*, (2nd Ed) The Penguin Press, London, England, 1990.

2 Centre for Learning in Primary Education. A Centre which offers advice, courses and workshops for teachers. It has a strong commitment to child centred education and a positive approach to how children learn. The Centre has also published books relating to children's literacy development and has an international reputation.

3 NC is the National Curriculum which lays down the statutory requirements that teachers and schools are to fulfil with regard to maths, science, and English as well as history, geography, music, art, PE, design and technology, and information technology.
4 Standard Attainment Tasks. Children at the ages of 7, 11 and 14 are to be administered these tests during the summer term. They are based upon the National Curriculum outcomes.

References

BUCK, M. and INMAN, S. (1993) *Curriculum Guidance No. 2: Re-affirming Values*, Centre for Cross Curricular Initiatives, London: Goldsmiths College.

SCAA (1996) *Desirable Outcomes for Childrens' Learning*.

Chapter 10

Researching Assessment Practice in PSE: A Secondary Case Study

Gill Pooley

Abstract

This chapter is a case study of a Personal and Social Education (PSE) department in a South London comprehensive school. It focuses on a piece of action research undertaken by the PSE coordinator in collaboration with PSE teachers and students. The purposes of this research has been to evaluate the current assessment practice within the PSE department and to highlight areas for change.

PSE as an element of PSD

As a PSE coordinator, I have worked with a team of PSE teachers to develop a particular perspective on this aspect of the curriculum. This perspective views Personal and Social Education as an element or strand of Personal and Social Development (PSD) and as an essential curriculum entitlement in a school committed to placing PSD at the centre of its purpose. As previous chapters have discussed, PSD is concerned with developing a range of knowledge, skills and attitudes and as such it is a vast area involving all staff and students and experiences within the school. My role has been to look specifically at the curriculum provision for PSE, which has meant attempting to identify the specific knowledge, understanding, skills and attitudes that ought to form a meaningful programme. The development of our current programme and assessment practice began five years ago. Our perspective on PSE has a very clear central focus on an explicit curriculum input which has intellectual rigour and status within the curriculum and that gives students the opportunity to develop their own values.

As such, the overall aim of our PSE programme is to provide a centre for the students' moral, social and cultural development. However, the main responsibility for students' PSD does not lie with the PSE curriculum alone, as it is central and integral to the purpose of all aspects of the school. The school's aims and values are clearly at the centre of our commitment to PSD and were drawn up by staff, students, parents/guardians and governors. These can be seen in Figure 10.1.

Figure 10.1: School's aims and values

As a school community of students, teachers, support staff, parents and governors, we value

An atmosphere characterized by calm, friendly and courteous behaviour, in which there is no tolerance of any kind of discrimination or unkindness and where young people have the right to be heard.

Classroom experiences in which young people and adults share responsibility for the task of learning within clear boundaries of order and discipline.

The variety of experiences, cultures, languages, needs and abilities that each person brings.

Students' who are confident, original, articulate, considerate and creative.

Our relationship with the local community and our involvement with local and borough affairs.

The breadth of cultural, social, sporting, pre-vocational as well as intellectual opportunities offered to all our students within and outside the timetabled curriculum, and the programme of guidance and support that accompanies their learning throughout their school life.

We aim, through the agreed policies of the school and their expression in activities and structures

To maintain a school environment which is clean and attractive and which displays students' work and school achievement with pride.

To provide enthusiastic and stimulating teaching and a classroom environment in which responsibility, humour, fairness and respect for the individual make it possible for students to develop skills and confidence.

To respect and appreciate difference, to live together without prejudice, to encourage self-esteem, to develop tolerance yet a critical awareness of society, to welcome the new perspectives brought by diversity, and to stimulate a sense of justice.

To encourage students to persevere and to be generous in recognition of each other's needs and achievements.

To make opportunities within and outside the curriculum to challenge and extend abilities and talents and to support learning and development.

To develop our policy of welcoming visitors and to become a resource for learning and social activity for the neighbourhood.

To develop our links with the community through school leaver employment and work experience.

To maintain a structured and a supportive programme offering appropriate guidance and encouragement, learning support and extension, and opportunities for our students to develop through responsibility, social interaction and decision making.

These aims are made public through the school's documentation and are reflected in other school policies such as equal opportunities, behaviour and sex education, as well as in school assemblies and display. In all areas of the curriculum, teachers have spent considerable time discussing ways in which they can contribute or may develop their contribution to students' spiritual, moral, social and cultural development through their curriculum content and teaching methods.

The role of the form tutor is also central to the implementation of the school's aims and whilst there is no formal tutor period, tutors have been given an extra free period in which to develop their pastoral role. The links between the PSE programme and the pastoral programme are, at present, informal but this is clearly an area for future development. The recent Ofsted report highlighted the way in which all these strands work together to promote students' PSD

> The personal development of the pupils is very good and is enhanced by the relationships with the teachers, the excellent PSE programme and the wide range of creative extra-curricular activities on offer. Overall the attitudes, behaviour and personal development of the pupils contribute to the school's strong learning culture and reflect most positively on the community as a whole. (Ofsted Inspection Report 27/9/96–4/10/96 paragraph 55)

The following aims of the PSE programme are intended to reflect the school's commitment to the personal and social development of every student.

- to integrate students' personal, social, moral and cultural education
- to empower students with the knowledge, skills and understanding necessary to take an active role in society and to make informed choices
- to develop students' sense of self-esteem and self-awareness
- to encourage students to become confident and assertive
- to develop students' ability to think critically and to question taken for granted assumptions
- to enable students to develop the skills to work collaboratively and autonomously
- to enable students to understand and, where appropriate, be sensitive to and respectful of the beliefs, values and way of life of others
- to give students the opportunity to develop ideas about fairness, justice and equality on a personal, societal and global level

There are many parallels between the whole school aims and the aims of the PSE programme. While the school's aims underpin the purpose of the PSE programme, the programme's aims have been developed with a curriculum focus. Within the PSE programme students are offered opportunities to consider issues of personal and social values and morals, issues of rights and responsibilities (on a personal, local, national and global level), social structures and the relationship between the personal and the social. Students are also encouraged to develop an understanding of the concept of culture and community.

The PSE programme has been developed as a spiral curriculum which endeavours to consider appropriateness and accessibility in terms of students' age, stage of development and needs. This can also allow for the revisiting of themes and topics at different stages throughout the school. It is taught for one lesson a week by a small department of specialist teachers. The PSE coordinator is responsible for coordinating and promoting the provision of the PSE programme throughout the school, managing its delivery and resourcing and leading a team of teachers. As such, the PSE team operate in some aspects as any small department within the school. We have long been committed to this approach for a number of reasons. In the first place, a specialist team enables teachers who value PSE and feel that they can make a contribution to its development to make this their main teaching commitment. It allows these teachers to spend time together reviewing and developing the programme and has given us the opportunity to focus on developing our assessment practice. Clearly this also avoids the difficulties that can arise when form tutors are delivering a PSE programme with limited time, facilities, training and interest. In the worst scenario PSE can become a burden on staff and negative messages about its perceived value are conveyed to students resulting in everyone dreading the PSE slot, period 1 on a Monday morning. The PSE teachers in this department have been appointed for their expertise in this area, but come from a range of backgrounds including, social studies, humanities and PE. The specialist approach allows teachers to attend relevant INSET and to share professional development within the department as well as with other staff, for instance through the school's NQT INSET programme. This has enabled us to become more successful PSE teachers and our Ofsted report reflected this, identifying the PSE department as 'a strength of the school' and a 'group of highly skilled teachers' (OFSTED Inspection Report, paragraphs 16 and 88). With this approach, the school is able to timetable PSE lessons as an integral part of the curriculum which makes resourcing PSE more manageable. The specialist approach also gives students the opportunity to develop a relationship with a member of staff who they know has chosen to teach PSE and is confident and knowledgeable about a particular range of issues. The links between the PSE teacher and the form tutor are, at present, largely informal although the role of the form tutor is, I believe, supported by the specialist approach to PSE. Tutors will often liaise with PSE teachers about aspects of a particular student's development. However, the form tutor has the day-to-day contact with their tutor group and as such has the key responsibility for monitoring students' welfare and academic progress. This approach has undoubtedly contributed to the success of our PSE programme and has enabled us to move ahead in many aspects, especially assessment.

Current assessment practice — why, what, how

Over the course of the last three years, the PSE team have looked at the issue of assessment and this has become a focus for a great deal of development work.

Initially, the question that we needed to address was 'why assess?', in other words, what is the purpose of developing assessment practice within PSE? This question raises all sorts of issues related to what we consider to be the role of PSE within the curriculum and how assessment practice would benefit students' personal and social education and development. It seemed clear that the purpose of assessment needed to be rooted in developing ways of monitoring students' progress that would enable students to plan and take control of their own learning. This would therefore need to involve communication between student and teacher on a formal and informal basis. Assessment practice would need to allow students and teacher the opportunity and time to reflect on students' learning, to set targets and to plan for the next stage of learning. Assessment practice ought to involve recognition of progress made and identification of issues that may need resolution or further thought. Other aspects of the assessment process should include gathering meaningful knowledge about students' progress that can be recorded and used to inform reports and for a range of audiences such as parents' evenings and tutor group reviews.

One of the main differences between PSE and most of the rest of the curriculum is that we don't have National Curriculum attainment targets or a curriculum outlined for us. In many ways this is a real advantage as it allows for creativity and imagination, but it also presents many difficulties in developing a programme with clear knowledge and skills development and one in which students' progress can be assessed. Instead of a National Curriculum document therefore, our starting point was our existing set of aims for PSE and our actual PSE programme as it then existed. The programme had been developed over several years and had been informed by various documents including the National Curriculum Cross Curricular Themes (health, careers, citizenship, economic and industrial understanding and to some extent environmental education) as well as more recently, Ofsted guidelines on spiritual, moral, social and cultural development (Appendix 1). As this programme was already set up and running it would not have been practical to abandon this and start from scratch and we also felt that much of what we were doing was valuable. The first step was to examine this existing programme to identify what we were currently assessing informally. At this stage our schemes of work did not have any identified assessment foci but they did have clearly explained aims. Looking at these in relation to assessment was very interesting and provided us with an opportunity to identify what might be the assessable aspects of our PSE programme. The achievement of some of these aims was already resulting in outcomes which could be assessable even though they might not produce right or wrong answers, e.g. to develop students' ability to think critically, to develop collaborative skills. As a result we have identified assessment criteria which include specific areas of knowledge and understanding and a range of skills. These are in Figure 10.2.

However, other aims such as encouraging self-esteem and ideas about justice are much more problematic as they refer to attitudes, values and personal qualities which the department discussed and at that time decided not to develop as part of a

Figure 10.2: Assessment criteria in the PSE programme

ASSESSMENT CRITERIA

Skills:

Listening	Discussion
Speaking	Explaining ideas
Writing	Being critical
Presentation	Organization
Group Cooperation	Analysing
Research	Working independently
Selecting information	Evaluation

Knowledge and understanding key concepts:

Change	Culture
Power/Authority	Community
Social differentiation	Childhood
Ideology	Health
Equality/Inequality	Race
Resistance	Gender
Self	Sexuality
Justice	Choice
Prejudice	Career
Responsibility	Need/Want
Rights	Relationships
Socialization	Safety
Puberty	

formal assessment policy. Whereas we have been able to develop ways to gather a range of evidence and therefore comment on the degree to which a student has developed a certain skill, or a level of knowledge and understanding, it was felt that it would be extremely difficult to measure a change in attitude, value or personal quality. Discussions around this issue raised many thorny problems. First, there is the issue of whose values do we teach and judge to be the 'right' ones and whose are to be seen as negative or problematic? Clearly there are some values which can be seen as common and indeed our 'school aims' outlines the school's own values. These might include honesty, respect for others, a sense of justice or equality, but when it comes to making a formal assessment of a student's progress in relation to such values we have yet to come up with an idea that as a department we would feel happy to implement. For example, if a student argues that they are against racism but supports the right of another student to make a case for the British

National Party, are they showing that they have developed respect for others? As a department we remain uneasy about this and we do not, at present, attempt formally to assess students' attitudes, values and personal qualities. It would be untrue to say that this does not happen on an informal basis through class discussion, comment and praise. As a department we would need to be much clearer about the purpose of making such assessments more formal before we would develop this. However, as a practical way forward we are beginning to look at our use of the PSE assessment profile (Appendix 2). This could provide an opportunity to reflect on students' attitudes and values and assessments relating to issues such as behaviour that might, perhaps, be recorded here. It has also been felt that for this sort of assessment to be meaningful it would need to be a whole school approach involving a large degree of information sharing across the curriculum. Clearly this is an area for further debate both within the department and across the school. The department felt that the way forward for PSE at this time was to focus on what it is that we do in PSE that we believe we can and should be assessing in. Consequently, we wanted to go forward to develop our ideas about what might constitute good practice in assessing PSE and to devise ways of recording assessment that would be practical within the constraints of the time that we spend with each class.

The process involved:

- reviewing schemes of work to make the assessment focus for each unit of work and then each lesson more explicit and ensuring that this is shared with students;
- considering how we would make sense of such a wide range of possible evidence for forming assessments and identifying the range of assessment opportunities in PSE (Appendix 3);
- looking at systems of assessment that already exist in the school and whole school assessment policy to ensure consistency across the school; and
- building in the process of target setting and review.

Clearly every unit of work has an incredible range of possible learning outcomes which would be unwieldy and possibly meaningless to assess. As a result, it was decided to develop an assessment focus for each unit of work. These include particular skills and areas of knowledge and understanding which have been drawn from our assessment criteria and which are made explicit to students at the beginning of each unit. This approach has been recognized as successful by our Ofsted report 'progress is better when pupils have clear expectations of what is to be taught in a unit of work with assessment criterion known at the outset as occurs in PSE' (OFSTED Inspection Report, paragraph 47). During a unit of work, evidence is gathered in usual ways — e.g. observing students, marking books, talking to students. In each unit of work we have developed an assessment task which is marked against a particular criterion (Appendix 4).

Underpinning the ways in which we have developed methods for putting assessment policy into practice, has been the notion that assessment should be an integral part of the learning process in PSE and that this should be recognized by student and teacher alike. Assessment ought to be part of normal activity. Therefore, assessment should not occur twice a year but frequently. The assessment practice within PSE is meant to be formative, to give both students and teachers a chance to focus on the students' learning, to monitor progress and check and set targets. Assessment in PSE lessons occurs in many ways, formal and informal, including peer and group assessment, student self-assessment, teacher assessment including the marking of written work and the evaluation of oral contributions.

In an attempt to pull these strands together, to endeavour to be explicit about the assessment practice and to involve students in this practice, we have developed an internal profile system (Appendix 2). This is designed to provide a focus for and a record of assessment and to give regular feedback to students about their progress. This profile was piloted with Year 7 and Year 10 groups in September 1995 and was extended across the school in September 1996. At regular intervals, the student and teacher will complete a section of the profile, with some discussion about the assessment focus and negotiation around target completion and setting. Since September 1996 we have tried to allocate one lesson at the end of each unit as an evaluation lesson in which to focus on the profile. Our aim has been to enable students to set realistic and achievable learning targets. Meaningful target setting needs to include the process of monitoring and review and as such the intention has been that teachers refer to students' targets when marking their books or when talking informally. Concerns have been felt within the department over the issue of target setting and how well we have been able to achieve this aim.

A further aspect of our assessment practice has been the development of monitoring methods to allow us to look at how well we assess. This has included work sampling to look at consistency within the department. As a result of a programme of work sampling that took place in January 1996, the department embarked upon the development of an Assessment Portfolio. This consists of examples of students' work covering a range of work and response levels. The intention is that this is used to enable us to review and monitor marking and assessment in PSE and as part of the induction for new staff. The process of selecting work to go into the portfolio is intended to allow us to review our own practice and to look critically at levels of achievement in PSE.

Over the last three years we have looked into ways of formally accrediting students' achievements in PSE at Key Stage 4. As PSE is taught for only one hour a week there have always been serious limitations on formal accreditation. However, it has been felt by all staff that it was important to find some way of rewarding students for their achievements and that this should ideally be external. For two years we used the City and Guilds Diploma in Vocational Education. This was being developed in other areas of the school as an alternative or in addition to GCSE accreditation. This qualification had three main elements, a vocational area (such as business studies, manufacturing and design etc.) work experience and an element entitled 'Self and the Environment'. The Vocational Education Coordinator at the school helped also to develop the PSE programme at Key Stage 4 to meet the requirements of the City and Guilds 'Self and the Environment' element and arranged for students to be accredited for their work in PSE alone. This was quite successful particularly in terms of students' motivation, however the DVE has since been superseded by GNVQ. Fortunately the school has piloted GNVQ at Key Stage 4 and so the Vocational Education Coordinator was able to look at accrediting the PSE programme. At present this is happening through GNVQ Communication (see Appendix 4) which means that PSE enables most students to achieve part of a GNVQ. This not only accredits their achievements but can also be used if they go on to take a full GNVQ in future. This form of accreditation has involved us in mapping our own programme against GNVQ criteria and reflecting these in our methods of assessment at Key Stage 4. Although as a department we have found these two forms of accreditation reasonable to manage and helpful in rewarding students' achievements, we would welcome developments that would seek to accredit PSE itself either on a local or national level.

Researching assessment practice — purposes and method

In September 1996 I began to develop ideas about evaluating our current assessment practice in PSE. The approach described above had begun three years ago and has been part of usual practice in the department since September 1996. It seemed an appropriate time to take stock and so I embarked upon designing a small scale research project. The aim has been to evaluate and monitor current assessment practice to determine whether the new practice meets the purposes of assessment we have identified and consequently to enable the department to revise our practice. In order to do this it was necessary to go back to our stated purposes of assessment to identify some criteria upon which to base this research. Consequently, the research has concentrated on a number of key questions outlined below, for the purposes of this book I will focus on only some of these.

Key questions

- Do teachers feel that they have any better knowledge of students' strengths and weaknesses and learning needs as a result of current practice?
- Are the records created by current practice useful and used?
- How manageable do teachers find current assessment practice?
- Do teachers feel that current assessment practice has had any impact on students' perception of PSE?
- Do students feel that they have a clear understanding of how they are assessed and of the progress they are making in PSE?
- To what extent do students feel involved in the assessment process?
- Are there some elements of current practice that are more useful than others for students?

- How well does current practice enable meaningful target setting and target review?
- Should we be assessing any other aspect of PSE e.g. attitudes and values?
- What are the strengths and weaknesses of current assessment practice in PSE?

The general purpose of these questions has been to examine our assessment practice in relation to four key areas — manageability, appropriateness of methods, quality of information and effectiveness.

As a teacher using research to examine and improve practice in my own department I felt it would be inappropriate and unrealistic to attempt to use quantitative methods of research. In many ways this research project has simply been a more explicit form of what all teachers do continuously as part of their job, rather than an attempt to find any large scale answers to universal problems. Consequently, this project has taken the form of a small scale piece of action research involving both staff and students in collaboration. Both teachers and students were aware and supportive of the purposes of this research. One feature of action research is that it is cyclical, involving action followed by research followed again by action. We intend to follow up on the changes made as a result of the research by conducting a similar piece of research in a year's time.

The research strategies I used needed to enable me to gather useful in-depth information within the constraints of the school timetable and the other demands of school life. This ruled out observation of assessment practice and I believe that my presence in such a situation would have seriously affected behaviour and would not have given me any useful or reliable information. Instead I set up a series of interviews with teachers and students. The teacher interviews were set up with the two other staff who have a mainly PSE teaching timetable. I allowed for about one hour per teacher and conducted the interviews individually. I used a range of mainly open-ended questions that were designed to encourage discussion around the key areas I identified above. For the interviews with students I decided to focus on two year groups, Year 8 and Year 11 as these had been the pilot groups for some aspects of the development of our current assessment practice in September 1995. I felt that the students would respond more freely if interviewed in groups rather than individually and that this situation might facilitate greater discussion around the key areas with less direction or input from me. Like the staff interviews the questions were mainly open-ended and interviews were between 45 minutes and one hour in duration.

Research findings

The following is a summary of some of the most important findings of this research in relation to the four key areas of manageability, appropriateness of methods, quality of information and effectiveness.

Manageability

A major concern of this research was to identify any difficulties with the management of our assessment practice and to look at ways of improving this. Teachers all identified some organizational difficulties with assessment practice, in particular with the implementation of the assessment profile. Among the comments made about this were 'time is always the problem but this has been better in the second year of the profile' and 'we need to find more time to discuss the profile fully and to speak to all students individually about their progress'. However, teachers seemed to value the profile and were committed to making this work. In other respects all teachers seemed confident that management of the range of records created by assessment was quite straightforward and allowed for a greater flow of information. The marking scheme that the department developed to mark class and homework was seen by teachers as very useful, easy to manage and a real improvement on previous methods which included only comments which were not linked to assessment criteria. One teacher commented 'it ties me down to making more specific comments'. All areas of concern around the organization and management of our assessment practice focused on the limited time that teachers have with students to implement some aspects of current practice effectively.

Appropriateness of methods

As we have developed our assessment practice in PSE, we have endeavoured to use a range of methods by which to gather relevant information about students' progress. These include both formal and informal methods. The findings of this research have been useful in highlighting which aspects of this process work well and which do not. Overall, teachers said that our methods were appropriate and commented that 'a clear assessment practice can help create a positive status for PSE'. Teachers felt that students valued having their work assessed in PSE. All teachers and students commented very positively on the use of the marking scheme which differentiates between effort and attainment. One teacher said 'the marking scheme gives me flexibility when I'm marking students books'. Books marked in a specific and thorough way was seen as very helpful by all students as it helped them to identify their strengths and weaknesses after each piece of work set.

Having a clear assessment focus was also seen as useful by teachers, one said it was helpful in 'pinning down the purpose of our activities in PSE'. Teachers felt that individual assessment tasks were useful in that they gave students the opportunity to show their strengths as they were usually more open-ended than day-to-day activities. Teachers thought that students paid particular attention to teachers' detailed comments on these assessment tasks. However, group assessment tasks were seen as worthwhile but problematic to assess as it was often unfair to assess the contribution of all members of a group equally. This was identified as an area for further work. The assessment profile was seen as a good way of communicating with students when time permitted and one teacher thought that younger students especially took this very seriously. One Year 8 student said that she liked it when she got to write her ideas on to the profile before her teacher did, she explained that this was one way of 'telling the teacher what I think'.

The time spent explaining the aims of each unit of work with students was praised by Ofsted but, more importantly, was identified by students as very helpful. One Year 11 student said 'it helps us know why we're doing a piece of work and what we should be trying to achieve'. All students said that they valued time to discuss their progress with their PSE teachers and that if anything they would like more time to do this. Self-assessment was seen by students and teachers as a way of helping students take charge of their own learning.

The main area of concern regarding our current methods of assessment was around target setting. This was universally seen as worthwhile but not yet as effective as it might be. Teachers felt that students might find target setting meaningless as 'it happens quite often but we devote less time following it up'. It was suggested that we need to think about different and more imaginative ways of approaching target setting to make it more relevant and interesting. This might include more class discussion and sharing of targets and perhaps peer or group assessment and target setting. Year 8 students suggested that they would enjoy pairing up and taking some responsibility for monitoring each others' targets 'we could tell the others our targets and they would help remind us about them'. The same students also suggested that a list of examples of targets would help them set more meaningful and specific targets. This however, was not seen as appropriate by Year 11 students.

Teachers felt that current assessment methods clearly assess knowledge and understanding and a range of skills successfully. As part of this research I wanted to raise the issue of attitudes and values once more to identify whether it was felt that out methods needed to address this in the future. Both teachers expressed concern about extending formal assessment practice into attitudes and values. One teacher explained that attitudes and values may be implicitly assessed through informal comments made. She said 'assessing a value explicitly would be very difficult as we would need to be specific about what value was being assessed and it would be impossible to say how much of a value or attitude a student had developed'. It was felt that we could, as PSE teachers, comment on a range of areas such as the ability to work collaboratively, respect for others and so on and that these areas could perhaps be developed from the school's aims and values statement. Another teacher said that PSE gave lots of opportunities to discuss attitudes and values but that this could not form part of what we assess as it raises 'too many problems'. One problem mentioned was measurability, one teacher asked, 'Is an attitude measurable, does attitude development progress in one direction, does an attitude change last?' It was felt that our PSE programme at present should encourage debate around a range of attitudes and values. Students were also uneasy about teachers assessing their attitudes and values but were interested in discussing this. Clearly much more debate would be needed in this area and this would need to be at a whole school level with the school aims and values at the centre.

Quality of information

Some of the interview questions were designed to examine what sort of information our assessment practice was giving to both teachers and students. The aim of our practice has been to gain relevant information about students' progress in relation to our assessment criteria that can be used to help students progress and plan for their next stage of learning.

In terms of the marking of day-to-day written work, both students and teachers felt that this was usually thorough and detailed: all teachers said that 'this gives us the most useful information about students' achievement'. Students were very positive about the sorts of comments made by their PSE teachers in their books which were seen as specific and detailed and not bland comments such as 'keep it up' which one student explained was useless to her. Students also said that they valued the focused feedback they received on assessment tasks. Most students also said that they understood the written comments made by their teachers. This is clearly of great importance if this information is going to be used successfully by students to take charge of their learning. Year 11 students pointed out that they were much clearer about their progress when they had had time for personal discussion with their teachers. Students enjoyed being able to respond to teachers' comments and enter into some discussion about their work in PSE. The key issue that arose in respect of the quality of information was time. While the present arrangements for discussion of the profile were seen as useful, all students, and to some extent teachers, said that they would value even more space for this.

Effectiveness

The main reason for conducting this research has been to look at the effectiveness of current assessment practice in PSE. I decided that one way to identify this was to find out whether students had a clear understanding of how they were being assessed and of the progress they were making in PSE. Year 8 students were able to identify many aspects of the ways in which they are assessed in PSE and could explain that assessment happened through discussion with their teacher and with each other. These students were very clear about what sorts of skills were being assessed in PSE and some explained that this was because their teacher explained it to them. Year 11 students felt that PSE assessed different things from other curriculum areas and identified 'giving opinions . . . contributing ideas . . . communicating with people'. All students said that they were very clear about their strengths in PSE but were less certain about their weaknesses.

One teacher felt that our approach to assessment had been effective in raising standards in PSE over the last two years and she explained that 'because we now take it seriously, the students in turn take it seriously too'. The rise in standards was also put down to the ways in which students and staff are now more clearly focused on assessment criteria and teachers consequently had raised expectations of students' attainment in PSE. It was felt that this had also helped to reinforce the positive status that PSE enjoys in the school. Another aspect of assessment that was felt to be effective was student evaluation which gave teachers valuable information about how a unit of work has been perceived and where it has successfully achieved its aims. This has enabled teachers to identify changes needed.

Target setting had already been mentioned as an issue for attention in relation to methods of assessment. It was also felt by teachers and Year 8 students that there needed to be more guidance with this process if it was going to help all students make progress. Both stated that many students set bland targets, one student explaining that she had written 'I must work harder' more than once and that this had not been very useful. However, target setting seems to have had success with older students and one Year 11 student gave the example of her target 'to speak up more often in class discussions'. She explained that she had achieved this target to a large extent and felt better about herself as a result. She had been helped to achieve this by friends in the class reminding her and encouraging her.

The way forward

This research has highlighted a range of areas for future development within our PSE department. Two key issues seem to have been clearly raised, firstly that there are some changes needed which will include:

- investigating more imaginative approaches to self-assessment and target setting;
- developing ways to make target review more integral to lessons, looking at how to encourage students to take more responsibility for target setting and review;
- finding more opportunities for student teacher discussion within the present time allocation;
- modification of the assessment profile; and
- further discussion around attitudes and values assessment looking more closely at how our assessment practice relates to the whole school approach to students' PSD.

Secondly, the results of my interviews have at least reassured me that our efforts so far have been purposeful and are perceived to be so by students and teachers. The time we have spent on developing assessment practice has been worthwhile and endeavouring to get this right is central to the success of the PSE programme as a whole.

Appendix 1

The PSE Programme Years 7–11.

AT A GLANCE . . .

Unit Title and Description	*Relevant National Curriculum/DFE Guidance and School Policies*
YEAR 7:	
UNIT ONE: Starting Secondary School An introduction to school life. 2/3 weeks.	*NCC Curricular Guidance — X Curricular Theme: **Environmental Education**.
UNIT TWO: The Rights of the Child Introductory unit on issues of rights focusing on childhood and school. 10/11 weeks.	*NCC Curricular Guidance — X Curricular Theme: **Citizenship**. *School Equal Opportunities policy.
UNIT THREE: What is Health? a) A project to consider a range of health issues. 7 weeks. b) Changes — looking at physical changes during puberty male and female. 7 weeks.	*NCC Curricular Guidance — X Curricular Theme: **Health**. *ERA 1993 'Sex Education in Schools' Circular 5/94 *School Sex Education policy.
UNIT FOUR: Community An introduction to issues of the needs of a community — with a focus on the needs of older people. 14 weeks.	*NCC Curricular Guidance — X Curricular Theme: **Citizenship — Environment**. School Equal Opportunities policy.
YEAR 8:	
UNIT ONE: Roles and Relationships Looking at emotional/social changes during puberty — issues of friendship, family, love, roles and role conflict etc. 14 weeks.	*NCC Curricular Guidance — X Curricular Theme: **Citizenship — Health**. *ERA 1993 'Sex Education in Schools' 3/94. *School Sex Education policy.
UNIT TWO: Safety A range of issues around personal safety and assertiveness. 12 weeks.	*NCC Curricular Guidance — X Curricular Theme: **Health — Citizenship**. *School Equal Opportunities policy.
UNIT THREE: Drugs Awareness Introduction to issues of legal and illegal drug abuse. Focusing on personal, social and political aspects. 7 weeks.	*NCC Curricular Guidance — X Curricular Theme: **Health — Economic and Industrial Understanding and Citizenship**.

The PSE Programme Years 7–11.

AT A GLANCE . . .

UNIT FOUR: Development Looking at issues of sustainable development and global relationships. 7 weeks.	*NCC Curricular Guidance — X Curricular Theme: **Citizenship** — **Environment**.
YEAR 9:	
UNIT ONE: Civil Liberties Developing understanding of concepts such as politics, government, citizenship, justice, rights, responsibilities. etc. 7 weeks.	*NCC Curricular Guidance — X Curricular Theme: **Citizenship** — **Economic and Industrial Understanding**. *School Equal Opportunities policy.
UNIT TWO: Power and Prejudice Concepts such as power, prejudice, resistance. Focusing on racism. 8 weeks.	As above.
UNIT THREE: Gender Looking at the role of women and men. Developing ideas about how roles are created and looking at women's achievements. 7 weeks.	As above.
UNIT FOUR: Work and Careers Developing understanding of women in the workforce. Includes issues of legislation, choices etc. 7 weeks.	*NCC Curricular Guidance — X Curricular Theme: **Careers** — **Economic and Industrial** — **Citizenship**. *School Equal Opportunities policy.
UNIT FIVE: Sex/sexuality Developing an understanding of sexuality and sexual relationships. Includes issues of rights and responsibilities, sexual health, contraception. 14 weeks.	*NCC Curricular Guidance — X Curricular Theme: **Health** — **Citizenship**. *ERA 1993 'Sex Education in Schools' *School Sex Education policy.
YEAR 10: **UNIT ONE: Women's Health** Focusing on the range of factors that can influence our health — physical, social and psychological. The unit will consider a range of health issues. 7 weeks.	*NCC Curricular Guidance — X Curricular Theme: **Health** — **Citizenship**. *ERA 1993 'Sex Education in Schools' *School Sex Education policy.

The PSE Programme Years 7–11.

AT A GLANCE . . .

UNIT TWO: Violence Towards Women Developing knowledge and awareness of issues of domestic violence. Including possible causes and legal rights etc. 7 weeks.	*NCC Curricular Guidance — X Curricular Theme: **Citizenship**. *School Equal Opportunities policy.
UNIT THREE: Disability in the Community Looking at issues related to disability and equality — particularly access. 10 weeks.	*NCC Curricular Guidance — X Curricular Theme: **Citizenship — Environmental Education**. *School Equal Opportunities policy.
UNIT FOUR: The World of Work Linked to work experience, considering a number of work related issues. Developing understanding of concepts ie. work, economy, employment etc. 10 weeks.	*NCC Curricular Guidance — X Curricular Theme: **Careers Ed. — Economic and Industrial**. *School Equal Opportunities policy.
<u>YEAR 11:</u>	
UNIT ONE: HIV/AIDS A recap on issues of HIV transmission and safer sex. Focusing on the presentation of HIV and AIDS by the media. 12 weeks.	*NCC Curricular Guidance — X Curricular Theme: **Health Ed. — Citizenship**. *ERA 1993 'Sex Education in Schools' *School Equal Opportunities policy *School Sex Education policy.
UNIT TWO: 16+ — Careers Guidance Focusing on choices and decision making. Developing a range of skills related to getting a job/on a course. Developing understanding of issues affecting personal finance. 12 weeks.	*NCC Curricular Guidance — X Curricular Theme: **Careers Ed. — Economic and Industrial**.
UNIT THREE: This is left fairly flexible for us to respond to the needs of our students. It may be sensible to spend a few weeks looking at revision planning, skills and techniques.	For detailed programmes of study see folders years 7–12 in room 162. G.Pooley. May 1995.

Appendix 2

PSE Student Assessment Profile

Name: ________________ **Tutor Group: 7** ______ **PSE Teacher:** ________________

This is to be completed at the end of each unit by student and teacher. Students will also have completed a detailed evaluation of the unit in their books.

<table>
<tr><th>UNIT</th><th>ASSESSMENT FOCUS</th><th>Merit</th><th>Satisfactory</th><th>Needs Improving</th><th>COMMENTS AND TARGETS</th></tr>
<tr><td rowspan="4">1. Childhood</td><td>Group work</td><td>✓</td><td></td><td></td><td rowspan="2">STUDENT TARGET SET: My work is fine but I get distracted easily. I need to do all the H/W set for me. Do not be distracted by others.
Signed ....</td></tr>
<tr><td>K & U of Childrens' Rights</td><td></td><td>✓</td><td></td></tr>
<tr><td>Oral participation</td><td></td><td>✓</td><td></td><td rowspan="2">TEACHER: Some good work especially at the beginning of the unit. Try to concentrate carefully in class.
Signed ....
EFFORT M BEHAVIOUR M
ASSIGNMENT 6/10</td></tr>
<tr><td>Homework</td><td></td><td>✓</td><td></td></tr>
<tr><td rowspan="4">2. Healthy Lifestyle</td><td>Group work</td><td>✓</td><td></td><td></td><td rowspan="2">STUDENT TARGET SET: I enjoyed this project very much and I think we've done well. Do all H/W.
Signed ....</td></tr>
<tr><td>Presentation</td><td></td><td>✓</td><td></td></tr>
<tr><td>Research</td><td></td><td>✓</td><td></td><td rowspan="2">TEACHER: You worked well in your group but you need to keep your exercise book more up to date.
Signed ....
EFFORT S BEHAVIOUR M
ASSIGNMENT 7/10</td></tr>
<tr><td>K & U of factors contributing to health</td><td></td><td>✓</td><td></td></tr>
<tr><td rowspan="4">3. Changes</td><td>K & U—changes during puberty</td><td>✓</td><td></td><td></td><td rowspan="2">STUDENT TARGET SET: I think this project is my favourite It's interesting. My writing has to improve.
Signed ....</td></tr>
<tr><td>Discussion</td><td>✓</td><td></td><td></td></tr>
<tr><td>Group Work</td><td></td><td>✓</td><td></td><td rowspan="2">TEACHER: A really excellent unit. Well done for meeting your target.
Signed ....
EFFORT M BEHAVIOUR M
ASSIGNMENT 8/10</td></tr>
<tr><td>Homework</td><td>✓</td><td></td><td></td></tr>
<tr><td rowspan="4">4. Community (Optional)</td><td>Individual Work</td><td></td><td>✓</td><td></td><td rowspan="2">STUDENT TARGET SET: I enjoyed working in a group. I need to meet deadlines.
Signed ....</td></tr>
<tr><td>Writing</td><td></td><td>✓</td><td></td></tr>
<tr><td>Group Work</td><td>✓</td><td></td><td></td><td rowspan="2">TEACHER: Supportive group work but you also need to concentrate on completing individual tasks on time.
Signed ....
EFFORT M BEHAVIOUR M
ASSIGNMENT 7/10</td></tr>
<tr><td>K & U of culture & needs of a community</td><td>✓</td><td></td><td></td></tr>
</table>

PSE Student Assessment Profile

Name: ____________ **Tutor Group: 10** _____ **PSE Teacher:** ____________

This is to be completed at the end of each unit by student and teacher. Students will also have completed a detailed evaluation of the unit in their books/folders.

UNIT	ASSESSMENT FOCUS	Merit	Satisfactory	Needs Improving	COMMENTS AND TARGETS
1. Women's Health	Communication of ideas.	✓			STUDENT TARGET SET: I think I'm doing OK so far. I am enjoying it and I hope to do well. My target is to upgrade my planning. Signed ....
	K of women's health issues		✓		
	Planning and design		✓		TEACHER: A really good first assignment. You explained your ideas very clearly. Signed ....
	Presenting information		✓		EFFORT M BEHAVIOUR S ASSIGNMENT 7/10
2. Violence Against Women	K & U of issues of dom violence	✓			STUDENT TARGET SET: I worked hard on this topic. My target is to join in class discussion more. Signed ....
	Decision Making		✓		
	Research	✓			TEACHER: Your organisation has definitely improved and you researched this topic well. Signed ....
	Discussion & expressing ideas		✓		EFFORT M BEHAVIOUR M ASSIGNMENT 8/10
3. Disability in the Community	K & U of needs /rights of people with a disability		✓		STUDENT TARGET SET: I didn't really enjoy this unit. My target is to present my work neater. Signed ....
	Evaluation		✓		
	Presentation			✓	TEACHER: You have not put as much effort into this unit as others. Try to present your work in an organised way. Signed ....
	Group Work		✓		EFFORT S BEHAVIOUR M ASSIGNMENT 5/10
4. World of Work	K & U of concepts of work & career	✓			STUDENT TARGET SET: Work experience was interesting in some parts, but a bit boring. I coped well and my presentation was good. Target: to do well in my GCSEs. Signed ....
	Problem solving		✓		
	Communication	✓			TEACHER: Your report was very thoughtful. I am pleased you have met your last target. Think carefully about a careers target. Signed ....
	Group Work				
	Evaluation	✓			EFFORT M BEHAVIOUR M ASSIGNMENT 8/10

Appendix 3

Assessment Opportunities in PSE

observation of role play

close questioning

presentations

observation of group work

student's self-assessment

peer assessment

discussions

written work in book

special assignments

Appendix 4

PSE — GNVQ Communications

CASE STUDY ONE: Women's Health

Name: ______________________ **Tutor Group:** 10A

Date: 20–12–96

Assignment: **Newspaper Report on Eating Disorders:**

Teacher Assessment
Planning:
Your article is organised and well planned. Careful planning work earlier has certainly paid off.

Design/Layout:
Excellent! Your article is very authentic and looks extremely professional. You have selected your pictures well and your use of I.T. works well.

Use of Information:
(Written & video)
This is good. You cover all of the main points. I would like to have seen a little more detail in some areas e.g. the causes of eating disorders. Your 'true story' is very good and gives the reader an insight into the realities of an eating disorder. Well done for using a variety of sources.

Knowledge and Understanding of the topic:
You show a good understanding of the nature of eating disorders.

Other:
A well written article that is clear and easy to follow.
(Including targets for improvement)
Target: To research your next topic in greater depth.

[M] **Overall mark for Effort (SUMAX)**

[8] **Overall mark for Attainment (1–10)**

•SHOOTING STAR•

Volume 1 Issue 1 Month 1993

ANOREXIA AND BULIMIA KILLS THOUSANDS EVERY YEAR!!!!!!

LIFE IS NOT ALL BLACK &WHITE

14 Year old Louise Bell started feeling depressed since her parents had split up about three months ago. Her mother has recently found a new partner called Mark, and Louise's mother has no time for Louise anymore, because of work and social gatherings.

Louise was not happy with what was going on and was left alone in the house with Mark. Mark has on many occasions abused Louise, for the smallest mishaps. The only problem is this always happens when her mother is out at work or with friend and she will not believe what Louise says.

Also to add to Louise's upsetting situation, her father has gone on away on a business trip to America for a few months.

Louise says:

'I knew my parents were planning on getting divorced for quite along time now, I understood that they were not happy living with each other, and I just wanted what I thought was for the best

The only thing was I was not expecting a new man in the house straight away (I don't think my father was either). I suppose I still had my hopes up for my parents getting back together again.

His name was mark and all mum ever went on about was "Mark" this and "Mark" that, I hated him so much, I know it sounds selfish, but I could not deal with having both parents to myself and then sharing one parents with another person who I did not Know, and who abused me for no reason on earth.

Then my dad went away on a business trip and didn't come back after several months.

My life was gradually falling apart. I think that was when I started to lose weight.

Eventually Mum believed me about Mark, Dad came back from the business trip, and I had to go to see a councillor about my problems which soon sorted itself out.'

Sadly not all stories end like Louise's one. Louise was a lucky girl most girls are not so lucky!!

Page 2 SHOOTING STAR

What is Anorexia and Bulimia?

Anorexia nervosa and Bulimia are two extremely common diseases that teenage girls have when put under extreme stress, wanting of attention, family problems, pressure and many others.

Anorexia is when people are depressed or has been put under great pressure, so what people do is starve themselves and are determined not to eat anything, even though they really want to you will persist. Between 5 and 18 percent of known victims die of starvation every year, and the condition may lead to abnormalities in the menstrual cycle.

As anorexia is associated with depression and low self-esteem, and patients may benefit from treatment with antidepressant drugs, Psychotherapy, including family therapy often helps with these resolving their problem. Symptoms that you may notice with anorexia victims is under eating, excess loss of weight, fear of fatness, vigorous exercise, and monthly periods stop.

Bulimia is a disease that affects a slightly older woman in their mid-twenties are over-concerned with their body weight, which causes the person to vomit, use laxatives fasting, or excessive exercise to control weight. The symptoms that you may notice in bulimia victims is bad breath from vomiting and excess stomach acid disguised with chewing gum, irregular periods, fear of fatness.

'Between 5 and 18 percent of known victims die of starvation every year,'

Advice:

Eating Disorders Association
Sackville Place 44 Magdalen St
Norwich NR3 1JE
Tel 0603 621414

The Priory Centre
11 Priory Road, High Wycombe
Buck HP13 6SL
Tel 0494 21431

Facts on Anorexia and Bulimia......

- Anorexia and Bulimia happens to all kinds of young women, and happens to most girls who you would least expect it from.
- Most of the time people cannot tell if the person is Anorexic or Bulimic.
- The best way to help someone is to go through therapy or counselling as a family or with a friend, and take each day as it comes.

Postscript: Which Way Now?

Sally Inman, Martin Buck and Helena Burke

A number of changes have occurred during the course of writing this book. There have been changes both within the wider society and within the educational arena. In this postscript we attempt to look at some of these developments in relation to their possible implications for the future of PSD within the curriculum. We have already made reference to some of the developments from SCAA (now Qualifications and Curriculum Council) and Ofsted during 1995 and 1996. Despite our reservations about these developments, there is no doubt that they heralded a renewed interest and concern for an explicit place for PSD within the curriculum. This interest has continued; the SCAA consultation paper 'Broader thinking about the curriculum' (SCAA, 1996), gave particular attention to curriculum aims as set out in the 1988 ERA as part of the review of the National Curriculum. The DfEE is in the process of setting up a new advisory group on citizenship. In addition, during 1997 the National Association of Headteachers proposed a new curriculum model in which values and PSD were placed at the core of the curriculum, underpinning each aspect of the school's activities.

On the larger stage the May election of 1997 produced a new Labour government with an explicit commitment to the promotion of core societal values. Blair later articulated these values at the Labour Party conference in the autumn of 1997. In a speech to delegates he talked about 'Labour values for a new society'. These values included those of compassion, social justice, liberty, to struggle against poverty and inequality, and human solidarity. The overwhelming majority gained by the new Labour government seemed to indicate a desire for change and, furthermore, a change that embraced a commitment to a renewed sense of collectivity and shared citizenship. The Thatcherite belief that 'there is no such thing as society' seemed, at least temporarily, buried.

On the last day of August 1997 the public reaction to the death of the Princess of Wales appeared to underline this new sense of core values. The reaction to her death has been the subject of much analysis, and this will no doubt continue. However it is eventually understood, the public response during the week after the death highlighted a number of public issues and concerns that had been seemingly forgotten during the preceding years. Central to the concerns expressed were issues about common values and citizenship. There was much public debate and analysis of the importance of showing care, respect, and compassion towards others. It was as if people had woken up from the individualism of the years before, however temporarily.

It is too early to judge whether any of these events heralded fundamental change. However, there are already signs that the new values promoted by the Labour government are not quite so clear and strong as they might have appeared immediately before and after the election. In many areas — welfare, health, and employment, there are signs of policy and practice that do not fit entirely easily with the professed values. Perhaps this is what is meant by 'compassion with a hard edge'?

Education is clearly a stated priority of the Labour government, expressed through the slogan 'Education, Education, Education'. However, the Government's White Paper 'Excellence in Schools' (DfEE, 1997) is significant in its omission of any real debate about curriculum purpose. The White Paper is about excellence and yet offers little discussion of the kinds of excellence we might want to promote, or why we should want to promote it. These are taken as given, except in relation to enhancing national competitiveness. Given the stated values of the new Government one might have hoped for some discussion of the role of the school in promoting the values outlined by Blair and therefore some recognition of the centrality of PSD to the curriculum. The White Paper does have an implicit concern with empowerment and there are explicit references to the need for schools to ensure that they address ethnic diversity, but these are not explicitly linked to PSD. The White Paper also misses an important opportunity to acknowledge the different forms of young peoples' achievement and ignores the degree to which certain kinds of assessment shape the nature of the curriculum and the way it is delivered.

So which way now for PSD? The development of a more focused PSD curriculum and assessment practice will clearly remain uneven without a national impetus expressed through guidance and requirements. Nevertheless, schools do appear, despite the considerable pressures arising from a highly demanding subject curriculum and a predominantly testing culture, to be continuing to develop their PSD practice. Schools are examining their values through mission statements, aims and policies and are shaping environments in which spiritual, moral, social and cultural issues are more frequently explored, but there is still a question mark against the extent to which these practices permeate the whole curriculum. It remains difficult for many schools to raise the status given to PSD, particularly given their organizational structure (especially secondary schools), and the pressures from change overload since the 1988 Education Reform Act. Given this context we need to ensure that practice to promote and assess PSD is continued 'from below' by teachers and others, while at the same time arguing within the national context for a central place for PSD.

This book has attempted to explore issues in the assessment of PSD and to suggest ways in which we might move forward. However, we should remain mindful that a focus on assessment alone will not take us further. The key to developing our practice lies in the quality of what we provide for children. As Lyseight-jones reminds us 'The discussion on assessment in personal and social development cannot avoid including thoughts about the type of schools we want for our children and the kind of teachers we want children to be taught by'. It is our firm belief that, if schools are to prepare pupils to become effective participating citizens of the twenty-first century, then PSD must be central to their purpose.

Notes on Contributors

Martin Buck is Headteacher of Gayton High School in Harrow. He was previously Inspector with Ealing Education Department and has been a deputy headteacher in an inner London school. He is co-author (with Sally Inman) of *Curriculum Guidance No. 1: Whole School Provision for Personal and Social Development*, 1992 and *Curriculum Guidance No. 2: Re-affirming Values*, 1993. He is also co-author (with Sally Inman) of *Adding Value*? Published by Trentham Books in 1995.

Helena Burke is a Lecturer in Education at Goldsmiths' College where she convenes the PGCE secondary social studies course. Previous to this she worked in London schools for eight years, teaching sociology and humanities and coordinating PSE. Her particular interests are within the field of equality of opportunity. She is currently engaged in research into the quality of the inspection process with respect to personal and social development.

Alma Harris is Co-Director of the Centre for Teacher and School Development at the School of Education, University of Nottingham. Her professional interests are in the areas of teacher and school development, school improvement and middle management. She was a founding member of the 'Centre for School Improvement' at Bath University and is currently a Research Associate with the 'International Centre for School Effectiveness and School Improvement' at the Institute of Education, London.

Her most recent research work has included a DfEE 'School Improvement Project' entitled 'Effective Teaching and Learning in Work-Related Contexts'. Most recent publications include two books *School Effectiveness and School Improvement: A Practical Guide* (1995, Pitman Publishing) and *Organisational Effectiveness and Improvement* (1996, OU Press). Forthcoming publications include: *Teaching and Learning in the Effective School* (1997, Arena Press) and *Effective Teaching and Learning* (1998, Cassell).

Sally Inman is Senior Lecturer and Head of Professional Development within the Department of Educational Studies at Goldsmiths' College. She is also head of the Goldsmiths' Centre for Cross Curricular Initiatives. Sally is co-author (with Martin Buck) of *Curriculum Guidance No. 1: Whole School Provision for Personal and Social Development*, 1992 and *Curriculum Guidance No. 2: Re-affirming Values*, 1993. She is also co-author (with Martin Buck) of *Adding Value*? Trentham Books in 1995. Sally is currently engaged in research into the quality of the inspection process with respect to personal and social development.

Pauline Lyseight-jones is General Inspector: Curriculum Evaluation and Assessment for the London Borough of Ealing and has worked in primary, secondary and higher education and in the voluntary education sector. Her contributions to journals and books includes a chapter in *Assessment in the Multi-ethnic Primary Classroom* (Trentham Books, 1995).

Gill Pooley is currently the PSE and Work Experience Coordinator at a south London girls' comprehensive. She has been teaching in inner London comprehensive schools for nine years. She has taught PSE, sociology, integrated humanities and on GNVQ courses. Her interests include: Equal opportunities, active learning and work related curriculum.

Pam Slade currently teaches infants in an inner city school. She has taught in primary and secondary schools in Canada and the UK for many years. Pam is particularly interested in the role of personal and social development within the early years curriculum.

Roger Slee is currently Dean of the Graduate School of Education at the University of Western Australia. He was previously Professor of Education and Head of Educational Studies at Goldsmiths University of London. He has taught in a range of Australian Urban Schools and units for 'disruptive students'. He has written widely on student discipline and inclusive education. He is the editor of the International Journal for Inclusive Education.

Miles Tandy currently works as a Teacher Adviser in Warwickshire. Prior to taking up this post he worked as a teacher in a number of Nottinghamshire primary schools where he gained experience as both a deputy and headteacher. He has a wide experience in arts education, particularly in the fields of drama and storytelling.

David Trainor graduated in Economics and taught in four schools, rising to the rank of deputy head, before joining HM Inspectorate as a Curriculum Specialist. During his 20 years as HMI he held various posts including Staff Inspector for TVEI. He was Adviser to Ofsted on SMSC matters from 1992–1996 when he retired. He is now an Educational Consultant.

Index